More praise for Susan Tyler Hitchcock and *Mad Mary Lamb*

"Another deft portrait of the woman who murdered her mother and later joined with her better-known brother Charles to write *Tales from Shakespear*. Hitchcock (*Coming About*, 1998, etc.) dives into a deep and rich sea teeming with literary life. . . . Informed and sympathetic." —*Kirkus Reviews*

"Hitchcock's book is first-rate, an engaging work of scholarship lucidly written." —*Buffalo News*

"[Hitchcock provides] glimpses of 19th century London worlds not often visited: the Bethlehem hospital—'Bedlam'—and other facilities for the mentally ill; and the emerging industry of publishing books for children, where the Lambs found a tidy market niche among pre-adolescent female readers. . . . Presents Mary with feminist sympathy." —*Wall Street Journal*

"Susan Tyler Hitchcock's book, *Mad Mary Lamb*, has the thrills and chills of a novel, the careful documentation of a work of scholarship, and the sophisticated craft of a truly excellent piece of writing. She manages to combine these elements with grace and pizzazz. A 'must read,' and a major contribution."
—Frances Sherwood, author of
Vindication, *Green*, and *The Book of Splendor*

"With energy, clarity, compassion, meticulous research, and a deeply empathetic imagination, Susan Tyler Hitchcock has here summoned up from the shadowy past the life and times, at once tragic and triumphant, of the greatly gifted Mary Lamb. *Mad Mary Lamb* is a powerful story told with passion, authenticity, and grace, a significant contribution to our knowledge and understanding of the bygone age." —George Garrett,
author of *Death of the Fox* and *Entered from the Sun*

"*Mad Mary Lamb* is a wonderful book: a fascinating story, beautifully written, it is a superb account of the complicated intersection of insanity and literature. Hitchcock's portrayal of the dark but riveting world of Mary Lamb is excellent."

—Kay Redfield Jamison, author of *An Unquiet Mind* and *Exuberance: The Passion for Life*

"An absorbing account of madness, catastrophe, and creativity in early nineteenth-century England. The story's stars—mad but talented Mary Lamb and her devoted brother, the witty essayist Charles Lamb—come vividly to life in these pages."

—Sandra M. Gilbert, coauthor of *The Madwoman in the Attic: The Woman Writer and the Nineteenth-Century Literary Imagination*

"Susan Tyler Hitchcock's archival archaeology and sympathetic imagination combine powerfully to reconstruct a terrible, transforming moment in the life of a complicated woman who has received too little attention. With skill and sensitivity, Hitchcock makes a fully persuasive case for the importance of Mary Lamb to the history of intelligent, creative women."

—Stephen Cushman, author of *Nation of Letters: A Concise History of American Literature*

"Susan Tyler Hitchcock opens a window for us into the soul of a remarkable woman, sister of the essayist Charles Lamb, who killed their mother with a carving knife and then went on over several decades to read and write her way back toward something approaching sanity. This is a compelling tale of murder, mental illness, familial love, and literary redemption. Hitchcock's powerful narrative also provides wonderful insights into nineteenth-century literary London, the birth of children's literature in England, and the lives of a fascinating circle of women and men."

—B. Ashton Nichols, author of *The Revolutionary "I": Wordsworth and the Politics of Self-Presentation*

Mad
Mary Lamb

LUNACY AND MURDER

IN

LITERARY LONDON

Susan Tyler Hitchcock

W. W. NORTON & COMPANY

NEW YORK • LONDON

For information about permission to reproduce selections from this book, write to
Permissions, W. W. Norton & Company, Inc., 500 Fifth Avenue, New York, NY 10110

Manufacturing by The Courier Companies, Inc.
Book design by Brooke Koven
Production manager: Amanda Morrison

Library of Congress Cataloging-in-Publication Data

Hitchcock, Susan Tyler.
Mad Mary Lamb : lunacy and murder in literary London / Susan Tyler Hitchcock.—
1st ed.
p. cm.
Includes bibliographical references and index.
ISBN 0-393-05741-0 (hardcover)
1. Lamb, Mary, 1764–1847. 2. Literature and mental illness—England—History—
19th century. 3. Psychiatric hospital patients—Great Britain—Biography. 4. Women
and literature—England—History—19th century. 5. Authorship—Collaboration—
History—19th century. 6. London (England)—Intellectual life—19th century.
7. Mentally ill women—Great Britain—Biography. 8. Authors, English—19th
century—Biography. 9. Murderers—Great Britain—Biography. 10. Lamb,
Charles, 1775–1834—Family. I. Title.
PR4865.L2Z69 2005
824'.7—dc22

2004019753

ISBN 0-393-32753-1 pbk.

W. W. Norton & Company, Inc., 500 Fifth Avenue, New York, N.Y. 10110
www.wwnorton.com
W. W. Norton & Company Ltd., Castle House, 75/76 Wells Street, London W1T 3QT

1 2 3 4 5 6 7 8 9 0

To my mother

CONTENTS

Contents

ILLUSTRATIONS

1 Charles and Mary Lamb: Courtesy of the National Portrait Gallery, London.

2 Inner Temple, 1720s: Masters of the Bench of the Inner Temple.

3 Crown Office Row and Old Hall: Masters of the Bench of the Inner Temple.

4 New Morality: Courtesy of the National Portrait Gallery, London.

5 Milliners: Print Collection, Miriam and Ira D. Wallach Division of Art, Prints and Photographs, The New York Public Library, Astor, Lenox and Tilden Foundations.

6 House at 7 Little Queen Street: Reproduced by permission of the Huntington Library, San Marino, California.

7 William Godwin: After the 1802 portrait by James Northcote. From Ford K. Brown, *The Life of William Godwin* (London and Toronto: J. M. Dent & Sons; New York: E. P. Dutton & Co., 1926).

8 Mary Wollstonecraft: After the 1797 portrait by John Opie. From Ford K. Brown, *The Life of William Godwin* (London and Toronto: J. M. Dent & Sons; New York: E. P. Dutton & Co. 1926).

9 Samuel Taylor Coleridge, 1795: After the 1775 painting by Peter Vandyke. From Joseph Cottle, *Reminiscences of Samuel Taylor*

Coleridge and Robert Southey, London: Houlston and Stoneman, 1847.

10 William Wordsworth, 1798: By S. Arlent Edwards after a 1798 drawing by Robert Hancock. From Alfred Ainger, ed., *The Letters of Charles Lamb*, vol. 1 (Troy, N.Y.: Pafraets Book Co., 1901).

11 William Hazlitt: By S. Arlent Edwards after the portrait by John Hazlitt. From Alfred Ainger, ed., *The Letters of Charles Lamb*, vol. 2 (Troy, N.Y.: Pafraets Book Co., 1902).

12 Dorothy Wordsworth: By W. Crowbent after the 1835 painting by Samuel Crosthwaite. From David Watson Rannie, *Wordsworth and His Circle* (New York: G. P. Putnam's Sons; London: Methuen & Co., 1907).

13 Samuel Taylor Coleridge: From Ernest Hartley Coleridge, ed., *Letters of Samuel Taylor Coleridge,* vol. 1 (Boston and New York: Houghton, Mifflin & Co., Cambridge: Riverside Press, 1895).

14 William Wordsworth: By J. Skelton after a painting by H. W. Pickersgill. From Christopher Wordsworth, *Memoirs of William Wordsworth* (London: Edward Moxon, 1851).

15 New Bedlam in Moorfields: Courtesy of Bethlem Royal Hospital Archives and Museum.

16 "Melancholy" and "Mania" at Bethlem: Courtesy of Bethlem Royal Hospital Archives and Museum.

17 House at 45 Chapel Street: Reproduced by permission of the Huntington Library, San Marino, California.

18 Dove Cottage: From William Knight, ed., *Letters of the Wordsworth Family* (Boston and London: Ginn and Co., 1907).

19 Mackery End: Mary Evans Picture Library.

20 Charles Lamb standing: By Brook Pulham. Frontispiece, Richard Henry Stoddard, ed., *Personal Recollections of Lamb, Hazlitt, and Others* (New York: Scribner, Armstrong, and Co., 1875).

21 Letter from Mary: From *The Letters of Charles Lamb,* vol. 1 (Boston: Bibliophile Society, 1905). Reproduced by permission of the Huntington Library, San Marino, California.

Mad Mary Lamb

Prelude:

THE DREADFUL SCENE IMAGINED

It was a Thursday afternoon in London, September 22, 1796. Well-dressed men clattered through the cobbled streets, chatting with one another over the knotty cases of law they were tackling. They seemed to stand straighter and taller than those they passed: the woman hawking eggs on the corner, the street brats throwing old onions at one another. These men had grander things on their minds. They came out of cloistered quarters, the ancient Inns of Court, into the rabble of London. They noticed the autumnal change of seasons, more distinct this day than even a week before: the sun sinking nearer the Thames to the south, the clouds gathering thicker and lower, a gray chill in the air.

Just after the slow, hollow chime of the bells of Saint Clement's marked the hour of four, sounds of violence sliced through the quotidian scene. A chaos of shouting, shrieks, incomprehensible words, a high-pitched scream, then the gasp of an older woman, and a young girl's panicked calls for help as she ran from the scene. Passersby on Little Queen Street heard the unnerving noises, but most on the main street of Holborn carried on without notice. The cries seemed to come from quarters above the dusty little wig shop at 7 Little Queen Street.

The shop's proprietor could tell exactly where the sounds came from: upstairs, the rooms he had rented for the past few years to the Lamb family. They had always been so quiet—the daughter who did the housekeeping, the son who worked all day, and the three old people, father, mother, and aunt, none of whom had the energy to do or say much of anything.

Now and then he would hear the mother raise her voice, complaining, but that was to be expected from a woman so crippled she could no longer walk on her own.

The noise was not to be ignored. The landlord dashed out of his front door, around to the stairway at the side. Taking the steps two at a time, he met the family's apprentice girl flying down the stairs, her body akilter, face pinched in horror. She flung herself at him, pulled at him, called out, her eyes wide with fear; then, with an inchoate shriek, she flew past him down the stairs, escaping the scene.

The door to the Lambs' quarters stood wide open. The landlord hurried down the hallway to their front room. The smells of dinner—roast mutton and turnips—sweetened the air. The odor grew more pungent as the landlord looked in, and then the smell of warm blood stopped him short.

Elizabeth Lamb slumped unnaturally in her favorite chair at the window. A stain of red spread from a ragged tear in her white muslin bodice. Above her stood her daughter, Mary Anne, eyes gleaming, mouth a taut rictus. Suspended in a moment of thoughtless inaction, she held a bloody carving knife on high.

Beside the body knelt the dead woman's husband, John Lamb. He pulled desperately at her full skirts, helpless to undo the deed. Two trickles of blood ran down his face from a superficial wound above his left eyebrow. He glanced up at his daughter and cowered under the threat of the knife.

Gasps and wheezes came from the room's far corner as a fourth family member, John Lamb's older sister, backed away in terror. She drew one long, rasping breath and collapsed with a muffled thump, breaking the paralyzed silence. The murderess glanced around as if coming out of a trance. Her muscles relaxed. Her face fell. Her hand dropped, still gripping the knife. She stepped back and drew a long, slow breath. Her eyes softened. She blinked and looked around her.

At that moment a young man burst through the doorway. Pushing past the landlord, he cried out, "Good God! Mary! What has happened here? Why?" Then, quickly, Charles Lamb reached around from behind his sister, taking hold of the knife in her right hand. She succumbed to his grasp and gave up the weapon willingly. In that moment she rested in his strength. Gently he seated her in one of the dining chairs she had just arranged. The joint of meat meant for dinner sat untouched in the middle of the table. The gravy had started to coagulate. Gray turnip globes sat trapped in a thin white sheet of fat.

Charles Lamb placed the knife on the table, beyond Mary Lamb's reach, beside the leather case in which it was ordinarily stored. Slowly he moved around the room, assessing the chaos. All that could be heard were the meek sobs of his father, now crumpled on the floor and clutching his wife's left ankle, and tense chatter from the hallway, where the apprentice girl had returned and was heatedly describing to the landlord what she had seen. The air was electric with the smell of blood and held breath.

Charles Lamb gathered the utensils scattered all over the wooden floor. Bloodstains marked the carving fork's tines. From its position in the room, Charles determined it to be the object that had struck his father in the forehead. He did not have to look at his sister to feel her spirit in retreat. She sat silently, sidelong to the table, just as Charles had placed her, motionless, staring downward. Only her hands moved, folding and unfolding, one and then the other hand on top, fingers working madly. Seizing one quiet moment, Charles sat in a chair facing Mary and took those wild hands in his. He looked intensely into her eyes. She dared to look back at him, her face flickering with guilt and trepidation. Their eyes met, and for that one moment she felt saved.

THE STORY OF Mary Lamb and her act of matricide has lurked in footnotes for more than a century. If discussed at all by those who study English literature of the early nineteenth century, Mary Lamb plays the part of an albatross to her younger brother, Charles Lamb, who is considered one of the finest essayists in the English language. Never placed in the highest empyrean with Shakespeare and Milton, still Charles Lamb and his nimble wit stand for style and sensibility—utterly English, cunningly idiosyncratic, universally amusing. Contemporary essayist Phillip Lopate calls Lamb's *Essays of Elia,* his best-known work, "not only an essential text, but a near-buried treasure, an all-but-lost masterpiece."[1]

These days, as Lopate suggests, few but college students read the essays that brought Lamb his reputation. He is remembered as a beloved member of the Romantic circle of poets, an intimate of both Samuel Taylor Coleridge and William Wordsworth. His name is just as likely known, though, in combination with his sister's for their *Tales from Shakespear,* a retelling for children of Shakespeare's finest plays, first published in 1807 and still in print today. Through nearly two centuries now, countless parents have, with a combination of duty and pleasure, introduced Shakespeare's comedies and tragedies to their children through the writing of the Lambs. Few know of the matricide that had occurred ten years before the book was written. That is how Mary Lamb would have wanted it.

Silence muffles most of the evidence concerning Mary Lamb's murder of her mother. By and large the scene just described is a tissue of speculation, hung on a few firm facts. Charles Lamb lived until 1834, Mary Lamb until 1847, carrying for more than half a century memories of the deed she had committed at the age of thirty-one. Mary, Charles, and their friends conscientiously kept private any information they had regarding Mary's actions and state of mental health. They may have talked, but rarely did they write things down. Even the public record lacks a clear indication of the steps taken to extricate Mary Lamb from any painful legal consequences. What we do know is that she was put into a madhouse—the matricide deemed an act of lunacy—and Charles designated her guardian. It was a task he took on for life, recognizing that his sister had more promise than madness in her.

Things could not have turned out much better for her in that year of 1796. She was not tried for murder. She was not relegated to a prison like Bridewell or a mental hospital like Bethlem, that infamous icon, part asylum, part prison, part zoo, still recalled in the word "bedlam." Instead, under the gentle care provided by her brother, Mary Lamb lived as freely and productively as a woman of her time and temperament could expect—maybe even more so.

In some ways her times promised improvements for the working poor. Mary Lamb was twelve when the American colonies declared their independence; she was seventeen when King George III capitulated to the Sons of Liberty, calling troops and ships back across the Atlantic. She was twenty-two when French peasants stormed the Bastille, an exhilarating event for some London observers, excited by the political promise of democracy and ignorant of the cruelty and carnage yet to come. Mary Lamb lived in an age of fierce debate between aristocratic tradition and democratic revolution, acted out on the world stage and argued daily in the halls of Parliament and the streets of London. A new social order was emerging, founded on the principles of inborn human rights rather than the privilege of family heritage.

But extending rights to women was not the point for most radical intellectuals of the day. "Every individual is born equal in rights with his contemporary," wrote Thomas Paine in his *Rights of Man* (1791); still the prevailing opinion remained that women were "to be considered . . . so weak that they must be entirely subjected to the superior faculties of men," as Mary Wollstonecraft wrote in her groundbreaking *A Vindication of the Rights of Woman* (1792).[2] Now revered as one of the world's first feminist philosophers, Wollstonecraft was seen by many of her contemporaries as an irrational libertine and a threat to the social order.

The first expectation of a woman in those days was to be married; the second was to bear children. By September 1796, nearing the age of thirty-two, Mary Lamb had done neither. She had, however, met stiff responsibilities to her birth family. In her youth she cared for her brother Charles, ten years her junior. As he grew up, her attention shifted to the needs of her elders: her father, aged seventy, who likely suffered a stroke around 1792;

her mother, aged sixty and, suffering from some sort of arthritis or paralysis, growing ever less able to walk or stand on her own; and her aunt, her father's sister, aged about seventy-five. Considering that the average life expectancy in London around 1800 was only forty years, the Lambs lived long lives.

The murder of Elizabeth Lamb set Mary Lamb on a path altogether different from the one planned for her by her family and her society. Charles abided by his promise to watch over her, and the two of them lived in what he called a state of "double singleness" until he died in 1834. Mary lived twelve more years, to the age of eighty-two. She left a legacy of three books, all coauthored with her brother: *Tales from Shakespear,* published in 1807; *Mrs. Leicester's School,* a book of short stories, and *Poetry for Children,* both published in 1809. Not until 1838, though, did her name appear with Charles's on the title page of the perennially reissued *Tales from Shakespear,* but we have it from Charles's own letters that his sister contributed the larger share to it and to the other two books. In 1815 she made one foray into writing for adults, contributing an essay "On Needle-work" to the fashionable new *British Lady's Magazine.* After that Mary Lamb put down the pen.

Humble and self-effacing, insecure and doubtful of her capabilities, in many ways Mary Lamb followed the formula prescribed for a woman of her time. But by the force of her creativity and intellect—fired, perhaps, by her mental condition—she broke through the restraints of propriety. Her upstart act of matricide, as horrifyingly wrong as it was, freed her to explore the rights of women yet to come. Her life—and in particular the fruitful years between the matricide, 1796, and her last publication, 1815— allow a fascinating study of this turning point in history. Picture Mary Lamb as a Michelangelesque female figure emerging from the past into the modern world's future, in 1796 an unformed block of stone and by 1815 the closest she would come to the woman she could have been.

I

THE ONLY DAUGHTER

<hr />

MARY LAMB WAS the third child born to Elizabeth and John Lamb, both of whom served the well-regarded barrister Samuel Salt in the Inner Temple of London. According to Inner Temple records, Elizabeth Lamb gave birth to seven children in thirteen years' time. Only three survived: John Lamb, born June 5, 1763, claimed by his younger brother to be their mother's favorite; Mary Anne Lamb, born December 3, 1764; and Charles Lamb, born February 10, 1775. Mary likely recalled two of the siblings she lost: Edward, the baby boy born when she was five, and Elizabeth, the little girl born when she was four, whom Mary later remembered for her "pretty, fair face" framed in a little cap with a white satin ribbon.[1]

Since before Mary's birth, the Lambs had lived above the law office of Samuel Salt at 2 Crown Office Row in the Inner Temple, one of London's four hallowed Inns of Court, self-contained campuses for the study and practice of law. Her father performed services in the Inner Temple's Great Hall. Wearing the ancient garb of service, black robes adorned with a white collar, tie, and golden tassels, John Lamb and the other waiters stood at attention daily as the head porter blew the horn to call Temple members to the hall for dinner. Then they served up platters full of roast pork or pheasant to the barristers and their students, who were required to dine in the hall as part of their training for the bar.

Samuel Salt greatly favored the Lambs. A man widowed early, his one devotion in life was to his work as a bencher, one of the select few who governed the Inner Temple, and as undertreasurer, its chief financial administrator. He valued John Lamb's native intellect and paid him well for his services: from butler to scrivener, from preparing his wardrobe to copying out in a fine hand the reports he made regularly to the other masters of the bench. Elizabeth Lamb worked for Bencher Salt as well. She quietly ran the operations of his household. Food was prepared, linens and clothing laundered, desks and windowsills dusted, all presumably by Mrs. Lamb. In exchange for these kind services, Salt provided quarters for the Lamb family.

Although right in the center of London, between Fleet Street and the Thames, the setting in which the Lamb children grew up felt more like a monastery or a country green. Distinguished barristers, along with their families, students, and servants, lived within the walls of the Inner and Middle Temples. Occasionally an outsider seeking a quiet abode would rent Temple chambers. The great Samuel Johnson, author of the first English dictionary, had lived at 1 Inner Temple Lane from 1761 to 1765. That was too early for Mary to remember, but her father still pointed to the staircase and talked of spotting Mr. Johnson and of seeing his distinguished friends arrive, the great creative thinkers of the day: writer Oliver Goldsmith, painter Joshua Reynolds, political philosopher Edmund Burke, rising Whig leader Charles James Fox. Mary Lamb did remember, from the age of five, spying Goldsmith as he walked across the terrace. He, too, rented Temple quarters, and her father had told her that he was a great man for all the books he had published. Perhaps John Lamb took Mary into the Pope's Head, the Temple bookshop, now and then to show her books by Johnson and Goldsmith.

A quiet hush of importance and solemnity filled the Temple air. Children were expected to be quiet, even when they romped in the three-acre gardens that stretched down King's Bench Walk to the river Thames. Centuries before, the Knights Templar lived here, preparing for the Crusades, and the same righteous spirit of purpose and determination lingered still. The Temple maintained its own set of laws, distinct from those of the City of London. There was no threat of disorder among those living inside, but a criminal element crept about just outside the Temple walls. Vagabonds knew that in a pinch they could escape arrest by slipping into the Temple—climbing a ten-foot fence or dashing through gates left ajar. From Fleet Street, just outside the Temple, one could see the magisterial dome of Saint Paul's, but to reach the grand cathedral one walked past the Fleet prison and the Bridewell jail.

ONE MILLION people lived in London in those last years of the eighteenth century. It was the biggest city in the world, and with its size came the broad and colorful range of all human possibilities. Great writers and philosophers congregated there, fully aware that they shared these city streets with the spirits of Geoffrey Chaucer, William Shakespeare, and John Milton. George III's reign had lasted nearly forty years, which might have given Britons a sense of stability had it not been for the restlessness of other nations: the North American colonies in the 1770s and now France in the 1790s. In Parliament and in the newspapers, in coffee shops by day and public houses by night, the nervousness of social change, the tension that comes with the conflict of class and philosophy, infused the smoky air of London. The English were in the middle of a revolution, too, but theirs was taking place in people's minds and hearts, not in the street or on the battlefield.

Mary Lamb, thirty-one in 1796, may not have recognized it, though, as she went through the same dreary daily motions she had for the past few years. Most likely the biggest revolution she had experienced was the abrupt change that shook her family when Samuel Salt died in the winter of 1792. Immediately the family lost their home, and their income dropped precipitously. John Lamb remained first waiter in the Great Hall, a post he had achieved in 1772, but for it he received only fifteen pounds annually—not enough for a family of five to live on, especially since, without their benefactor, the Lambs could no longer live in Crown Office Row. Salt's will was generous to the Lambs, however. He left five hundred pounds of South Sea Company stock "to my servant, John Lamb, who has lived with me near 40 years," and two hundred pounds to Mrs. Lamb, "for her care and attention during my illness." He also left annuities for the family, assuring a small annual income.[2]

Salt had also provided for the Lambs during his lifetime in ways that remained after his death. He had recommended both their sons, John and Charles, for entry into Christ's Hospital, London's finest charity school, where boys of little standing but significant intellectual promise could attain the same education as those from aristocratic families. He had likewise used his influence on the board of directors of the South Sea Company to secure clerical positions for both boys as they came of age. By the momentous year of 1796, John Lamb had already advanced in his position. His salary—and his personality—were such that he no longer lived at home. By 1796 Charles had been clerking for five years, too, which meant that he had completed his apprenticeship and earned a salary of seventy pounds annually.[3]

Until 1792 the family had lived a serving-class life, but they had been supported adequately. With Salt's death they had reason to worry. Sometime soon after—records do not say just when— they moved out of the Temple and up the street, north and west of Lincoln's Inn Fields but just short of High Holborn, into quarters on Little Queen Street. They remained in the part of London familiar to them, with Lincoln's Inn and Gray's Inn, London's two other Inns of Court, not far away. But the move must have felt almost as if they had landed in the street.

The change bore down hard on both John and Elizabeth Lamb. There are hints that at this time John Lamb suffered a stroke, for he soon lost the use of his left hand, which threatened to jeopardize his work in the Great Hall. Lamb petitioned for a continuance of his post, and Inner Temple records still carry the decree returned by the masters of the bench: "Upon reading the Petition of John Lamb, First Waiter in the Hall, setting forth that he had been a servant to the House near Forty years, and that he had nearly lost the use of his left hand, and was otherwise very infirm, and praying that he might be permitted to find a person to attend for him, Ordered that a person be permitted to attend for him during the pleasure of the Table."[4] Some friend at the Inner Temple—perhaps Randall Norris, the Inner Temple librarian—stood in for John Lamb for the next few years. He continued to receive his annual fifteen pounds until his death in 1799.

During these same difficult months Elizabeth Lamb began to experience pain, perhaps arthritis, that ultimately affected her whole body. Finding it more and more difficult to walk, she must have leaned on Mary, the one able adult in the household during the day. By 1796 Charles described his mother as "entirely helpless (not having any use of her limbs)," and said that for that reason Mary was "necessarily confined from ever sleeping out, she being her bed fellow."[5] So daughter and mother had begun sharing a bed—not just because quarters were small, one imagines, but also because Elizabeth Lamb needed to know that if in the dark of night she needed to relieve herself or even turn from one side to the other, Mary would be there to help her.

Of the three elders, John Lamb's sister, Sarah, seems to have required the least care in 1796—ironically so, since she was the oldest of the three. For most of her childhood, Mary Lamb later told a friend, the two sisters-in-law had "made each other miserable." Their intolerance for each other built to a level of "bitter hatred," although their feelings softened as they aged. In retrospect Mary recognized Sarah Lamb to be "as unlike a gentlewoman as you can possibly image,"[6] but "Aunty," as she called her, may well have added some levity to the household, enchanting Mary with stories of times gone by, laced with saucy comments. In 1796 Sarah Lamb probably demanded little aside from the attention that any fragile, aging woman needs.

In 1796 it was the lot of both Mary and Charles Lamb to do all they could to take care of their aging elders. Their older brother, John, aged thirty-five, lived on his own. He probably shared some of his income with the family and visited occasionally, but he had by and large separated himself from the daily rigors of life at 7 Little Queen Street. Charles had left the South Sea Company and now worked at East India House, Britain's other pillar of imperial trade. Its headquarters were on Leadenhall Street, not a twenty-minute walk from Little Queen Street. He was diligent about getting to work in the morning and responsible about coming straight home at night, but even Charles must have caused Mary to worry. Late in 1795 he had suffered a mental breakdown, an episode in his life of which we know very little. He may have started talking too fast and too long, spouting poetry or gibberish, or he may have retreated into a depressive withdrawal: No one can know, for no records have been found that describe the behavior that led to his six weeks in a madhouse. Judging from his later struggles, the episode may have been triggered by overindulgence in alcohol. Whether Mary, a parent, a friend, or even Charles himself decided he should be committed, we do not know, but we do know that Charles Lamb spent the turn of the year, 1795 to 1796, as a patient in Hoxton House, London's best-known private madhouse.

Considering how much her family needed her, it was a good

thing that Mary Lamb never married. It was a good thing, too, that she had taken up the trade of mantua making, or seamstress work, for when the family needed to increase its income, from 1792 on, she could mend caps, trim edges with lace, and stitch together the occasional garment for paying customers. She could sew by candlelight late into the night, making profitable use of the hours after her father, mother, and aunt had gone to bed.

Early in the fall of 1796 someone in the Lamb family must have decided it was a good idea to find Mary an apprentice. In those days families in financial straits would often place their daughters at ten or eleven years of age in other households. For room and board the girls worked and, if they were lucky, learned a trade as well. Perhaps Charles, the most likely to be looking out for his sister's livelihood, suggested the nine-year-old girl, the unnamed apprentice who joined the Lamb family just days before the death of Elizabeth. It is fair to assume that she was expected to help Mary cook, clean, and care for the three elders and, as possible, begin to do the easy sewing jobs, like hems and straight seams.

Imagine the consequences of adding a nine-year-old to that household. She was young and unfamiliar with her surroundings, the people around her, and their expectations of her. She may have known little about cooking, and she may have been unable even to thread a needle. What if she cried into the night as she lay down on what little the Lambs could provide for her bed? She may have quickly turned out to be a burden, but the Lambs had made a promise to her family. If the task of turning such a girl helpful fell to anyone, it would be to Mary.

The expectations heaped themselves on Mary Lamb in September 1796. Her father no longer made sense when he talked. All he wanted was someone to play cribbage with him. Her mother needed help moving from one chair to another, but her mind and tongue were still as sharp as ever. Brother John did what he pleased, but early in the summer he had had an accident.

As he was out walking one day, a boulder fell off a stone wall and damaged his leg so severely that his family feared he would need amputation.[7] Ultimately it mended, but he had moved back in with his family for a while, too—it was so convenient to have someone feed and dress him.

Mary tried to keep from dwelling on her burdens. Sometimes their weight felt almost physical, though, like a beast in her heart or her stomach, clawing at her from the inside. Her head would throb so hard that she could barely see. She smelled the blood pulsing through her veins. It helped to imagine herself screaming.

It only took two days after the apprentice girl had moved in for those feelings to come back, harder and stronger than ever. Something inside her reminded Mary of the one time, years before, that she had just started crying and had not been able to stop for hours. It seemed like days. The elder Dr. Pitcairn had come to see her then, visiting her in her bed in their old Crown Office Row home. He had helped her sit up, spooned a thick, dark syrup into her mouth, then laid her head back down. She had slept a long time.

She wished she had a draught of that same syrup now. She would gladly have gone to sleep for hours, days, weeks, forever. But she had to stay awake. She had to keep taking care. She had to show this little girl how to set the table. The mutton had been roasting over the fire so long it was dry. The turnips would soon fall apart in the boiling water. Her mother was calling from the front room, asking where was dinner. The girl was wandering into the hall. Mary called her back in, pressed the flatware into her hands, even made sure that the girl's fingers gripped around it. She noted what was still needed on the table. She picked up the salt shaker, the carving fork, and the case knife. She turned to walk toward the table and nearly tripped over the apprentice girl, who had not moved an inch. She told the girl again to go and set the table. "Do you not know what I mean when I say set the table?" she asked impatiently. Those nine-year-old eyes looked blankly, sadly, dumbly, resentfully at her. She jerked the girl's body around and shoved her into the next room.

Her mother saw her do it. She shouted some angry words. Mary heard the noise but did not hear the meaning as she set the salt shaker and carving fork down on the table. She absentmindedly slid the knife out of its case, to be sure it had been sharpened. Her mother raised her voice again, this time haranguing that Mary must not be listening to her. Mary saw her world turn white, then red, then white again. Screams from deep inside filled her ears; then she realized they were filling the air around her. The apprentice girl was running away from her. Mary sensed herself motionless but saw that her arms were thrashing. The salt shaker flew across the room. The carving fork followed. Mary felt the bone handle of the knife, cold and strong against the skin of her palm. She was drowning in the sound of her mother's voice, and there was only one way to stop it. She moved forward, and the knife plunged down, slicing in an instant through cloth, skin, fat, muscle, bone, marrow, striking to the heart.

2

THEIR VERDICT: LUNACY

NGLISH LAW REQUIRED that on the occasion of any sudden death, witnesses were to summon the local coroner to investigate the circumstances *super visum corporis*—by viewing the body—at the place where the death occurred. The coroner's "enquiry is made by a jury from four, five or six of the neighbouring towns, over whome he is to presind [preside]," the law prescribed. "If any be found guilty by this inquest of murder, he is to commit to prison for further trial."[1]

In the case of Elizabeth Lamb the manner of death was not difficult to determine: a single knife wound to the chest. The perpetrator seems never to have been in question either. There were witnesses to the murder: the apprentice girl, Aunt Sarah, and John Lamb. Two others, Charles and the landlord, entered on the scene soon after, presumably witnessing circumstances that left no doubt. Mary Lamb seems never to have denied her act, although the written record contains no firsthand admission. The closest we come is the letter written on September 27 by Charles Lamb to his dear friend Samuel Taylor Coleridge, stating, "My poor dear dearest sister in a fit of insanity has been the death of her own mother. I was at hand only [in] time enough to snatch the knife out of her grasp."[2] The coroner's inquest did result in written records, a paragraph or two documenting their findings, but those records are long lost.[3] Since London newspapers drew directly from those inquest reports, the local account of Elizabeth Lamb's death is the closest we can come to reconstructing the deliberations of the jury.

On Monday, September 26, the four pages of *The Times* of London were rife with fear over war with France. Spain had just signed a treaty with the Directory, the governing body of the new French regime. The embargo on English trade vessels now extended to Spanish ports as well as French, and the court of Madrid was seizing merchandise from the few British vessels still harbored there. An emissary of the British government had recently returned to London, expelled from Paris without his passport. Troop movements near the Rhine suggested that General Jourdan and his French army might be retreating from Rotterdam, and General Bonaparte was leading a brigade of five thousand men and fifteen hundred horses, confronting Austrian troops in Mantua, northern Italy. *Leo,* a French privateering schooner captured by His Majesty's Royal Navy off the island of Cuba two weeks earlier, had arrived at Plymouth harbor, replete with weapons and gunpowder. Prussia was expected to follow Spain and establish an alliance with France.

Amid this grim news, at the bottom of the newspaper's third page, alongside other items of local interest—the navy's purchase of twelve thousand oxen and the "considerable contution on the thigh [sic]" received by the Marquis of Buckingham when he was thrown from his horse—appeared this untitled article:

On Friday afternoon the Coroner and Jury sat on the body of a Lady, in the neighbourhood of Holborn, who died in consequence of a wound from her daughter the preceding day.

It appeared by the evidence adduced, that while the family were preparing for dinner, the young lady seized a case-knife laying on the table, and in a menacing manner pursued a little girl, her apprentice, round the room. On the calls of her infirm mother to forbear, she renounced her first object, and with loud shrieks approached her parent. The child, by her cries, quickly brought up the landlord of the house, but too late. The dreadful scene presented to him the mother lifeless, pierced to the heart, on a chair, her daughter yet wildly standing over her with the fatal knife, and the old man her father weeping by her side, himself bleeding at the forehead from the effects of a severe blow he received from one of the forks she had been madly hurling about the room.

For a few days prior to this, the family had observed some symptoms of insanity in her, which had so much increased on the Wednesday evening, that her brother, early the next morning, went to Dr. Pitcairn, but that gentleman was not at home.

It seems the young lady had been once before deranged. The Jury of course brought in their verdict, *Lunacy*.[4]

Identical reports appeared in the *Morning Chronicle,* the *Gentleman's Magazine,* and elsewhere. The *Whitehall Evening Post* included more information, again likely culled from the coroner's inquest report, about the cause of this event. It corrected misinformation found in other papers; concerning Dr. Pitcairn, the Whitehall paper commented, "had that gentleman been met with, the fatal catastrophe had in all probability been prevented." This writer included the information that "the young lady had been once before, in her earlier youth, deranged from the harrassing fatigues of too much business," and concluded—still presumably quoting from the coroner's report—"As her carriage towards her mother was ever affectionate in the extreme, it is believed, that to the increased attentiveness which her parents infirmities called for by day and night, is to be attributed the present insanity of this ill fated young woman." The Whitehall newspaper, unlike the others, identified the killer: "The above unfortunate young person is a Miss Lamb, a mantua-maker, in

Little Queen-street, Lincoln's-inn-fields. She has been, since, removed to Islington mad-house."[5]

For centuries English common law had held that the state of mind of the person wielding the weapon had legal bearing in determining the gravity of the crime, or indeed whether the act was a crime at all. So did the relationship of the killer to the victim. Historical records name five eighteenth-century women who killed their husbands, the last as late as 1789, who were burned at the stake, their crimes considered acts against the social order and hence petit treason.[6] Women who killed their own children were sometimes exonerated, sometimes put to death. But no statute or common law specified a punishment for parricide.

By the end of the eighteenth century the murder of a child, a parent, or oneself was increasingly interpreted as an act of lunacy. Tracing the history of the insanity defense in Britain, one researcher determined that between 1760 and 1843, almost one in three acts of personal offense (murder, assault, or kidnapping) was officially attributed to insanity.[7] Lunacy replaced moral defect as an explanation for violence in extraordinary circumstances, as in this case, reported in a women's magazine in 1815: "The bodies of a young woman and her infant were lately found drowned in the river Mersey. On the coroner's inquest it appeared, that she had been slighted by a young man, the father of her child; and that, destitute of protection, she drowned herself and her infant in despair. The verdict returned was, *Lunacy*."[8]

The term "lunatic" was an ancient legal designation. A lunatic experienced periods of lucidity, whereas an idiot never had done so and never would. The very word—from *luna*, Latin for "moon"—conveyed the concept of rationality that waxed and waned. Hence a person like Mary Lamb—acting irrationally at times but normally at others—would be called a lunatic. She was, in the words of *Blackstone's Commentaries*, the touchstone of English common law, "one who hath had understanding, but by disease, grief, or other accident hath lost the use of his reason," a category that included those acting "under frenzies." Care of lunatics was to be entrusted to the Lord Chancellor, by authority from the king, who then "usually commits the care of his person, with a suitable allowance for his maintenance, to some friend"—specifically not an heir with an interest in the lunatic's death. English law considered the "defected or vitiated understanding" of a lunatic a "deficiency in will," and "in criminal cases therefore idiots and lunatics are not chargeable for their own acts, if committed when under these incapacities: no, not even for treason itself."[9]

ON THESE PRINCIPLES the insanity plea was founded, but decades after the case of Mary Lamb. Most legal historians date its establishment to a famous decision in 1843. Parliament articulated the McNaughton rules, as they are still called today, after a twenty-nine-year-old Scottish woodworker, Daniel McNaughton, shot and killed Edward Drummond, believing himself to be assassinating Sir Robert Peel, the prime minister and Drummond's employer. Investigators learned of McNaughton's history of depression and delusions, and they verified his condition through extensive examinations by the physicians in London most highly regarded for their knowledge of mental aberrations. From McNaughton's case on, in English and American law, the question of guilt has ridden on the question of intellectual capability, a person being liable to punishment "if he knew at the time that he was acting contrary to the law of the land."[10] Medical experts were to be consulted to determine the person's mental state, and anyone found incapable of discerning right from wrong was found not guilty but kept in court custody for medical treatment.

The McNaughton case forms the basis of our modern-day insanity plea, but such legal concepts were not fully formed in 1796. In fact, when a coroner's jury pronounced a verdict of lunacy, no clear path of action followed. Interesting cases that precede Mary Lamb's, historical precursors to McNaughton's, show judicial authorities responding to irrational acts of violence with compassion for the perpetrator.

In 1784 a man named William Walker killed his wife with one knife stab to the chest, then invited his neighbors in to see what he had done. The judge advised the jury that if they found evidence "that he was not in possession of his right senses, and of his right mind, but that it was done under the pressure of some disorder of mind, occasioned by something that you and I cannot get to the bottom of," such discoveries would "make him nothing more than a mere instrument in the hands of Providence, . . . not at all answerable to the laws of God or man for what he has done, any more than the simple knife could be answerable that gave the fatal blow." To this judge clarity of mind and purpose was the deciding factor: "[H]e is either guilty of the crime of willful murder, or he is a mere machine." The jury swiftly found Walker not guilty, and to that verdict the judge attached the proviso that he be kept in custody for "proper care."[11]

On August 2, 1786, King George III climbed out of his carriage in front of St. James's Palace, when from out of the crowd, a middle-aged woman sprang forward and lunged at him, a sheaf of papers in one hand and a well-worn butter knife in the other. Guards grabbed her and foiled her attempt to stab the king. "I am not hurt," George III is reported to have said, adding, with sympathy toward his assailant, "Take care of the woman—do not hurt her, for she is mad."[12]

Interrogations revealed that Margaret Nicholson, an unmarried housemaid in her forties, had for a week been contemplating an attack on the king, to persuade him to give her "property due to her from the Crown of England." She seemed a worthy citizen: She worked reliably as a maid and seamstress; she could read and write and in fact owned a dictionary. The attending physician stated, though, that "he never in his life had seen a person more disordered" or "a clearer case of Insanity."[13] Attempted regicide constituted treason, a crime punishable by death. Yet in 1786 the will of the Crown was not to execute but to hospitalize her. She was sent to London's Bethlem Hospital, where she lived until her death in 1848.

EVOLVING LEGAL OPINIONS reflected changing views in the general public. It took a king to make the people feel differently about madness.

On June 11, 1788, King George III—then fifty years old and in the twenty-eighth year of his reign—doubled over in pain. As one of the queen's court confided to her diary, "The King was seized with a bilious fever, attended with violent spasms in his stomach and bowels." Sir George Baker, the royal physician, encouraged a retreat to Cheltenham, a Cotswold village known for its healing waters. For two months George lived in Cheltenham, taking laxative rhubarb pills, drinking and bathing in the waters, and eating a diet of mutton and potatoes, all measures designed to reduce an excess of bile.[14]

The Times first reported the king's condition as something inconsequential: "His Majesty being much indisposed with a cold, did not attend the drawing-room yesterday, but set off in the morning for Kew-Palace," read an article on June 13. When a more concerned report appeared in the *Morning Herald,* it so infuriated Queen Charlotte that she ordered the paper burned and the printer charged with treason.[15] But the king's subjects missed his public presence, and, on August 1, when he attended the theater, "the loudest acclamations continued for the space of seven minutes."[16] Any lingering disappointment over his part in the loss of the American colonies was replaced by genuine concern for his health.

Intestinal spasms returned in mid-October. This time George III asked for an opium pill, then a common remedy for pain and fever. His physician also prescribed castor oil and senna, botanicals identified in the eighteenth-century pharmacopoeia as purgatives, to flush intruding fluids from the body. Some attributed the king's illness to his own misadventures. He had taken a long walk through tall grass, they said, then kept on wet stockings all the rest of the day. To top that off, he had eaten four large pears in one sitting.[17]

Then George's symptoms turned mental. Frances Burney, the queen's lady-in-waiting—better known as Fanny, a novelist and friend of Dr. Johnson's, whose family would befriend Mary and Charles Lamb in years to come—feared "a total breaking up of the constitution." The king's body grew weak but his behavior grew manic: "[H]e walks like a gouty man, yet has such spirits that he has talked away his voice," Burney wrote in her diary.[18] He chattered on, incoherently and incessantly, once for nineteen hours straight, according to Robert Fulke Greville, the king's groom, who kept notes on the king's illness. By November, Greville considered him "entirely deranged."[19]

Rumors flew through aristocratic circles. It was impossible to keep George III's incompetence out of the public eye. To discuss the king's malady, court spokesmen used the word "fever," which in those days had the fortunate ambiguity of meaning both an elevated body temperature and a prolonged state of nervous agitation. On Saturday, November 15, *The Times* reported that "His Majesty's disorder has yet had no favourable turn, and . . . there is the greatest apprehension to fear it is now settled in the brain."

Whatever his illness, George III could not conduct business. Fierce debates ensued over whether the power of the throne should remain with him or be vested in the Prince of Wales, first of George III's eleven children and heir to the throne. The son's personality did not encourage faith in his leadership potential. He was a twenty-six-year-old brat, scornful of his father, tradition, and authority. Many believed he was secretly married to a

Catholic woman, Maria Fitzherbert. Worse than profligacy, it was against English law for a royal to marry a Catholic.

More significant to parliamentary leaders than the Prince of Wales's love life, though, was the question of who held the power to declare a regency. At the crux of the debate was the irony of the king's mental condition. When lucid, he argued passionately against a regency. But then he would slip into a period of irrationality, behaving with complete disregard for protocol and confirming the need for an alternate monarch. A team of medical experts reported regularly to the queen and the prime minister: specialists including Lucas Pepys, a member of the Royal College of Physicians' Madhouse Commission, which inspected and licensed private madhouses; Sir William Fordyce, an expert on the symptoms of insanity; and the legendary Reverend Dr. Francis Willis.

Ordained in the Church of England and educated in medicine, Willis had since 1776 operated a private madhouse in Lincolnshire. While his contemporaries saw madhouses as final repositories for the untameable, Willis considered his a treatment center. He augmented physical techniques with what today we might call a psychotherapeutic approach. He was famous for staring intently into the patient's eyes to win attention and control. He would outright command an unruly patient to stop offensive practices, and he enforced daily routines, curing his patients by shaping their behavior. The social historian Roy Porter called Willis the world's first psychiatrist.[20]

King George III at first resisted, but Willis swiftly broke the will of his royal patient. Just as when breaking an untrained horse, Willis told Greville, repeated physical submission was essential to the cure. "I hate all Physicians but most the Willises," George III said. "They treat me like a Madman." When the king was rational enough to pay attention, Willis lectured against his ravings. When George ranted back, Willis stuffed a handkerchief into his mouth and kept on lecturing. Willis also ordered a cornucopia of medicinals, including calomel (mercury chloride, a mineral prescribed then for fevers), digitalis (a botanical still used in heart medicines today, known then to lower the pulse), salt water, and senna bark.[21]

One observer suspected that George III took some pleasure in his madness. Frances Burney recalls that in February 1789, the king encountered her in the garden, kissed her on the cheek, then talked and talked, inquiring after her health, extolling her father, explaining his political plans. "It was but the joy of a heart unbridled," Burney believed.[22]

George III was declared cured in the spring of 1789, just in time to moot the regency vote in Parliament. The royal family returned in full regalia to Windsor Castle on March 14. "All Windsor came out to meet the King," wrote Burney, cheering with "a joy amounting to extacy [*sic*]."[23] Celebratory medals were struck in honor of the cure. Some historians now believe that King George suffered from porphyria, a genetic disease of the nervous system, exacerbated by manic-depressive disorder.[24] He would reign in good health for more than a decade after his first bout with madness, although by 1810 the disease would overtake him permanently.

The British public never knew the full story, but they knew enough. Their king lost his mind for a few months and then, thanks to a "mad-doctor," regained his full and glorious being. Madness, a condition into which both high and low could fall, was reversible, a disease of the mind, not the body, and certainly not of the soul. George III's publicly recognized bout with mental illness mitigated many stigmas associated with the condition called lunacy.

CHARLES LAMB understood that he had to become his sister's advocate. With the laws unformed and prevailing opinion compassionate toward the lunatic, he negotiated a system open to manipulation. His family had already identified, perhaps consulted with,

Dr. David Pitcairn, a second-generation physician in Islington, now part of London but then a village outside the city. Pitcairn was the nephew of and successor to William Pitcairn, long a member of the elite Royal College of Physicians and known for his four-acre botanical garden. When William Pitcairn died in 1791, David Pitcairn took over as physician to St. Bartholomew's, London's ancient and revered charity hospital. Both uncle and nephew served on the Royal College's Madhouse Commission. It was Pitcairn, as one newspaper account stated, that Charles Lamb hoped to consult on the morning of Mary's precipitous act. It was probably through Pitcairn that Charles Lamb learned of Fisher House, the privately operated madhouse where Mary Lamb was swiftly confined. There Pitcairn could pay frequent visits to his patient, since he lived just minutes away. Recently retired as physician at London's St. Bartholomew's Hospital, Pitcairn may have had a professional affiliation with Fisher House.

Charles seems to have harbored little doubt that he had to remove Mary from the house where the murder had occurred. Having taken that definitive step, he found himself surprisingly calm on the night of his mother's death, shored up by the realization that the responsibility for his family now rested on him. "I felt that I had something else to do than to regret," he wrote a week later.

> On that first evening my Aunt was laying insensible, to all appearance like one dying,—my father, with his poor forehead plaisterd over from a wound he had received from a daughter dearly loved by him, & who loved him no less dearly,—my mother a dead & murder'd corpse in the next room—yet was I wonderfully supported. I closed not my eyes in sleep that night, but lay without terrors & without despair.[25]

So when on Friday afternoon, September 23, the coroner and his jury arrived at 7 Little Queen Street, Mary Lamb was already living at Fisher House. The coroner's jury performed its duties: to inspect the body of Elizabeth, now laid out on her bed, and to inquire into the circumstances of her murder. The evidence was so clear that they probably did not need to talk with Mary. They questioned Charles and the landlord, certainly; perhaps the apprentice girl and Sarah. They may only have paid regards to John Lamb who, according to his son, "was playing at cards, as tho' nothing had happened, while the Coroner's Inquest was sitting over the way!"[26] Presumably satisfied to hear that the young man of the family had already made the responsible decision to place his sister in a madhouse, the inquest concluded. It was an act of lunacy, and so they wrote in their report.

One can only wonder, as the circle grew of those who mourned Elizabeth Lamb, how many knew how she died. Family friends, Mr. and Mrs. Norris—not, it appears, the Inner Temple librarian, but another Mr. Norris whom the Lambs knew from Christ's Hospital—provided such solace that they felt like father and mother to Charles.[27] Samuel Le Grice, one of his classmates, ended up staying with the family for several days. He was particularly kind to Charles's father, agreeing to endless rounds of cribbage.

John Lamb, the elder brother, seems conspicuously absent from the scene. "I had the whole weight of the family thrown on me," Charles wrote a week later, "for my brother, little disposed . . . at any time to take care of old age & infirmities had now, with his bad leg, an exemption from such duties." Apparently John railed at his brother when he heard that Mary had already gone to Fisher House, though. "I know John will make speeches about it, but she shall not go into an *hospital*," wrote Charles. For the older brother, rather distant from his sister, the obvious solution was to send her to Bethlem. Although by doing so they would be giving up control and perhaps even access, that was just the advantage for someone like John Lamb. Furthermore, Bethlem would not cost them the 50 or 60 pounds a year that Fisher House would charge.[28] John Lamb argued the point vigorously just after his mother's death, but he soon relented—and thereby provided himself a rationalization for leaving the burden of Mary's care with Charles for the rest of their lives.

Through the weeks just after his mother's death, Charles Lamb wrote intimate letters to his friend, Samuel Taylor Coleridge. They reveal how much his mind dwelled on his sister. At times he felt guilty that his worries about Mary overshadowed his sorrow about the death of his mother. Questions of blame and guilt, cause and effect, haunted him. He shared one key psychological insight with Coleridge: "Poor Mary," he wrote, "my mother indeed *never understood* her right."

> She loved her, as she loved us all with a *Mother's love*, but in opinion, in feeling, & sentiment, & disposition, bore so distant a resemblance to her daughter, that she never understood her right. Never could believe how much *she* loved her—but met her caresses, her protestations of fillial affection, too frequently with coldness & *repulse* . . .[29]

He mourned his mother, but there was some sense—never spoken, of course, maybe never even brought fully to consciousness, because it was so antithetical to anyone's sense of right and wrong—that Elizabeth Lamb had it coming. To put it more delicately, perhaps years of maternal scorn and indignities preceded Mary Lamb's one swift and ultimate act of matricide.

Their mother, Charles wrote,

> would always love my brother above Mary, who was not worthy of one tenth of that affection, which Mary had a right to claim. But it is my Sister's gratifying recollection, that every act of duty & of love she could pay, every kindness (& I speak true, when I saw to the hurting of her health, & most probably in great part

to the derangement of her senses) thro' a long course of infirmities & sickness, she could shew her, *she ever did*.

The syntax of this passage is difficult, as if the author is not comfortable enough with the content to clarify his ideas. He seems, though, to blame Mary's infirmities—the "hurting of her health" and the "derangement of her senses"—on her long, selfless devotion to her mother, repaid only with "coldness & repulse" and maybe even worse.

Such dark thoughts surely clouded Charles Lamb's conscience, and they may explain why he mourned his sister as intensely as his mother in those last days of September 1796. "One little incident may serve to make you understand my way of managing my mind," he wrote Coleridge in early October:

Within a day or 2 after the fatal *one*, we drest for dinner a tongue, which we had had salted for some weeks in the house. As I sat down a feeling like *remorse* struck me,—this tongue poor Mary got for *me*, & can I partake of it *now*, when she is far *away*—a thought occurrd & relieved me,—if I give into this way of feeling, there is not a chair, a room, an object in our rooms, that will not awaken the keenest griefs, I must rise above such weaknesses—. I hope this was not want of true feeling. I did not let this carry me tho' too far.[30]

Charles Lamb's decisions meant that the responsibility for Mary's future lay in his hands. They were decisions he made out of devotion and naïveté both. Mary, eleven years his elder, had been his surrogate mother. Most of his fondest memories included her. Charles's mother taught him how to behave, his father taught him how to read and write, but his sister taught him joy and human kindness. Even when they were adults, she was his best friend. The only other person who came close was Coleridge, to whom he had written just months before, "You are the only *correspondent* & I might add the only friend I have in the world."[31] His friend was equally devoted. Charles Lamb, Coleridge told a Cambridge acquaintance that winter, was his "dearest Friend" and Mary Lamb was "dear to me as an only Sister."[32] Now those bonds really mattered.

A SMALL CROWD—relatives from Hertfordshire and friends from Christ's Hospital and the Inner Temple, one supposes— gathered in the Lamb household on Saturday, September 24, in memory of Elizabeth Lamb. Her body was to be laid to rest two days later, in the graveyard of Saint Andrew's, Holborn. The gathering upset Charles, though. He found socializing difficult. Forty-eight hours after his mother's abrupt death, its finality was weighing on him. The steely grip he had on his feelings loosened. With grief and fury mixed, his tears finally flowed. "On the very 2d day (I date from the day of *horrors*)" he wrote Coleridge,

as is usual in such cases there were a matter of 20 people I do think supping in our *room*—. They prevailed on me to eat *with them* (for to eat I never refused) they were all making merry! in the room,—some had come from friendship, some from busy curiosity, & some from *Interest;* I was going to partake with *them,* when my recollection came that my poor dead mother was lying in the next room, the very next room, a mother who thro' life wished nothing but her children's welfare—indignation, the rage of grief, something like remorse, rushed upon my mind in an agony of emotion,—I found my way mechanically to the adjoining room, & fell on my knees by the *side* of her coffin, asking forgiveness of heaven, & sometimes of her, for forgetting her *so soon.* Tranquillity returned, & it was the only violent emotion that master'd me, & I think it did me good.

3

IN THE MADHOUSE

WE CAN ONLY imagine how Mary Lamb was feeling the night she killed her mother. While Charles released his feelings through long letters to Coleridge, Mary did not write anything down—or if she did, nobody saved it. The most difficult challenge in discovering Mary Lamb's story is hearing her own voice.

The *Morning Chronicle,* probably following the coroner's report, had reported that "the family had observed some symptoms of insanity in her." Judging from patterns in years to come, though, she may have noted the symptoms herself. She may have warned Charles that she felt worried and uncomfortable, afraid that her behavior might erupt in ways she could not control, prompting his morning search for Dr. Pitcairn. She may well have been experiencing the classic symptoms of anxiety: shaking hands, racing heart, shallow breathing, lightheadedness, an aversion to eating, lack of focus, vague feelings of panic and dread.

Physicians of her day regarded a woman experiencing such symptoms as nearing a state of delirium, caused by "inequality in the excitement of the brain," as explained by William Cullen, a Scottish physician and author of *First Lines of the Practice of Physic* (1777), then a standard medical reference. Although it was considered a disease, delirium revealed itself through intellectual aberrations, "a false or mistaken judgment," for example, different from the judgment formed by "the generality of men" or even from that which "the person himself had before usually formed."[1]

In telling Charles about her feelings of anxiety, Mary Lamb was asking for help. She was, Charles wrote Coleridge, "conscious of a certain flightiness in her poor head oftentimes, & mindful of more than one severe illness of that Nature before."[2] Maybe Mary already knew those feelings, that progression from inward anxiety to manic expression that was to plague her all her life. Medical experts of her day recognized the pattern. "A hurry of mind," as Cullen wrote, can lead "to some action which is always pushed with impetuosity and violence," and "often with respect to their former dearest friends and relations."[3]

Noting such symptoms, the well-informed doctor of the late eighteenth century responded first and foremost with physical restraint. "Angry passions are always rendered more violent by the indulgence of the impetuous motions they produce," Cullen advised. "Restraint, therefore, is useful, and ought to be complete; but it should be executed in the easiest manner possible for the patient, and the strait waistcoat answers every purpose better than any other that has yet been thought of."[4]

Building upon the concept of "an inequality of excitement in the brain," Cullen reviewed every technique already in practice to treat manic behavior. Bloodletting was a valuable method for balancing body fluids, he believed, but cutting open the jugular vein "is very often inconvenient." He proposed opening a vein in the arm instead. Enough blood should be let that the patient experiences a "deliquium animi"—that is, faints—"which is always a pretty certain mark of some diminution of the fulness [sic] and tension of the vessels of the brain."[5] Purgatives relieved not only the bowels but also the "fulness and tension of the vessels," while vomiting might actually "do harm by impelling the blood too forcibly into the vessels of the brain."[6] Better that the physician practice cupping, or blistering, Cullen advised, by applying heated glass cups or irritating ointments to the critical body part. Blisters and sores draw the patient's blood toward them, thus rearranging bodily fluids.[7]

Since heat excites, cold must do the opposite, posited Cullen. From that principle he advised that "maniacs have often been relieved, and sometimes entirely cured, by the use of cold bathing"—especially when practiced by "throwing the madman in the cold water by surprise; by detaining him in it for some length of time; and pouring water frequently upon the head, while the whole of the body except the head is immersed in the water. . . . This, I can affirm, has been often useful."[8] Cullen considered opium "a powerful remedy of mania." The most effective cure, though, was fear. "A very constant impression of fear," Cullen advised, will "inspire them with the awe and dread of some particular persons, especially of those who are to be constantly near them."[9] With well-read physicians following Cullen's advice, Mary Lamb could fall victim to treatments even more painful and humiliating than those George III had suffered a decade before, and all in the name of medical science.

LONDON OFFERED a number of possible residences that cared for the mentally infirm: two mental hospitals, at least sixteen private, licensed madhouses, and an untold number of smaller, unlicensed madhouses. We have some records from a few of London's late-eighteenth-century private madhouses, but many have disappeared. The choices really came down to the dichotomy expressed by the poet Andrew Marvell a century before. In 1672, arguing against a dogmatic Anglican, Marvell said that the cleric had raved so long, "he is fit for nothing but *Bedlam* or *Hogsdon*."[10] Bethlem or Hoxton—a hospital or a private madhouse: Mary Lamb faced the same alternatives.

The process of enrolling her in Bethlem would have been quite straightforward. A family member put forth a petition to the governors of the hospital, certifying that the candidate was a lunatic. In Mary Lamb's case, with the coroner's decision, there would have been no argument. Further information to be offered during the application procedure was the person's age, how long her senses had been disordered, the first instance of such, whether or not she had attempted mischief, and her condition of health. A Bethlem subcommittee met every Saturday morning at eleven to consider the week's petitions. If the Lambs had applied, a witness to their circumstances—someone who could certify that the family deserved charity—would appear before the committee. If all went well at this stage, the committee would invite Mary herself to meet with them the following week, at which point they would determine if her case appeared suitable for the hospital.[11]

England's first residence built specifically to house the insane, Bethlem replaced an earlier Bishopsgate facility that started as a priory in 1247, became a hospital in the 1330s, and as early as 1403 was quartering *sex viri mentecapti:* six insane men.[12] For centuries the same body of governors ran Bethlem Hospital and Bridewell, London's infamous palace-turned-poorhouse-turned-prison, an indication of how the English tended to lump the poor and the insane together as similar civic challenges.

The Bethlem Hospital building of Mary Lamb's time had once been called a palace for lunatics, though by 1796 it was falling into ruin. Designed by Robert Hooke, a sometime collaborator of Sir Christopher Wren, Bethlem spread grandly, 550 feet from one end to the other, just outside London's city wall and facing Moorfields, a public green. The original building was erected in 1676. Wings on either end were added in the 1730s, male and female quarters for the incurables. After that it could accommodate as many as 250 inmates.[13]

Ornamented like a palace of olden days, as grand as a museum of our time, Bethlem was built for viewing. Londoners could stroll the green, edge the sailing pond, and gaze through Bethlem's filigree fences at the inmates' exercise yard, which stretched the full width of the building. They could stroll down the tree-lined entry for a closer look at the two massive stone sculptures of Melancholy and Mania, Bethlem's Gog and Magog, who greeted every inmate and visitor. Melancholy stretched out sensuously, as if languishing in his supine state, belly loose and vacant visage limply smiling. Mania clenched his fists and tightened every muscle, lifting the chain and wrist manacle, neck taut, face wrenched by agony.

Past Bethlem's two gruesome gatekeepers strode many a curious gentleman and lady, for a visit to Bethlem was a popular Sunday outing. One visitor recalled how, during Easter week in 1753, "to my great surprise, I found a hundred people at least, who, having paid their two pence apiece, were suffered, unattended, to run rioting up and down the wards, making sport and diversion of the miserable inhabitants."[14] Officials banned gawkers in 1770, but the curious could still take a tour. All Britain used the hospital's name—"Bedlam"—to speak of chaos and disorder. Today, administrators at Bethlem Royal Hospital, relocated south of London in Beckenham, Kent, carefully avoid the word.

One hundred twenty years after its glorious construction, Bethlem at Moorfields was run-down and filthy. Built on fill dirt piled over rubbish in an old City ditch, designed without proper architectural foundations, the whole building was sinking. Not a floor was level, and many interior walls were giving way. A survey of the building in 1791 found conditions "in such a state as to endanger the Health of the patients."[15] Eight years later, inspectors still found the building "dreary, low, melancholy, and not well aired."[16] The condition of the building alone would have been reason for Charles Lamb to insist, against the will of his older brother, that their sister not be sent there.

Mary Lamb could instead have entered St. Luke's Hospital,

founded in 1751 through public subscription as an alternative to Bethlem. This new facility positioned itself opposite Bethlem both geographically and philosophically. It stood on the north edge of Moorfields, facing Bethlem to the south. At St. Luke's the mad received treatment based on medical principles, declared the hospital's founding physician, William Battie. A child of the Enlightenment, Battie argued that the treatment of insanity, just like the treatment of any other disease, should be guided by knowledge and study. His claims implicitly called into question the treatment that madmen and madwomen received just across the green. These philosophical differences became the subject of public debate.

For a century and a half, a family dynasty of physicians had been managing Bethlem Hospital. James Monro, Bethlem physician from 1728 to 1752, believed that the treatment of the insane was "a subject that can be understood no otherwise than by personal observation."[17] He neither referred to the medical principles of others nor articulated his own. His reputation as one of London's great eighteenth-century mad doctors stood primarily on his valiantly long tenure at Bethlem. His son John took over on his father's death and served even longer. John in turn raised his youngest son into the trade, and Thomas Monro became physician at Bethlem in 1792. He had a deep interest in art: He himself both painted and collected paintings, but, more important, he held a weekly "academy" that drew young artists, notably J. M. W. Turner, whose own mother was Monro's patient at Bethlem.

Monro's aesthetics instilled a respect for the art of the insane that is still integral to the Bethlem tradition today. But in other ways his practices were archaic, as revealed in the public debates he waged with Battie, the physician at St. Luke's. William Battie had articulated his new ideas on mental patient care in his *Treatise on Madness* (1758). "Madness, though a terrible and at present a very frequent calamity, is perhaps as little understood as any that ever afflicted mankind," it began. "The names alone usually given to this disorder and its several species, *viz. Lunacy, Spleen, Melancholy, Hurry of the Spirits, &c.,* may convince any one of the truth of this assertion."[18]

Influenced by Locke's Enlightenment philosophy of the mind as a blank slate on which incoming impressions accumulate into known ideas, Battie defines madness as "the too lively or the too languid perception of things." Treatment should begin with "the patient's being removed from all objects that act forcibly upon the nerves." He argues against every technique in his contemporaries' repertoires—bleeding, blistering, purges, vomiting, opium, mineral waters for drinking or bathing. These treatments tend to clog or strain "the vessels of the brain or nervous integuments" and "endanger a rupture or further disunion, instead of a deliverance from their oppressive loads." Management, not medicine, is madness's best treatment.[19]

Goaded into a public debate against his will, Monro grudgingly published his *Remarks on Dr. Battie's Treatise.* "I should rather define madness to be vitiated judgment," he argued. He assumed a righteous tone and simply stated the obvious rather than arguing from first principles, as Battie had done so well. Evacuation, vomiting, bleeding, and blistering had shown their effectiveness simply by having been used successfully over and over. "Why should we endeavour to give the world a shocking opinion of a remedy, that is not only safe, but greatly useful?"[20]

The Battie-Monro argument set the parameters for a generation of debate over the treatment of the mentally ill. Techniques of physical restraint, "fluid evacuation" (to use Monro's term), and severe drugging continued into the nineteenth century, not only in Bethlem but in the private madhouses as well. Worse than that, some madhouses—and to some extent, even Bethlem—operated simply as holding tanks or prisons, as became more evident when conscientious citizens and then government officials began investigating them. As late as 1814, inspectors visiting Bethlem reported seeing room after room of patients chained by their arms or legs to the wall. Women wore "blanket-gowns" and men were naked. The inspectors reported that some rooms conveyed "the complete appearance of a dog-kennel," odor and all.[21]

Battie and St. Luke's exemplified a new idea, the moral management of the mentally ill. Just as Francis Willis had looked George III in the eye and talked about his behavior, so the late-eighteenth-century innovators in mental care believed in engaging the minds, hearts, and wills of their patients, not just restraining their bodies and manipulating their fluids. Moral management blossomed in full not in London but in York, where William and Samuel Tuke, grandfather and grandson, ran the Retreat, founded in 1792 under the auspices of the Society of Friends, or the Quakers.

CHARLES LAMB sought a setting where Mary would be treated with kindness. He could not afford to place Mary in Whitmore House, the madhouse for aristocrats, reputed to be the city's best. Whitmore House was owned and operated by Thomas Warburton, the magnate of London-area madhouses. Warburton began his career as the Whitmore House gatekeeper, married its owner's widow, and ultimately became the paterfamilias of three generations of madhouse keepers. Whitmore House was located in an aging Hoxton mansion called Balmes House (whence, some believe, our word "balmy"). Care there cost as much as fifteen hundred pounds a year. For that an aristocratic madman lived in a private wing, tended by a personal keeper, secure in the knowledge that his presence there would be kept secret. Neither money nor rank could protect him, though, from the strait waistcoat and bed chains.

Charles must have considered Hoxton House, one of London's largest and longest-established private madhouses. It was "a large brick house" with "extensive grounds at the back," recalled Londoner John Hollingshead, who grew up nearby.[22] In the 1790s Hoxton House was operated by Jonathan Miles, a sheriff and alderman of the City of London who had taken over for his father in 1772. Records from 1815 show 486 patients living at Hoxton House, although there may have been fewer twenty years earlier. Many were paupers, whose parishes sent them for about seventy pounds a year. Many others were naval patients, for from 1792 on, the Admiralty sent lunatic officers and sailors to Hoxton House at the government's expense.[23] When the inspector of naval hospitals visited Hoxton House in 1815, he reported conditions to be "exceedingly bad." Patients were not categorized: the violent roomed with the introverted, the sick with the well. Some shared beds. The exercise grounds were tiny for the numbers, with no shade or furniture. Inmates stood during meals and were allowed no implements.[24]

Rooms full of battle-scarred, fever-riddled sailors—it was a scene from which Charles Lamb would have wanted to protect his sister. Such conditions don't seem to have bothered Charles himself, though. Charles knew Hoxton House from the inside out, since this was where he had been a patient. In fact, he claimed to have rather enjoyed his six weeks there: "At some future time I will amuse you with an account as full as my memory will permit of the strange turn my *phrensy* took," he promised Coleridge. "I look back upon it *at times* with a gloomy kind of *Envy*. For while it lasted I had many many hours of pure happiness." Opiates may have influenced Charles's blissful madhouse experience, which he said was touched with "all the grandeur & wildness of *Fancy*."[25]

With such sentimental memories, Charles Lamb knew that the right madhouse setting could be good for his sister Mary. He followed David Pitcairn's advice and took her to Fisher House, a modestly priced, smaller private madhouse in Islington. There

Mary would be somewhat far away—about a two-hour walk from Little Queen Street or East India House—but she would be in quiet, countrified surroundings. Islington was a village that Charles already knew and liked. "To me 'tis Classical ground," he had told Coleridge just two months before.[26]

With its high ground and open air, Islington had for centuries been regarded as the place to go for health and refreshment. At town center stood (and still stands) Canonbury Tower, built in the early sixteenth century, home to a lord mayor of London and then, from 1616 to 1625, to essayist and philosopher Sir Francis Bacon.[27] When Oliver Goldsmith wasn't residing in the Temple, he was in his country quarters in Islington. All these uplifting connections made Fisher House, and Islington, the right choice.

Islington was a green expanse beyond the edge of the city when Mary Lamb moved there in 1796. The town center still had a village feel to it, with the Angel Inn the favorite gathering place. A nursery and a vegetable market anchored the community in its agricultural past, but surrounding pastures were being eyed for metropolitan development. A tea and muslin warehouse provided employment, distributing imports brought in by the East India Company. Brick estates now skirted the village's northern edges, the first signs that Islington was becoming a suburb. A brick factory now operated northwest of town, providing materials for the burst of middle-class residences going up in villages all around London.

Fisher House, where Mary Lamb went to live, lorded over the village center near the Angel. Rumored to have cost four thousand pounds when built in the early 1600s, Sir Thomas Fisher's house was once the largest in the parish.[28] By 1796 Fisher House had declined and crumbled. It was a sign of the times that enterprising middle-class owners revived it by turning it into a residence for the insane.

OVER THE COURSE of Mary Lamb's first week at Fisher House, Charles Lamb met and talked with the mother and daughter who operated the madhouse. They appeared to be goodhearted, hardworking, earnest, and compassionate, yet they were almost certainly uneducated. The primary job of a madhouse staff was simply to watch over the residents and rein in their behavior. Government licensure required nothing more than an annual visit by the attending physician. If a patient needed attention from a doctor or an apothecary, the family made those arrangements.

It is possible that in her first few days as a patient at Fisher House, Mary Lamb received some of the standard treatments: physical restraint, seclusion, intimidation, bloodletting, blistering, purgatives. She may have been diagnosed with fevers and made to take tartar emetic—potassium antimony tartrate, a poison given in small doses to cause vomiting. She likely spent early hours, maybe days, strapped into a strait waistcoat, her arms shoved into sleeves with no openings, the laces cinched down her back, her arms folded across her chest, tied down securely by straps stitched onto the sleeve ends and wrapped around her middle. If her manic behavior continued—if she fought physical restraint or other treatments—the madhouse keeper may have administered opium, most likely in the form of laudanum, an alcohol solution or tincture.

The first small doses of opium would calm the patient. Only after repeated use, accelerating into an addiction, would opium bring on the sort of physical and mental agonies that Samuel Taylor Coleridge later experienced. Ironically, just six weeks after Mary's Fisher House confinement, Coleridge took his first dose of opium, treatment for a severe onset of neuralgia: "I was seized with an intolerable pain from my right temple to the tip of my right shoulder," he wrote on November 5, 1796, "but I took between 60 & 70 drops of Laudanum, and *sopped* the Cerberus just as his mouth began to open."[29] That incident marked the beginning of painful decades in Coleridge's life, cycles of illness cured, then caused, by overuse of opium—decades during which his addiction evoked both sympathy and anger in his friends, Mary and Charles Lamb.

WITH HIS MOTHER buried, his sister in Fisher House, his aunt revived, and his father still playing cribbage, Charles Lamb established a new routine. He could rise early, walk north for a visit to Islington, and get to the East India Company by ten. Or he could leave his office at four with a detour to Islington, arriving home for a late supper. One presumes he visited faithfully, although Mary's caretakers may not have allowed him to see her in the early days of her confinement, a common practice in madhouses large and small.

"I have seen her," he wrote to Coleridge on October 3, letting the ink spread broadly. "I found her this morning calm & serene, far very very far from an indecent forgetful serenity." She was not, in other words, drugged into oblivion, nor had she slipped into so deep a depression or so deranged a state of mind that she could ignore the seriousness of the act she had committed. "She has a most affectionate & tender concern for what has happend [*sic*]," Charles wrote. Two strengths saved her, so he believed: "her strength of mind, & religious principle."[30]

Despite that comment the Lambs were not a particularly religious family, nor did religion play much of a part in the recovery and continuing life of Mary and Charles Lamb. Charles may have wanted the help of religion, as he wrote Coleridge soon after the death of his mother. Devotions seemed the proper way to respond, but he needed his friend to guide him through them. "Write,—as religious a letter as possible—," Charles Lamb had desperately asked.[31]

"You bid me write a religious letter," answered Coleridge. A young man who had considered a career in the pulpit, he wrote a letter with more sermon than sympathy. "I am not a man who would attempt to insult the greatness of your anguish by any other consolation. The Comforter that should relieve you is not far from you." Charles responded with thanks, calling Coleridge's letter "an inestimable treasure"[32] and reading it and others out loud to Mary. But while Charles Lamb saw the value of religion, he never truly belonged. "I want more religion," he once wrote Coleridge.[33] A Victorian biographer ascribed to him a "wayward, fitful, disturbed piety,"[34] and his sister likewise seems to have respected religion without practicing it. The friends who became closest to them included religious dissenters, Unitarians, Quakers, and atheists.

Ten days after her collapse, Mary Lamb was already returning to herself. "The Lady at this Mad house assures me that I may dismiss immediately both Doctor & Apothecary, retaining occasionally an opening draught or so for a while," Charles wrote. Once the madhouse keepers determined how compliant and altogether helpful Mary Lamb was, they were willing, so Charles reported, to transfer her into a less expensive group room with a shared nurse. The charge for these services would be about sixty pounds per year—just the amount that Charles had carefully determined he could afford. The lowered cost of keeping her there depended as well on Mary's willingness to do household chores at the madhouse. She probably spent some time each day mending the strained seams of the stiff white canvas strait waistcoats.

In what little time she had to herself, Mary Lamb read. Charles brought books to Fisher House, but she outstripped him in the speed with which she read them. "I am rather at a loss sometimes for books for her," he wrote a month into her Fisher House stay. "We have nearly exhausted our London library. She has her hands too full of work to read much, but a little she must read; for reading was her daily bread."[35]

Mary quickly ingratiated herself with her keepers at Fisher House. "She will, I fancy, if she stays, make one of the family, rather than of the patients," Charles wrote Coleridge. "The old & young ladies I like *exceedingly,* & she loves dearly, & they, as the saying is take to her *very* extraordinaryily, if it is extraordinary that people who see my sister should love her. Of all the people I ever saw in the world my poor sister was most & throughly devoid of the least tincture of *selfishness.* [*sic*]"[36] That was the sort of comment often made about Mary Lamb. Throughout her life those who knew her repeated Charles's portrayal of a humble, unprepossessing woman, the furthest one could imagine from a maniac or a murderer.

"Dressed with Quaker-like simplicity in dove-coloured silk, with a transparent kerchief of snow-white muslin folded across her bosom," wrote one acquaintance later in life, "she at once prepossessed the beholder in her favour, by an aspect of serenity and peace."[37] "Her manner was easy, almost homely, so quiet, unaffected, and perfectly unpretending was it," wrote another.[38] Skeptics might ascribe Mary Lamb's lifelong amiability to mental vacantness. Often those who choose to relegate her to the footnotes characterize her as dimwitted or mentally incompetent. But her contemporaries would argue otherwise. "Beneath the sparing talk and retired carriage, few casual observers would have suspected the ample information and large intelligence that lay comprised there," continued the friend above, as if to counter that very assumption. "In the modest-havioured woman simply sitting there, taking small share in general conversation, few who did not know her would have imagined the accomplished classical scholar, the excellent understanding the altogether rarely-gifted being, morally and mentally, that Mary Lamb was."[39]

Others—in particular feminist scholars—argue that Mary Lamb's madhouse experiences damaged and muffled her. Sarah Burton, the recent Lamb biographer, hypothesizes that in a later confinement Mary Lamb may have experienced and no doubt witnessed abuses ranging from force-feeding to whipping.[40] Bonnie Woodberry extrapolates from imagery in Mary Lamb's writing evidence that she experienced bloodletting, dunking, blistering, and purges—all madhouse methods intended to effect "a general silencing of madness."[41]

But the very fact of being female in the year 1796 was enough to keep a woman silent. Mary may have undergone harsh physical treatment when she first arrived at Fisher House, and in subsequent madhouse settings as well. It was the standard medical practice of her time, and it probably did compound the demoralizing messages she had already received since birth as a serving-class woman of the eighteenth century. But Mary Lamb thrived, too, in Fisher House. Through time alone and time with other women, she came back into her own as a productive and worthwhile individual, connecting, human to human, with those around her. "The good Lady of the Mad house, & her daughter, an elegant sweet behaved young Lady, love her & are taken with her amazingly, & I know from her *own* mouth she loves them, & longs to be with them as much,"[42] Charles reported.

In less than a month at Fisher House, Mary Lamb reached a state of self-acceptance. Her act of murder, while undeniably bad and wrong, did not undo the hours, days, and years of kindness she had devoted to her mother. She talked with Charles about these thoughts. She assured him that her conscience rested easily in the knowledge that, all told, she had been a good daughter. "It is my Sister's gratifying recollection," Charles wrote, "that every act of duty & of love she could pay, every kindness . . . thro' a long course of infirmities & sickness, she could shew her, *she ever did*."[43] These are the memories that helped Mary Lamb stay afloat amid guilt over killing her mother. Never do we hear her express, never does Charles report, an outright statement of remorse for the act. Some see this omission as a sign of Mary's dementia. It may as likely reflect their acceptance of the larger justice of her act and its consequences.

Through Charles, we can almost hear Mary Lamb's own voice, telling us how she felt after a month in Fisher House. "Mary continues serene & chearful [*sic*]," he wrote to Coleridge in mid-October.[44] "I have not by me a little letter she wrote to me, for tho' I see her almost every day yet we delight to write to one another (for we can scarce see each other but in company with some of the people of the house), I have not the letter by me but will quote from memory what she wrote in it:

> I have no bad terrifying dreams. At midnight when I happen to awake, the nurse sleeping by the side of *me,* with the noise of the poor mad people around me, I have no fear. The spirit of my mother seems to descend, & smile upon me, & bid me *live* to enjoy the life & reasons which the Almighty has given me——. I shall see her again in heaven; she will then understand me better."

4

READING, WRITING, AND MANTUA MAKING

FTER SIX MONTHS in Fisher House, Mary Lamb moved out of the madhouse and into a room of her own. "I have taken her out of her confinement," Charles wrote on April 7, 1797, "and taken a room for her at Hackney, and spend my Sundays, holidays, &c., with her. She boards herself."[1] We know nothing more about her circumstances. Chances are good that she was placed in the care of kind householders who were willing to watch over her for any recurrence of irrational behavior. Even if she had caretakers, her new circumstances were a far cry from living in a madhouse.

From Islington to Hackney was a move east from village to village, both about the same distance from Charles in London. Hackney was a tolerant community, a gathering place for those with religious views other than Anglican. No record remains of the address where Mary Lamb lived, but it was probably a room above a little business establishment along Church Street, the main north-south thoroughfare. The bells in the thirteenth-century church tower rang their hollow sounds on the hour. Just after Mary moved to Hackney, the antique church shut its doors. Crowds gathered for the consecration of the new Saint John's, built to accommodate a good two thousand worshipers. Perhaps, waking at dawn, Mary would cross the bridge over Hackney Brook and walk by the moon's last light down to Morning Lane and the watercress beds, where crisp greens were picked daily, spring and fall, and carried to the London markets.

Not many single women in their thirties would want to live by themselves in turn-of-the-nineteenth-century London, but Mary Lamb was not the sort of woman to worry about appearances. An acquaintance from later in life wrote that she stood under middle height, with brown eyes, well-cut features, and a winning smile. "There was a certain catch, or emotional breathingness, in her utterance," a "yearning, eager effect in her voice" that made people listen more closely. She tended toward plumpness and dressed in simple clothing, tucking her brown hair into a mobcap long after these gathered cloth headpieces went out of style.

Taking a step back out into the world, Mary Lamb likely returned to the trade she knew best. As a mantua maker she worked at home on garments for women and men, sewing and mending. The English derived their word "mantua" from the French for "coat," *manteau*. One hundred years before, a lady called her loose overdress her mantua and wore it over her bone-ribbed and bodice-cinched dress.[2] As ladies' fashions loosened up, so did the meaning of the word, which came to designate women's garments in general and, occasionally, a particular sort of silk out of which they might be made. By 1797 "mantua" covered all sorts of clothing, at least when used to name the trade of mantua making. Over Mary Lamb's years of work as a mantua maker, the record shows her making gowns and petticoats for ladies, waistcoats for gentlemen, and caps for infants. Coleridge once asked her to stitch him some silk slippers, but she demurred, saying that the cloth would not work for soles.[3]

In the realm of needlework, as in so many other aspects of English life at the time, a hierarchy prevailed. A mantua maker fell somewhere between a journeyman tailor and a seamstress who made shirts and smocks.[4] Ready-made clothing was beginning to appear in London shops, shipped in from newly industrial cities like Leeds, so custom-made clothing had become a sign of distinction. Everyone who mattered could tell the difference at a glance.

A milliner, distinguishable from a mantua maker, operated a storefront. (Not until the late nineteenth century was the term limited to hatmakers.) Milliners not only sewed clothing but sold the fabric for it—silk, serge, lawn, cambric, calico, muslin. Political strife had caused American cotton and French silk and satin to disappear from the shops, but by 1797 plenty of cotton from India and silk from China were coming in, thanks to the East India Company. Brilliant dyes colored the white cloth—cochineal red, indigo blue. In the cotton mills new roller printers pressed colorful patterns onto yards of fabric in one pass. Silk thread arrived regularly at the docks of London, destined for the Hackney silk mills.

A mantua maker neither operated a shop nor stocked fabric. Customers brought her clothing that needed mending or alterations, or they bought fabric from a milliner or mercer for her to make into a garment. Every mantua maker in London was expected to be "a perfect Conoisseur [*sic*] in Dress and Fashion," as noted in an eighteenth-century commentary on the tradesmen of London.[5] She would be expected to know the styles of the time, so that when a customer brought in lengths of taffeta and muslin asking for a sacque dress, she knew just how to fashion it—and knew to suggest a few tucks or flounces, a line of buttons, or an edging of lace to make the dress unique. A mantua maker who stitched ladies' dresses or gentlemen's trousers needed to have an ample curtained closet, if not a separate changing room, for the sake of modesty.

Milliners and mantua makers had to behave with extreme discretion in order to compensate for the reputation they had acquired over the years. Comedies through the eighteenth century capitalized on the stereotype of the lascivious dressmaker. Robert Drury's 1737 play, *The Rival Milliners*, titillated audiences by dramatizing a shop full of chattering young apprentice dressmakers, all eager to win over their gentlemen customers. An engraving made to illustrate a 1770 printed edition of the play echoed the insinuation. Two milliners dote on a well-dressed gentleman, both taking the liberty of touching his body in ways that would not be proper in any other setting. One encircles his wrist with her hands, measuring for cuffs, while the other holds a ruler against the breadth of his shoulders. Flirtatious glances dart among the threesome. For extra titillation the artist draped a length of lace on the milliners' worktable, with one end falling between the gentleman's legs and drawing the eye to the bulge in his crotch.[6]

Through the eighteenth century, women read novels spun of the same stereotype. In Eliza Haywood's 1751 novel, *The History of Miss Betsy Thoughtless,* the naive main character is pressed by her mantua maker, Mrs. Modely, to marry a man who has spied on her during a fitting. Betsy Thoughtless's passion for the finest in clothing signals a shallow character and moral vulnerability. *The Cherub,* published anonymously in 1792, promised in its subtitle to be a "Guardian of Female Innocence, Exposing the Arts of," among other things, "corrupt Milliners and apparent Ladies of Fashion." Part advisory and part bawdy narrative, the book warned female readers that its omniscient character, the "Cherub," had often "observed the secret scenes, the nocturnal orgies of sensuality, the midnight immolations of female virtue, which are made, and celebrated behind the folding shop doors of a millinery deception."[7]

Drama, art, and fiction pick out tendencies and exaggerate them, but they also affirm those stereotypes in the public mind. Every time Mary Lamb measured a customer's waist or shoulders, she risked an action that could be misconstrued. It was an anxiety she never mentioned, but it must have irritated her nonetheless. Only when economics reorganized the clothing industry—first when middle-class women took up the needle for their own families, then when factory-made clothing became the norm—did the stereotype dissolve. Those social advances brought on other problems for the working class of women who depended on mantua making for a living, as Mary Lamb would later argue in her essay "On Needle-work."

MARY LAMB may well have read *Miss Betsy Thoughtless* and *The Cherub*. They are titles little known today, but then many of the books that fascinated an avid female reader in 1797 are lost to all but a few scholars, collectors, and librarians. Women may not have gained gender equality on many fronts, but books and magazines they had in number.

By the end of the eighteenth century the majority of English women and men knew how to read. Evangelicals, who believed that reading Scripture could lift the poor in spirit and living condition, taught reading in Sunday schools and evening classes across Britain. In 1797 there were at least two privately run lending libraries in the little village of Hackney alone and dozens in London, although the great blooming of commercial libraries would not occur until the 1830s and '40s.[8] Reading was becoming a daily practice for everyone, women and men, aristocrats and merchants, even servants and tradespeople. Later in life Mary Lamb fondly watched as a friend's adolescent daughter taught her maid to read.[9]

Printers worked hard to keep pace with the demand, and the volume of material printed in London grew tremendously through the eighteenth century. Seventy printing presses operated in London in 1724; thirty years later that number had tripled.[10] Annual English newspaper sales totaled 7.3 million copies in 1750, up to more than sixteen million in 1790.[11] In 1793 sixteen different daily newspapers covered London alone, along with some fifty other provincial newspapers across the country.[12] A newspaper wasn't cheap. One day's issue of *The Times* cost four and a half pence, the equivalent of more than one pound today.[13] Many Londoners read the news at local coffeehouses and taverns or passed each day's issue around among friends.

Londoners chose from scores of different magazines as well, some specifically for women. London's first women's magazine appeared before 1700. As a female readership grew, the choices proliferated. The *Lady's Weekly Magazine,* most successful of all, was established in 1770, and after that came the *Lady's Curiosity,* the *Old Maid* (which lasted only six months), the *Young Lady,* and the *Lady's Museum.* When a "Society of Ladies" began in 1798 publishing the *Lady's Monthly Museum* (subtitled *A Polite Repository of Amusement and Instruction*), they announced their intent to publish "an assemblage of whatever can please the fancy, interest the mind and exalt the character of the British Fair."[14] Women's magazines reported on political events, profiled great women of history, and offered mildly moralistic advice. Fashion, food, and sex—mainstays of today's women's magazines—appeared rarely. Fashion too haughtily drew attention to one's self; food was the concern of the serving class; and sex was on the one hand unmentionable but on the other every wife's duty, needing no discussion.

Women were reading more books than ever, creating a growing demand for, as John Stuart Mill called it a few decades later, "a literature of their own."[15] Some have argued that at the end of the eighteenth century, the British woman was a more commercially important reader than the British man.[16] In Mary Lamb's era women read nonfiction—travelogues, almanacs, and conduct books like *Letters on the Improvement of the Mind, Addressed to a Young Lady* (1773) and *An Inquiry into the Duties of the Female Sex* (1797). Written by both women and men, these books about courtesy and morals guided daughters, wives, and mothers on the path to domestic happiness.

And women read fiction—"that branch of the literary trade" represented by novels and romances, "almost entirely engrossed by the ladies," writers and readers alike, according to a 1773 article in the *Monthly Review*.[17] One modern researcher concluded that between 1780 and 1830, women dominated among published novelists.[18] Traditionalists of the time worried that a passion for fiction would lead a woman astray. Women deserved equal education not to increase their amusement but to improve their behavior as wives and mothers. As author and reading advocate Hannah More explained,

> The chief end . . . in cultivating the understandings of women, is to qualify them for the practical purposes of life. Their knowledge is not often like the learning of men, to be reproduced in some literary composition, and never in any learned profession; but it is to come out in conduct. A lady studies, not that she may qualify herself to become an orator or a pleader; not that she may learn to debate, but to act. She is to read the best books, not so much to enable her to talk of them, as to bring the improvement which they furnish, to the rectification of her principles, and the formation of her habits. The great uses of study to a woman are to enable her to regulate her own mind, and to be instrumental to the good of others.[19]

The act of a woman reading was charged with moral and political ambiguity. A reading woman could take the opportunity to improve herself—or she could succumb to temptations and overstep social bounds. Coleridge advised men, when reading to their wives and daughters, to edit any language that might "offend the delicacy of female ears, and shock feminine susceptibility."[20] Curious and gullible women might be swayed by the democratic and atheistic ideas expressed in books like Thomas Paine's *The Rights of Man* (1771), Mary Wollstonecraft's *A Vindication of the Rights of Woman* (1772), or William Godwin's *Enquiry Concerning Political Justice* (1773). In 1799, the *Lady's Monthly Museum* printed a letter from a worried mother, warning that reading Wollstonecraft's book had ruined all three of her daughters. One lost "all that softness so amiable in a woman"; one "applies herself to books," ignoring all her womanly chores; and one became so interested in studying the human body that she began attending anatomy lectures disguised as a boy![21]

Romances could turn a woman reader's head. A compulsive reader might even go mad, like the main character in Charlotte Lennox's popular novel, *The Female Quixote, or the Adventures of Arabella* (1752). Raised in rural seclusion, Arabella based her worldview entirely on the French romances she read. She shaped her behavior and judged that of others according to expectations appropriate only within the exaggeratedly courtly and melodramatic world of the romance. Her story is unrealistic, probably satiric of prevailing attitudes of the times, but nevertheless a mirror of contemporary concerns.

Toward the end of the eighteenth century, plot overtook moral message. Writers began to explore more realistic characters and situations and tackled more ambiguous questions of conscience. Mary Wollstonecraft wrote in the preface to her novel *Maria, or the Wrongs of Woman* (published posthumously, 1798) that she intended to portray passions, not manners. The consummate art in the novels of Jane Austen, published a decade or two later, was her ability to portray both.

Books like these were the blockbusters of the late eighteenth century, and bibliophiles like Mary Lamb read them all. Throughout her life Mary Lamb preferred a domestic novel or a passionate adventure to just about any other kind of book—especially the old tracts and antique tomes that her brother favored. In his essay "Mackery End, in Hertfordshire," Charles Lamb teasingly distinguishes his sister's reading habits from his own inclination to pore over books like the seventeenth-century *Anatomy of Melancholy* by Robert Burton, a work he admired and cribbed for contemporaries.

> We are both great readers in different directions. While I am hanging over (for the thousandth time) some passage in old Burton, or one of his strange contemporaries, she is abstracted in some modern tale, or adventure, whereof our common reading-table is daily fed with assiduously fresh supplies. Narrative teases me. I have little concern in the progress of events. She must have a story—well, ill, or indifferently told—so there be life stirring in it, and plenty of good or evil accidents.

Booksellers paid more attention to the demand among female readers for a story than they did to the moralistic naysayers. The 1790s represented a decade of swift growth in both the numbers of readers and the volume of publicly available reading material, even though the political climate set booksellers on edge. The king and Parliament were inclined to identify any freethinking author—like Paine, Wollstonecraft, or Godwin—as a Jacobin, a radical, a supporter of the French Revolution, likely to incite rebellion on British soil. The booksellers who cranked out such incendiary works—in cheap editions, clearly intended for the masses of new middle- and working-class readers—bore equal responsibility.

Reformers had been rabblerousing for years, since the time of the American Revolution. They argued that the gain of England's Glorious Revolution of 1688, a truly representative Parliament, had never been fully implemented. But as the threat of a French invasion loomed, officials cracked down on antiestablishment messengers. John Thelwall, son of a London silk mercer, took up the reform cause, lecturing throughout the country and drawing thousands to the cause. In 1794, when he and two compatriots, shoemaker Thomas Hardy and linguist John Horne Tooke, organized a convention on parliamentary reform, they were arrested for treason. They escaped conviction, but the high-profile hearing clearly conveyed a message to everyone inclined to wield the pen on behalf of democracy in Britain. And now Thelwall's lectures were being printed on cheap stock, for all to read. In 1795 Parliament first suspended habeas corpus, so officials could arrest suspects without showing cause, then it passed the Treasonable Practices and Seditious Meetings Act, vastly broadening the field of actions that could be called crimes against the Crown.

The streets were tense with the awareness of the power of the written word. No one could enter a lending library or a bookseller's shop without sensing it. Although the political censors cared little about novels and romance, Mary Lamb absorbed it all. Years later, writing her own works of fiction, she dramatized the power of reading on an unformed mind in the story, "The Young Mahometan." The story is narrated by Margaret Green, an only child who, after her father's death, moves into the grand country house of her widowed godmother, where her mother has been hired as a companion to the elderly woman. Margaret roams the vast house for "solitary amusement." Soon she dares to unlock the door to a "so-long-desired room": "It proved to be a very large library. This was indeed a precious discovery. I looked round on the books with the greatest delight. I thought I would read them every one. I now forsook all my favourite haunts, and passed all my time here. I took down first one book, then another."

Margaret discovers a book titled *Mahometanism Explained,* full of stories that she knows from the Bible, but told from a different perspective. Like a forbidden fruit, it tempts her into reading.

I know it was very wrong to read any book without permission to do so. . . . I forgot what was right and what was wrong. . . .

When I had almost learned the history of Ishmael by heart, I read the rest of the book, and then I came to the history of Mahomet, who was there said to be the last descendant of Abraham. . . . His history was full of nothing but wonders from the beginning to the end. The book said that those who believed all the wonderful stories which were related of Mahomet were called Mahometans, and True Believers:—I concluded that I must be a Mahometan, for I believed every word I read.

Margaret finds herself seeing the world through Mahometan eyes, but ultimately her secret devotions get the better of her, and "anxiety" develops into "a fever." "I was so ill that my mother thought it necessary to sleep in the same room with me," says Margaret. One night she nervously awakens her mother, reveals her fascination, and begs her to become a Mahometan. Declared "delirious," Margaret is put in the custody of a doctor and his wife.

What finally saves Margaret from her Mahometan madness is a trip to the Harlow fair—a return to the simple pleasures of English country life. The kind doctor's wife buys her a workbasket, complete with needle case and pincushion, introduces her to other children, and informs her that the author of *Mahometanism Explained* "did not mean to give the fabulous stories here related as true," but rather to share the fallacies of the Turks, "a very ignorant people." In a switch back to standard expectations, Mary Lamb ends by recanting Margaret's discoveries: "Perfectly cured of the error into which I had fallen," Margaret admits to be "very much ashamed of having believed so many absurdities."

By taking a book too seriously, Margaret Green adventured into a thrilling foreign and forbidden land, where she explored new boundaries between right and wrong. She is a childlike counterpart to the young heroines in the novels Mary Lamb devoured during her first months of independence in Hackney. In the long run both Margaret Green and Arabella, the "female Quixote," returned to a proper ladylike existence, but normal routines had been breached. Their minds had been opened. These characters dared to skirt the limits set by society, and they would never be the same. That could also be said of Mary Lamb.

5

CHARLES ALONE

I N AUGUST 1798 a cartoon appeared in the new and decidedly Tory *Anti-Jacobin Review and Magazine*. It spread across two pages, brimful of caricatures. Bat-winged raptors and scaly sea monsters (the largest of all a recognizable Prince of Wales, heir to the throne) join a throng of donkeys, toads, monkeys, and half-humans to worship at the altar of three grotesque hags labeled Justice, Philanthropy, and Sensibility. Dozens of pamphlets spill out of the "Cornucopia of Ignorance," and the ministers at the altar all hold printed works from which they appear to be reading aloud. "NEW MORALITY," reads the title below, "or The promis'd Installment of the High Priest of The Philanthropes, with the Homage of Leviathan and his Suite."

The foremost rider atop the central sea monster carries *Thelwall's Lectures*—it is the radical lecturer himself. A little donkey brays out, reading *Political Justice*—that's William Godwin. Among the books spilling out of the cornucopia is Mary Wollstonecraft's novel *Wrongs of Woman*. Another donkey, flourishing with his hand, reads *Coleridge Dactylics*. In the middle of the crowd, a pair of toads read together from a pamphlet titled *Blank Verse*. Beneath runs a poem in rhyming couplets, mocking the congregation of "the Men without a God," washed up on Egypt's shores where "Buonaparte's victor fleet" would protect them. The rhyme hints at identities, naming one of those toads as L_____B: Charles Lamb.

To understand how Charles Lamb found his way into the center of a political cartoon, identified with the most notorious radicals of the times, we must begin with Samuel Taylor Coleridge. The son of a North Country grammar school teacher, Coleridge was headed into the ministry. He preferred books to games and won acclaim for his precocious schoolwork. Like Charles Lamb he was recommended for entry into Christ's Hospital, the London charity school for boys. Lamb and Coleridge both entered in 1782. Coleridge was two years older and stayed at the school longer, until he was nearly nineteen, while Lamb withdrew at age fourteen and started to work.

At Christ's Hospital, Coleridge found himself far from home in a rigid and unfamiliar setting. Devotion to study was his main consolation, and he began to write poetry as well. Although he would spend years wandering, seeking some other occupation, he had already found his calling in life as a scholar, a philosopher, and a poet. He entered Cambridge University in October 1791.

Coleridge followed events unfolding in Paris. Crowds stormed the Bastille in 1789, taking the French Revolution to the streets. He read in detail Burke's 1790 pamphlet, *Reflections on the Revolution in France*—a manifesto written by the eminent parliamentarian, the man who had so boldly advocated independence for the American colonies but who now seemed to be quashing the democratic impulse among his own countrymen. "The people of England will not ape the fashions they have never tried," wrote Burke, as if revolution were a passing fancy, "nor go back to those which they have found mischievous on trial. They look upon the legal hereditary succession of the crown as among their rights, not as among their wrongs; as a benefit, not as a grievance; as a security for their liberty, not as a badge of servitude." To Burke (and, he believed, to all loyal British subjects), "the undisturbed succession of the crown" guaranteed the "stability and perpetuity" of the British empire.

Coleridge took great intellectual pleasure in the responses to

Burke that soon rolled off London presses. Mary Wollstonecraft's *A Vindication of the Rights of Men* (1793), then Thomas Paine's *The Rights of Man*, and many more—Samuel Taylor Coleridge surely read them all, honoring their principles even as efforts in France were going awry. Many intellectuals still spoke out on behalf of their country's own poor, calling for rights and equality. But now, in wartime, anyone who appeared to sympathize with the French Revolution—even if only in the realm of ideas—was seen as a traitor. When William Frend, Unitarian Fellow at Queen's College, Cambridge, urged reconciliation with France in his pamphlet, *Peace and Union Recommended* (1793), he was tried for sedition. Students stood up on his behalf—including Samuel Taylor Coleridge, who risked arrest by exuberantly supporting his professor.

From his Cambridge days Coleridge had already shown his tendency toward a peripatetic lifestyle. He briefly joined the dragoons, briefly returned to Cambridge, traveled from town to town and walked hundreds of miles through the countryside, wrote poems, met people, and harangued them with his intellectual acrobatics. He was concocting a plan for a utopian society he called "Pantisocracy." "The leading Idea of Pantisocracy is to make men *necessarily* virtuous by removing all Motives to Evil—all possible Temptations," he wrote to a prospective convert in 1794.[1] The primary temptation to be removed was private property. He earnestly invited friends, male and female, to move to America and become part of his newly conceived democratic and communal society.

When French Revolutionary leader Maximilien Robespierre was executed by his own people in July 1794, Coleridge partnered with a fellow poet, Robert Southey—Britain's poet laureate twenty years later—and created a dramatic rendition of events in France. Coleridge wrote the first act, Southey the second and third, of a play called *The Fall of Robespierre*. "The tempest gathers," it begins. "All—all is ours!" speaks Tallien, plotting to overthrow Robespierre; "E'en now the vital air / Of Liberty, condens'd awhile, is bursting."[2] They completed the play in record time and by late September, Coleridge had five hundred copies printed and was selling them to raise money for his utopia.

Coleridge's pantisocratic plans faded, but his passion for ideas and poetry did not. He cobbled together a living by contributing poems to newspapers and journals and by lecturing on politics and religion to paying audiences. Reconnecting with his school acquaintance Charles Lamb during the winter of 1794, Coleridge spent about a month in London. He rented a room at the Salutation and Cat, a public house near Christ's Hospital at 17 Newgate Street, where the two young men met evening after chilly evening to drink, smoke, and philosophize.

Back home in the North, Coleridge impulsively married Sara Fricker in October 1795, certain of neither her nor his future. He founded *The Watchman,* a journal of democratic and Unitarian ideals whose motto was "That all might know the Truth and that the Truth might make us free," but he managed to finance only ten issues. Hoping to collect enough poems to make a volume worth printing, Coleridge asked friends to contribute. One who did so was Charles Lamb.

The schoolboy friendship between Charles Lamb and Samuel Taylor Coleridge evolved into a lifelong exchange of poetry. When Coleridge published his first collection of *Poems on Various Subjects,* he included four "effusions" in sonnet form by Charles Lamb. "Independently of the signature their superior merit would have sufficiently distinguished them," Coleridge stated in his preface.[3] Charles's are all cleverly constructed sonnets, two love poems addressed to an idealized woman named Anna, one lyric addressed to the actress Sarah Siddons, and one a situational lyric inspired by the ocean. All read as if they were written more for practice than from passion.

Soon discussing a revised and expanded edition, Charles Lamb and Samuel Taylor Coleridge sent poems back and forth to each other through the spring and summer of 1796. Their letters brimmed full of minutely detailed commentary on rhythm, rhyme, diction, and innuendo. Lamb's intention was to build a corpus of works that Coleridge would agree to publish alongside his own. "The sonnet I send you has small merit as poetry," he wrote in May 1796, "but you will be curious to *read* it when I tell you it was written in my prison house in one of my lucid Intervals." He titled it "to my sister," little knowing the irony of its madhouse origin or the poignancy of its brotherly dedication in those months before September 1796:

> *If from my lips some angry accents fell,*
> > *Peevish complaint, or harsh reproof unkind,*
> > *Twas but the Error of a sickly mind,*
> *And troubled thoughts, clouding the purer well,*
> > *& waters clear, of Reason: & for me*
> > *Let this my verse the poor atonement be,*
> *My verse, which thou to praise: wast ever inclined*
> > *Too highly, & with a partial eye to see*
> *No Blemish: thou to me didst ever shew*
> > *Fondest affection, & woudst oftimes lend*
> *An ear to the desponding, love sick Lay,*
> > *Weeping my sorrows with me, who repay*
> *But ill the mighty debt, of love I owe,*
> > *Mary, to thee, my sister & my friend—*[4]

Clearly the nexus between brother and sister was already close, and complicated, in the spring before Mary's fateful act.

IN DAYLIGHT HOURS Charles Lamb performed the duties of an assistant accounting clerk. He must have stood for hours at a desk in the dark labyrinth of hallways inside the magnificent new East

India House headquarters, just opened on Leadenhall Street. Neoclassical columns towered above all who entered, and larger-than-life statuary, the gods and goddesses of commerce and industry, stood guard on the roof. Thanks to firms like East India House and the South Sea Company, London was Europe's busiest commercial seaport. Charles Lamb was a tiny cog in that massive and influential machine. He duly noted numbers all day long: goods shipped out of the warehouses, on to the docks, and then aboard the company's fleet of Indiamen, bound around the cape of Africa for destinations east. He likewise noted in large ledger books the quantities of goods arriving from the East: pepper and spices, chintz and muslin, coffee and tea, cups and saucers, platters and bowls. Goods sold, income received. Goods purchased, prices paid. For someone with a sparkling imagination and a taste for the odd, it must have been an odious job.

Every evening Charles returned from East India House and relieved the housekeeper of responsibility for his aunt and his father. Sarah Lamb never fully recovered from witnessing the violent event, so she could not assume the role of matriarch, nor was she the sort of woman who would. She was eccentric, never having smoothed off the edges of her coarse country ways. Unlike her sister-in-law, she had no aspirations to become a middle-class lady. Yet she had a kind heart, significant to both niece and nephew. In his schoolboy days, Charles remembered, his aunt had been "the kindest goodest creature," visiting him at school midmorning with some kitchen tidbit for a snack. At the time Charles "despised her for it, & used to be ashamed to see her come,"[5] but as he matured into his own eccentricities, he held the memory dear.

Within days of Elizabeth Lamb's untimely death, a relative identified by Charles as "an old Lady, a cousin of my father & Aunts, a Gentlewoman of fortune," came forward and offered "to take my Aunt & make her comfortable for the short remainder of her days."[6] That arrangement didn't last long, however. Within six weeks the generous cousin had turned into "an old Hag" in Charles's estimation. She called Sarah Lamb "indolent & mulish," with an attachment to her former household that was "so strong that she can never be happy apart." Pulling out all stops, the "Hag" told Charles that he must be a hypocrite if he did anything but rejoice at his aunt's return. The beleaguered Sarah moved back to 7 Little Queen Street in December 1796, and Charles found himself again "beset with perplexities."[7] To lighten his load he moved father, aunt, and household out of London and into the village of Pentonville, north of the city, considerably closer to Islington and Mary. They lived at 45 Chapel Street on a busy little corner, a short walk from an open market.

On February 9, 1797, Sarah Lamb died. "This afternoon I attend the funeral of my poor old aunt, who died on Thursday," Charles wrote Coleridge. "I own I am thankful that the good creature has ended all her days of suffering and infirmity. . . . Good God, who could have foreseen all this but four months back!"[8] On the day of her funeral Lamb composed a poem, uniting in death two women who rarely got along while living. "Go thou," he wrote, addressing Sarah Lamb, "and occupy the same grave-bed / Where the dead mother lies."[9]

To add to Charles's burden, Mary fell ill in late December 1796, suffering from "a sore throat, & a slight [attack] of Scarlet fever,"[10] as he told Coleridge. At least she was then still in Fisher House, where attendants could care for her and Dr. Pitcairn could visit. Charles's thoughts dwelled on his sister, because in the same letter to Coleridge, written on January 2, 1797, he shared a poem he had written to her. Mild and resigned, it begins:

> *Friend of my earliest years, & childish days,*
> *My joys, my sorrows, thou with me hast shared,*
> *Companion dear; & we alike have fared,*
> *Poor pilgrims we, thro' life's unequal ways.*

It ends:

> *And we will sometimes talk past troubles o'er.*
> *Of mercies shewn, & all our sickness heal'd,*
> > *And in his judgments God remembring love:*
> *And we will learn to praise God evermore*
> > *For those "glad tidings of great joy" reveal'd*
> > > *By that sooth messenger, sent from above.*

The rhetoric of Christmas carols and devotionals muffles the cries of sorrow and fear—an indication of how Charles Lamb sought support through traditional religion in these times of trouble. "My sister, I thank God, is nigh recover'd," Charles wrote less than a week later. "She was seriously ill."[11]

Charles's responsibilities might have been simplified if he had moved Mary back home after Sarah died, but he was adamant that she "must not, I fear, come to live with us *yet* a good while. In the first place, because at *present* it would hurt her, & hurt my father, for them to be together." Lamb had a second, more personal motive in keeping Mary at a distance: "from a regard to the world's good report, for I fear, I fear, tongues will be busy *whenever* that event takes place."[12]

As if the double responsibility was not enough, Charles Lamb's father was so beyond reason that he in no way lightened his son's load. "I get home at night o'er wearied, quite faint—," Charles, now nearly twenty-three, reported, "& then to *Cards* with my father, who will not let me enjoy a meal in peace."[13] Sometimes Charles satisfied his father by reading out loud from the small collection of poems the elder Lamb had written in years past, particularly "The Sparrow's Wedding":

> *A sparrow, youthful, airy, gay,*
> *Chirp'd and danc'd his time away;*

His thatch'd retreat he did forsake,
Of ev'ry pleasure did partake:
He swore he always would live free,
A mighty bird for gallantry;
Made love to all the feather'd race,
Was fond of ev'ry youthful face;
In ev'ry field, in ev'ry grove,
His chief employ was making love. . . .[14]

It was a poem Charles had undoubtedly heard since boyhood. Reading it aloud could not have been much more amusing than a round of cribbage—rather sad, in fact, considering his father's depleted state. What Charles really needed was some time to himself, but circumstances did not allow it. "After repeated games at Cribbage," he reported, his father would finally relent, but not without a stinging comment such as, "If you won't play with me, you might as well not come home at all!"[15]

At an age when other young men were either courting or carousing, Charles Lamb had little opportunity to live a normal social life. Even before the family tragedy, though, he felt like an outsider. "I go no where & have no acquaintance," he wrote Coleridge in June 1796. "*Slow of speech,* & reserved of manners, no one seeks or cares for my society & I am left alone."[16]

Like his sister, Charles Lamb stood under middle height. A childhood case of smallpox had left him with a diminutive body and an uneven gait, "advancing with a motion from side to side,"[17] as one observer put it. But he could walk fifteen miles or more in a day and would do so simply for the pleasure of it. His black hair curled above a face whose dark eyes, large nose, and olive complexion made many, including Lamb himself, say he looked Jewish. His features and expressions, one admirer wrote, were "varied and almost contradictory in appearance"; in him "the pride and solemnity of the philosophic observer of human nature, melting into the innocent playfulness of the child, and the mad fun of the school-boy."[18] Charles Lamb was "thin even to mea-greness, spare and wiry as an Arab of the desert," wrote Thomas De Quincey, another essayist among the Romantics.[19] Lamb tended to dress in black: black knee breeches, black stockings, black shoes, covered with high black gaiters.[20] His head and body seemed out of proportion. He had, as one man put it, "a head worthy of Aristotle . . . placed upon a *shadowy stem,*" a combination so awkward that his early teachers knew he would never perform well in the pulpit.[21] They may have based that judgment on Charles Lamb's stutter as well, which plagued him all his life but which he learned to use to his advantage. "No one ever stam-mered out such fine, piquant, deep, eloquent things in half-a-dozen sentences as he does," wrote his friend Bryan Waller Procter. Lamb's compulsive punning was, recalled another friend, "greatly heightened in effect by his stammer, which delayed and kept the mind in suspense for the joke which the eye plainly told you was coming."[22]

CHARLES LAMB'S ambitions flew far beyond his accounting desk in Leadenhall Street. He aspired to be a poet, and he eagerly shared his works with the friend who helped them find their way into print. His plans went awry on September 22, 1796, and Charles's letters to Coleridge became, instead of poetic commen-taries, the diary of a matricide and its aftermath.

Sobered by the responsibilities suddenly falling on him, Charles lashed out against poetry, sanctimoniously declaring it "unprofitable to my soul. . . . these questions about words, and debates about alterations, take me off, I am conscious, from the properer business of *my* life," he wrote Coleridge.[23] In December 1796, in an act of purgative self-denial, he came close to burning

all his poems and anything else related to literature or philosophy—or so he said in a letter to his friend:

> I almost burned all your letters,—I did as bad, I lent 'em to a
> friend to keep out of my brother's sight, should he come and
> make inquisition into our papers, for, much as he dwelt upon
> your conversation while you were among us, and delighted to
> be with you, it has been his fashion ever since to depreciate
> and cry you down,—you were the cause of my madness—you
> and your damned foolish sensibility and melancholy—and he
> lamented with a true brotherly feeling that we ever met.[24]

In the eyes of Charles's no-nonsense brother, poetry and the life
of the imagination were pure indulgences, escapes and distrac-
tions from the rigors of work and family obligation. But for
Charles poetry would soon become even more precious.
Coleridge would not let him leave the fold. He responded to
Charles's resolution with—of course—a poem, which included
the exhortation, "Oh! for shame return!"[25] Soon Charles realized
that he needed poetry. It was the one way he could express feelings unutterable amid the grief and demands of everyday, and
everynight, life.

Another young poet contributed poems to Coleridge's second
volume. Charles Lloyd became fast friends with Charles Lamb at
this time, although in the long run his brother Robert would turn
out to be the more important friend to both Mary and Charles.
The Lloyds came from a wealthy banking family in Birming-
ham, devoutly Quaker, the founders of the enterprise that
would become Lloyds of London. After meeting Coleridge at
Cambridge, Charles Lloyd reverentially attached himself to the
budding philosopher, for a short time living with him as his student, even though both were still in their early twenties. The tute-

lage was Lloyd's way of distancing himself from his family and expressing skepticism about their strictly religious ways, and it was Coleridge's ill-conceived effort to embark on a moneymaking venture and meet family obligations. His first child, Hartley David Coleridge, was born on September 19, 1796, a week before the death of Elizabeth Lamb.

Knowing little about Charles Lloyd beyond his connection to Coleridge, Lamb was surprised to hear from him in January 1797. Lloyd was rooming at the Bull & Mouth Inn in St.-Martins-le-Grand, just north of Saint Paul's Cathedral, and ended up spending many an hour with Charles, sharing "Welch rabbits, punch, & poesy."[26] Lamb wrote a poem at the time, portraying himself as "Alone, obscure, without a friend, / A cheerless, solitary thing," and thanking Lloyd for bringing "a gleam of random joy." They celebrated together when, in October 1797, booksellers began to offer *Poems, by S.T. Coleridge, second edition, to which are now added Poems by Charles Lamb and Charles Lloyd*.

Lloyd's poems included a pair that hinted at his own mental instabilities. "Why does the tear unbidden start, / And why those sighs that wildly swell?" he wrote in "The Melancholy Man." A companion poem, "The Maniac," expressed ambivalent longing for the state of madness. "Poor Maniac, I envy thy state," Lloyd wrote. "When shall I be *wise*—and forget! / For 'tis *madness* to feel and to think!"[27] In fact Charles Lloyd suffered from seizures even at the time he was befriending Charles Lamb. He ultimately succumbed to his own form of mental illness and was twice admitted for care to the Retreat, the asylum in York operated by the Society of Friends.[28]

The pages containing Charles Lamb's poetic contributions to the new volume were introduced with their own dedication:

> *The few following poems,*
> *creatures of the fancy and the feeling,*

> *in life's more vacant hours;*
> *produced, for the most part, by*
> *Love in Idleness*
> *are*
> *with all a brother's fondness*
> *inscribed to*
> *Mary Ann Lamb*
> *the*
> *author's best friend and sister*

He contributed fourteen poems, including the sonnet written to Mary from Hoxton, "If from my lips some angry accents fell," and the lonely poem written to Charles Lloyd.

Charles Lloyd's friendship, as diverting as it might have been, ultimately troubled Lamb's conscience. "The truth is," Lamb reflected,

> he tried to force my mind from its natural & proper bent, he continually wished me to be from home, he was drawing me *from* the consideration of my poor dear Mary's situation, rather than assisting me to gain a proper view of it, with religious consolations——. I wanted to be left to the tendency of my own mind in a solitary state, which in times past, I knew had led to quietness & a patient bearing of the yoke——he was hurt, that I was not more constantly with him——.[29]

Lloyd may well have seconded Charles's older brother, arguing that Mary should be institutionalized for life. Charles was more inclined to champion Mary, holding fast to his attitude that "what she hath done to deserve, or the necessity of such an hardship I see not."[30]

Charles saw in his sister an intelligent, potentially productive, gentle, and sympathetic individual. He carried that sense of her through the aftermath of her crazed act of murder and through every relapse. History has by and large limited its view of Mary Lamb to one irrational act; but to her brother, her daily habits formed the fabric of who she was: her kindnesses to those around her, her passing commentary on the world and on her condition, the books she read, the thoughts and feelings with which she responded to them. These features of her character are nearly invisible to us today, yet—if we trust her brother—they more clearly reflect who Mary Lamb was than the one spectacular exception to the rule.

The three-way friendship among Lamb, Lloyd, and Coleridge got complicated. Lloyd's moods and ill health made him more a handicap than a profit-making venture in the Coleridge household, and restless Coleridge ended the tutoring relationship, writing to one friend that he had "determined not to take the charge of Charles Lloyd's mind on me."[31] He wrote Lloyd's father about his change of heart, saying that now he considered his son "merely as a lodger and a friend."[32] Lloyd soon spent a few months in a hospital. While there, he wrote a short novel, *Edmund Oliver,* its main character based on Coleridge: A rapturous religious philosopher and his devotee and their wives ultimately form a sylvan utopia where "we have banished the words *mine* and *thine.*"[33] Lloyd dedicated the volume to Charles Lamb. Coleridge, annoyed at having been mimicked, returned the blow by publishing three sonnets in the *Monthly Magazine,* exaggeratedly imitating the styles of Lloyd, Lamb—and himself.

Meanwhile Lamb and Lloyd produced another volume of poetry. *Blank Verse* came out early in the summer of 1798, with Coleridge conspicuously absent. Soon thereafter the two poets found themselves in the congregation of infidels on the pages of the *Anti-Jacobin Review.* The Tory cartoonist paired "L___D and L___B": two amphibious creatures squatting side by side, mouths wide open as if singing in an atheistic choir, reading from "Blank-Verse by Toad &

Frog." While Lloyd and Lamb had clearly associated themselves in print and in society with others of a more radical tint, little that they published in *Blank Verse* warranted such an extreme political characterization. Granted, Lloyd had included his celebratory "Lines to Mary Wollstonecraft Godwin," introducing the poem with a sympathetic statement on behalf of the iconoclastic feminist. Otherwise it was guilt by association for the two budding poets.

Charles Lamb bared his soul and sorrows in *Blank Verse* more than ever before. He wrote no dedication, but of his seven pieces in the volume, four related specifically to his sister and her murderous outburst, including "The Old Familiar Faces," his best known poem. It appears time and again in literary anthologies, always footnoted with the family history that lurks between the lines.

Where are they gone, the old familiar faces?

I had a mother, but she died, and left me,
Died prematurely in a day of horrors—
All, all are gone, the old familiar faces.

I have had playmates, I have had companions,
In my days of childhood, in my joyful school-days—
All, all are gone, the old familiar faces.

I have been laughing, I have been carousing,
Drinking late, sitting late, with my bosom cronies—
All, all are gone, the old familiar faces.

I loved a love once, fairest among women,
Closed are her doors on me, I must not see her—
All, all are gone, the old familiar faces.

I have a friend, a kinder friend has no man.
Like an ingrate, I left my friend abruptly;
Left him, to muse on the old familiar faces.

Ghost-like, I paced round the haunts of my childhood.
Earth seem'd a desert I was bound to traverse,
Seeking to find the old familiar faces.

Friend of my bosom, thou more than a brother!
Why wert not thou born in my father's dwelling?
So might we talk of the old familiar faces.

For some they have died, and some they have left me,
And some are taken from me; *all are departed;*
All, all are gone, the old familiar faces.

When he first penned this poem, during the winter of 1797–98, Charles sent a copy to Marmaduke Thompson, the East India House chaplain, along with a letter that told the story of its composition. He had been socializing, probably at the pub he and Coleridge also haunted, the Salutation and Cat, with Charles Lloyd. "Lloyd had been playing on a pianoforte, till my feelings were wrought too high not to require Vent," wrote Lamb. "I left em suddenly & rushed into ye Temple, where I was born, you know." One imagines him, pacing the stone court-yards of his childhood, his footsteps echoing through the colonnades, then wandering the King's Bench Walk, into the gardens and down to the night-blackened waters of the Thames. Words and verses must have tumbled around in his imagination, "& in ye state of mind that followed [I composed these] stanzas. They pretend to little like Metre, but they will pourtray ye Disorder I was in."[34]

It was a disorder that mingled isolation and despair. That winter night Charles Lamb felt himself alone, without a mother, without childhood friends, without romance, with neither old friends like Coleridge nor new friends like Lloyd, and without his sister, who had been "taken from me." It is telling that in 1818, when Charles Lamb published his collected works, he chose not to include the first full stanza, beginning "I had a mother."

DESPITE THE SENTIMENTS in this poem, Charles Lamb soon realized that in some practical ways his sister had not been taken from him. Quite the contrary: Even when living apart, whether at Fisher House or in Hackney, she was very connected to her brother. He had made a lifelong commitment and would honor it until the day he died. In another poem in *Blank Verse*, he likened that commitment to marriage, describing Mary's absence as his widowhood. "Written on Christmas Day, 1797" is a revealing poem, poignantly descriptive of his sister a year after the matricide:

> *I am a widow'd thing, now thou art gone!*
> *Now thou art gone, my own familiar friend,*
> *Companion, sister, help-mate, counsellor!*
> *Alas! that honour'd mind, whose sweet reproof*
> *And meekest wisdom in times past have smooth'd*
> *The unfilial harshness of my foolish speech,*
> *And made me loving to my parents old,*
> *(Why is this so, ah God! why is this so?)*
> *That honour'd mind become a fearful blank,*
> *Her senses lock'd up, and herself kept out*
> *From human sight or converse, while so many*
> *Of the foolish sort are left to roam at large,*
> *Doing all acts of folly, and sin, and shame?*
> *Thy paths are mystery!*

Charles sent this poem, as if it were a New Year's confession, to Marmaduke Thompson as well. He warmly acknowledges Mary's "honour'd mind" and commends her for correcting in "sweet reproof," with "meekest wisdom," his "unfilial" tendencies. It was Mary who exhorted him to love his "parents old." Only those who knew the family story well would see the piercing irony in these lines. Charles Lamb asks the existential question, Why? Why should the one person who has been his moral guide now turn, her mind a "fearful blank," her "senses lock'd up"? Shifting his address from Mary to God, Charles finds no answers. "Thy paths are mystery."

Blank Verses contained one other veiled poem of mourning, "Written a twelvemonth after the Events"—Lamb's only contribution that was, as the book's title promised, blank verse. It is remarkable that Charles Lamb would so bare himself on the printed page. Perhaps he felt comfortable, hiding behind conventional sentimental imagery and overwrought language.

> *Alas! how am I chang'd! where be the tears,*
> *The sobs, and forc'd suspensions of the breath,*
> *And all the dull desertions of the heart,*
> *With which I hung o'er my dear mother's corse?*

Charles addresses God, thankful that Mary, "my long-loved Friend," came back to her senses: "Thou didst not keep / Her soul in death." He apologizes for his own behavior, and yearns for the simpler days, when he was a child beloved by his mother.

> *Forgive it, Oh my* Maker,
> *If, in a mood of grief, I sin almost*
> *In sometimes brooding on the days of long past,*
> *(And from the grave of time wishing them back)*
> *Days of a mother's fondness to her child,*
> *Her little one.*

For consolation, he envisions a heavenly scene, where all three—mother, daughter, and son—are reconciled:

Thou and I, dear friend,
With filial recognition sweet, shall know
One day the face of our dear mother in heaven,
And her remember'd looks of love shall greet
With answering looks of love, her placid smiles
Meet with a smile as placid, and her hand
With drops of fondness wet, nor fear repulse.

In these maudlin lines, Charles borrows from Mary's sparer vision, shared nearly a year before: "The spirit of my mother seems to descend, & smile upon me . . . I shall see her again in heaven; she will then understand me better." The poetic collaboration between sister and brother was just beginning.

THE ROW WITH Coleridge did not last long. The friendship was too long-standing, too deep, and too important. Knowing that Lamb was haunted by the bleak prospects for his sister's future, Coleridge invited Mary to come stay with him and his family, perhaps as nursemaid to his fifteen-month-old son, Hartley. Charles responded negatively but with gratitude. While he was seeking a permanent situation for his sister, he knew she needed a calmer setting than the Coleridge household could provide. He said so delicately in his answer to his friend's generous offer:

Mary is recovering . . . but I see no opening yet of a situation for her—your invitation went to my very heart—but you have a power of exciting interest, of leading all hearts captive, too forcible to admit of Mary's being with you—. I consider her as perpetually on the brink of madness—. I think, you would almost make her dance within an inch of the precipice—she must be with duller fancies, & cooler intellects. . . . I know a young man of this description, who has suited her these twenty years, & may live to do so still—if we are one day restor'd to each other—.[35]

The "young man" in question—someone with "duller fancies, & cooler intellects" than Coleridge—was Charles Lamb himself.

6

Double Singleness

THE ELDER JOHN LAMB, father to John, Mary, and Charles, the beneficent Inner Temple first waiter and scrivener to bencher Samuel Salt, was buried on April 13, 1799. To Charles his death came as a relief. It meant more time on his own, and it meant that Mary could come home. So later that month, when Mary was thirty-four and Charles twenty-four, they embarked on a life together that would ultimately last nearly four decades. "We house together, old bachelor and maid, in a sort of double singleness," Charles was later to say of the arrangement.[1]

They committed themselves to each other and to the single life, for better and for worse. For Mary Lamb to have remained unmarried so long was a likely indication that she would remain so for the rest of her life. The record shows none of her family yearning to find a mate for her. Perhaps the Lamb family lore about insanity made them hesitate, although one could imagine its propelling them in just the opposite direction. She never mourned the lack of suitors, and indeed in 1806 called marriage "a hazardous kind of an affair."[2] She seemed wisely aware of the situation in which a wife could find herself. Whether or not she had heard such warnings from her mother, she could look around and see the true nature of many a marriage, as her contemporary Mary Wollstonecraft described in *A Vindication of the Rights of Woman*:

Women are told from their infancy, and taught by the example of their mothers, that a little knowledge of human weakness, justly termed cunning, softness of temper, *outward* obedience, and a scrupulous attention to a puerile kind of propriety, will obtain for them the protection of man; and should they be beautiful, everything else is needless, for at least twenty years of their lives.[3]

Mary Lamb was wary of how marriage could transform a man. "I have known many single men I should have liked in my life (if it had suited them) for a husband: but very few husbands have I ever wished was mine," she wrote to a friend who was going through a stormy courtship. "One never is disposed to envy wives their good husbands. . . . So much for marrying."[4]

Friends and biographers have blamed Mary for Charles's life-long bachelorhood, but he seems to have developed a taste for it as well. "There is a quiet dignity in old-bachelorhood," he wrote Robert Lloyd, "a leisure from cares, noise &c., an enthronization upon the armed-chair of a man's feeling that he may sit, walk, read, unmolested, to none accountable."[5] Charles's life story includes several instances of unrequited passion: toward the woman to whom he addressed early sonnets, mentioned in "The Old Familiar Faces," and toward a woman who rejected his proposal of marriage later in life. Mary's history seems to include no such liaisons, leaving one to wonder about the force and direction of her libido. It may be that, given family expectations early in life and then social strictures and self-doubt later, she was able to quash that urge, or at least its outward expression.

Life together seemed to suit both sister and brother well, a balance of intimacy and independence, mutual care and respect. Certainly there were times of tension, periods of exasperation and frustration. Neither was an easygoing person. Each was demanding. "I know my dismal faces have been almost as great a draw back upon Charles comfort, as his feverish teazing ways have been upon mine [*sic*]," Mary wrote a friend in 1806. "Our love for each other has been the torment of our lives hitherto."[6] She could say that only because she knew that the same love was the solid center of their life together.

THROUGHOUT 1799 Mary Lamb maintained her equilibrium. "My sister Mary was never in better health or spirits than now," Charles observed at the beginning of the year.[7] In April she joined him in Pentonville. Between the daytime presence of Hetty, their housekeeper, and his evenings at home, Mary had company. Charles was always on the alert, aware of a "perpetual liability to a recurrence in my sister's disorder, probably to the end of her life."[8]

Hetty fell ill in April 1800, and Mary found herself caring for an invalid once again. She bucked up and managed but fell apart once Hetty died. "I dont know why I write except from the propensity misery has to tell her griefs," Charles Lamb wrote Coleridge on May 12. "Hetty died on Friday night, about 11 o Clock, after 8 days illness. . . . Mary in consequence of fatigue and anxiety is fallen ill again, and I was obliged to remove her yesterday." No record remains of where Mary Lamb spent the next month, but it seems fair to assume that she returned to Fisher House. Nor do we have, beyond the words "fatigue" and "anxiety," any details of the symptoms that led Mary and Charles to believe it was time for another confinement.

The scene was to recur again and again through the lifetime Mary and Charles Lamb shared. She would sense the warning signs and recognize that she needed the seclusion and care found only in a madhouse. Years later a friend described the pattern. "Miss Lamb experienced, and full well understood premonitory symptoms of the attack, in restlessness, low fever, and the inability to sleep; and, as gently as possible, prepared her brother for the duty he must soon perform."[9] Thus alerted, Charles would chaperone her to a madhouse. Another friend recalled the typical scene. "Whenever the approach of one of her fits of insanity was announced, by some irritability or change of manner, Lamb would take her, under his arm. . . . It was very affecting to encounter the young brother and his sister walking together (weeping together) on this painful errand; Mary herself, although sad, very conscious of the necessity for temporary separation from her only friend. They used to carry a strait jacket with them."[10]

The turn of events in May 1800 left Charles bereft, the scene vaguely reminiscent of September 1796.

—I am left alone in a house with nothing but Hetty's dead body to keep me company. . . . Tomorrow I bury her, and then I shall be quite alone, with nothing but a cat, to remind me that the house has been full of living beings like myself.—My heart is quite sunk, and I dont know where to look for relief—. Mary will get better again, but her constantly being liable to such relapses is dreadful,—nor is it the least of our Evils, that her case & all our story is so well known around us. . . . We are in a manner *marked*.

In theory Charles must have understood that Mary could suffer a relapse, but this first one overwhelmed him. "I am completely shipwreck'd," he wrote.[11]

After a year together, Mary had regained the status of helpmate and caretaker, with echoes of the days when, as a child, she watched over Charles. "Our servant is dead, and my sister is ill—," he wrote a few days later.

I have been left *alone* in a house, where but 10 days since living Beings were, &—Noises of life were heard. I have made the experiment & find I cannot bear it any longer——. Last night I went to sleep at White's [a schoolmate of Lamb and Coleridge] with whom I am to be till I can find a settlement——. I have given up my house, and must look out for lodgings. I expect Mary will get better, before many weeks are gone—but at present I feel my daily & hourly prop has fallen from me. I totter and stagger with weakness, for nobody can supply her place to me.[12]

In less than a month, another Christ's Hospital schoolmate, John Mathew Gutch, helped Charles find new quarters in the Southampton Buildings, Chancery Lane, not ten minutes from his childhood home.[13] It was a relief to Charles that Gutch knew their family secret. He understood Mary's vulnerability and invited them to rent his rooms anyway. "I have got three rooms (including servant) under £34 a Year,"[14] he reported to Coleridge—probably a stretch financially, given that Charles could not have been earning even one hundred pounds annually. By the end of July his sister came home, this time to Chancery Lane.

Just west of the City proper, with the dome of Saint Paul's still in view, Chancery Lane connected the major commercial thoroughfare of Holborn Street with London's legal district. It was in that neighborhood that Mary and Charles Lamb had forged their worldviews, and to it Mary and Charles soon returned—to that cloistered world in the thick of the city yet isolated from crowds, stench, and crime. In early 1801, when Number 16 Mitre Court Buildings, in the Inner Temple, became available for rent, Mary and Charles Lamb moved again.

"I am going to change my Lodgings," wrote Charles in February. "I have partly fixed upon most delectable Rooms, which look out (when you stand a Tip toe) over the Thames & Surrey Hills; at the upper end of King's Bench walks in the *Temple*." The view down the Inner Temple's long green to the Thames gave a glimpse of countryside from the midst of the metropolis. "By my new plan I shall be as *airy,* up 4 pair of stairs, as in the country; & in a garden in the midst of enchanting more than Mahometan paradise *London*."[15]

DELIGHTING IN CITY LIFE, Mary and Charles Lamb were bucking a trend of the times. Samuel Taylor Coleridge and his friend William Wordsworth had just declared a pastoral poetic revolution with their *Lyrical Ballads.* Published in 1798, then expanded and reissued in 1800, *Lyrical Ballads* is taken by most literary historians as the starting point of the Romantic movement, so influential was its new respect for nature, simple language, and the sensibility of plain country folk. It included Coleridge's "Rime of the Ancient Mariner" and Wordsworth's "Tintern Abbey." It contained poems about gathering hazelnuts, a pet lamb, an "old Cumberland beggar," and an "Idiot boy"—matters of indifference to the sophisticated city dweller, but that was just the point. In nature and naïveté, one came closer to "the power / Of harmony, and the deep power of joy," as Wordsworth expressed it. To be a "worshipper of Nature" was to approach whatever divinity this world offered.

By the time of the publication of *Lyrical Ballads,* Charles could call both authors his friends. With Mary securely in Hackney, he had taken a week in July 1797 to visit Nether Stowey, Somerset, where Coleridge and his wife, Sara, had recently moved with their baby, Hartley. William Wordsworth and his sister, Dorothy, were visiting the Coleridges at the same time. Soon their names became as "familiar in my mouth as household words,"[16] Charles put it, consciously echoing Shakespeare's Henry V.

Charles felt uneasy about the way he had behaved during the visit, however. He had always stuttered, but he turned completely tongue-tied in Wordsworth's presence. "My silence was not sullenness, nor I hope from any bad motive; but, in truth, disuse has made me awkward at it," he explained. "Company and converse are strange to me."[17] Far from faulting his friend for not talking, Coleridge viewed the visit as a landmark event. It inspired his poem, "This Lime-Tree Bower My Prison," published in 1800 with the subtitle, "Addressed to Charles Lamb, of the India House, London."

Just as Lamb had arrived at Nether Stowey, a pan of hot milk had spilled and burned Coleridge's foot, making it nearly impossible for him to walk. He stayed behind while his wife showed their visitors a splendid waterfall not far from their home. Imagining them on their way, Coleridge composed a poem that became an anthem of the Romantic poet's faith in nature. "Well, they are gone, and here must I remain, / This lime-tree bower my prison," the poem begins. The poet imagines his friends emerging from woods to view the open sky:

> Yes! they wander on
> In gladness all; but thou, methinks, most glad,
> My gentle-hearted Charles! for thou hast pined
> And hunger'd after Nature, many a year,
> In the great City pent, winning thy way
> With sad yet patient soul, through evil and pain
> And strange calamity!

Coleridge sees his friend as needing spiritual rejuvenation, and he paints the scene he hopes Charles will see: the sun setting against the purple heath, clouds on the ocean horizon. Imagining the effect such views would have on the spirit of his troubled city friend, Coleridge breaks forth in poetic lines that could be considered a Romantic manifesto:

> *Henceforth I shall know*
> *That Nature ne'er deserts the wise and pure;*
> *No plot so narrow, be but Nature there,*
> *No waste so vacant, but may well employ*
> *Each faculty of sense, and keep the heart*
> *Awake to Love and Beauty!*

The poem ends anchored not only in nature's beauty but in the character of Charles Lamb, who can see goodness even through "strange calamity."

As flattering as they may have been, the lines did not sit well with their subject. When the poem was published, Lamb wrote Coleridge, "For God's sake (I never was more serious), don't make me ridiculous any more by terming me gentle-hearted in print, or do it in better verses."[18] A week later he was still harping on the point and gave Coleridge a list of alternative adjectives to choose from: "In the next edition of the Anthology, (which Phoebus avert, and those nine other wandering maids [the Muses] also!) please to blot out *gentle hearted,* and substitute drunken dog, ragged head, seld-shaven, odd-ey'd, stuttering, or any other epithet which truly and properly belongs to the Gentleman in question."[19] At the age of twenty-five Charles Lamb was learning to take life, or at least himself, less seriously—a coping tactic he used for the rest of his days. His essays sing with self-mockery, and his uncontrollable laughter during solemn ceremonies drew many a frown. "He could not restrain his wit, even upon the most solemn subjects," a fellow East India House worker said of Charles Lamb. "Any thing awful makes me laugh," he said of himself a dozen years later.[20] His irrepressible wit showed his consummate strength and his deepest weakness.

IT WAS DURING the first year of their life together that Mary and Charles Lamb first met William Godwin. A friend had just given them a turkey, "the Largest I ever saw," exclaimed Charles, and they decided to share it with someone of distinction. "*Philosopher* Godwin! dines with me on your Turkey this day," Charles wrote the friend who provided the bird. "I expect the roof to fall and crush the Atheist."[21]

Born in 1756—hence eight years older than Mary and almost twenty years older than Charles—William Godwin in the year 1800 was a tarnished celebrity. He struck an odd figure, with a frame "low of stature" but "surmounted by a massive head," and first impressions belied his greatness since, as one who knew him wrote many years later, "his countenance was rarely lighted up by the deep-seated genius within."[22]

Godwin's reputation preceded him, though, and prepared expectations wherever he went. He had grabbed the attention of his countrymen, high and low, with his *Enquiry Concerning Political Justice* (1793), in which he argued that the best government is the least government. The errors of inequality are imposed by political institutions, wrote Godwin. Without institutions, men would conduct themselves according to truths deep within human nature and, through a natural democracy, achieve cooperation without government, leaders, or laws. "Monarchy and aristocracy . . . undermine the virtues and the understandings of their subjects," he wrote. "The thing most necessary is to remove all those restraints which hold the mind back from its natural flight."[23]

"Perhaps no work of equal bulk ever had such a number of readers," a contemporary biographer of Godwin's wrote of *Political Justice* in 1799—in part a tongue-in-cheek reference to the tome's eight hundred pages—"and certainly no book of such profound inquiry ever made so many proselytes in an equal space of time."[24] Despite its size, its price (one pound sixteen shillings, about two weeks' workers' wages), and its erudition, *Political Justice* became so important to workers in England, Scotland, and Ireland that they banded together to share copies and organized meetings to read it aloud. Pirated, then cheap, then abridged editions appeared, and the book circulated even more widely. Whether at home in London or traveling the West Country, Godwin quickly discovered, "I was nowhere a stranger." Explaining the book's instant acceptance, he believed that its doctrines "coincided in a great degree with the sentiments then prevailing in English society."[25] The authorities did not want to agree. Edmund Burke said it was full of "extravagant and absurd theories." William Pitt the younger, the prime minister, considered prosecuting Godwin for sedition but decided that the book's high price would limit its impact.[26]

Another book by Godwin appeared just a year after *Political Justice*. *Things as They Are; or, The Adventures of Caleb Williams* (1794) explored the opposite of the democratic ideal. It is at once an adventure story and a moral tale, as the honest and unassuming Caleb Williams suffers social injustices, becomes "a mark for the vigilance of tyranny," and is hunted down as a criminal. By writing a novel Godwin thought he could avoid the political searchlights, but in fact he moved more centrally into public view. "Those in the lower classes saw their cause espoused, & their oppressors forcibly & eloquently delineated," recalled his daughter years later. At the other extreme George, Prince of Wales, read the novel avidly.[27]

So Godwin held a place of honor among antiaristocratic radicals in 1794, when Pitt and the Tories clamped down hard. Hardy, Thelwall, Horne Tooke, and Thomas Holcroft—intellect and playwright, one of Godwin's best friends—were accused of treason. Godwin visited, defended, and supported in writing many of those brought to trial. After Holcroft's case was dismissed, he and Godwin sat side by side in the courtroom, noting every turn of argument. All accused won acquittal for lack of evidence. Cheering crowds waved pamphlets written by Godwin. The trials in 1794 represented the pinnacle of his popularity. Six years later, when the Lambs met him, his star was falling.

William Godwin's turn of fortune was due in part to his love for a woman: Mary Wollstonecraft. When Godwin first met her, Wollstonecraft was living her own idiosyncratic life. Determinedly independent and quick to argue gender inequity, in her personal life she epitomized the victim of a male-dominated culture. After traveling to Scandinavia and back on behalf of her American lover, in 1795 Wollstonecraft found herself abandoned with a year-old child. She survived a desperate suicide attempt. The radical publisher Joseph Johnson took her in and hired her to write and edit. They had known each other since 1786, when Johnson had bought her first book, *Thoughts on the Education of Daughters,*[28] for ten guineas, a guinea equaling one pound plus one shilling.

Godwin's first impression of Mary Wollstonecraft was not positive. In November 1791, Joseph Johnson hosted Godwin, Wollstonecraft, and Thomas Paine, the consummate revolutionary pamphleteer, at dinner. It was the only time Godwin ever met Tom Paine. Though Godwin later granted that the woman among them added a few "shrewd and striking remarks," to his annoyance, Wollstonecraft dominated the conversation. At the time, he later revealed, he felt "little curiosity to see Mrs. Wollstonecraft, and a very great curiosity to see Thomas Paine. Paine is no great talker. . . . I, of consequence, heard her, very frequently when I wished to hear Paine."[29] During the next five years Mary Wollstonecraft mellowed and William Godwin grew more interested in female companionship. First they became philosophical partners. Then they became lovers.

By 1796 Mary Wollstonecraft had established her own sort of celebrity. She first drew public attention with her *Vindication of the Rights of Men,* a hastily written argument against primogeniture and aristocracy. Her next book was rued in her day and is still valued in ours: *A Vindication of the Rights of Woman,* published by Joseph Johnson in 1792. In it Wollstonecraft applied the principles of the American and French Revolutions to the other half of the human race: women. "Contending for the rights of woman, my main argument is built on this simple principle, that if she be not prepared by education to become the companion of man, she will stop the progress of knowledge and virtue," she wrote in the book's introduction. "Truth must be common to all, or it will be inefficacious with respect to its influence on general practice."[30]

The book sold fast. It was reviewed with favor and swiftly translated into French and German. Intellectuals welcomed the message, but many raised their eyebrows. "The gentry of Pembroke are shocked at M.'s book," one of Wollstonecraft's sisters wrote to the other from Wales. "Every one declares it is the most indecent Rhapsody that ever was penned by man or woman."[31] By turning her readers' attention from male-dominated politics and philosophical abstractions to gender equality and practical matters, such as the right to own property, Mary Wollstonecraft trod into the realms of propriety, morality, and sexuality. It made her readers uncomfortable, especially those finally attaining middle-class comfort by following the rules of tradition.

Neither Godwin nor Wollstonecraft believed in marriage, but when they discovered that they had conceived a child, they succumbed to social pressures. They were married on March 29, 1797, at Saint Pancras Church in London. Mary and her three-year-old daughter, Fanny, moved into William Godwin's home. Another daughter was born on August 30, named Mary Wollstonecraft Godwin, but the mother never arose from the bed in which she gave birth. Despite the efforts of physicians, bits of placental tissue remained in her womb, and Mary Wollstonecraft died of an infection on September 10. Her threefold legacy persisted: in the revolutionary feminist volume she left behind; in the memorials soon composed by Godwin; and in the daughter whose birth caused her death, known to the world decades later as Mary Shelley, author of *Frankenstein*.

Godwin was grief stricken at his wife's death: "This light was lent to me for a very short period, and is now extinguished for ever!"[32] He assuaged his distress by immediately editing Wollstone-craft's unpublished works and by writing for her the *Memoirs of the Author of a Vindication of the Rights of Woman*. Believing that he was commemorating his beloved wife, Godwin bared many of her secrets: her liaison with a married man, her unmarried relation-ship with another, her two attempts at suicide. To Godwin these details showed how society wounded a woman of intellect. To his readers, though, they confirmed suspicions. The *European Magazine* predicted that the book would be received "with disgust by every female who has any pretensions to delicacy; with detes-tation by every one attached to the interests of religion and morality; and with indignation by any one who might feel any regard for the unhappy woman, whose frailties should have been buried in oblivion." The *Anti-Jacobin Review* indexed their review under the word "prostitution."[33]

Godwin's reputation plummeted, but he did not forsake his ideals. He was left with two children, Mary and Fanny. While most men would have shipped both girls out to relatives, nurse-maids, or nannies, William Godwin accepted his responsibility, seeing it as a challenge to practice the theories he and his wife had articulated concerning the education of daughters.

"Godwin I am a good deal pleased with—," Charles reported to the friend who had sent the turkey. "He is a well behaved decent man, nothing very brilliant about him or imposing. . . . I was well pleased to find he has neither horns nor claws, quite a tame creature I assure you."[34] The turkey dinner was the start of a growing friendship among William Godwin and Mary and Charles Lamb. Five years later, remarried, Godwin would start a new publishing venture, the Juvenile Library, hoping to turn his passion for democratic education and his experience of raising two daughters into some sort of livelihood. His good friends the Lambs would find themselves integral to the plan.

7

The Circle Forms

ARY AND CHARLES LAMB moved to Number 16
Mitre Court Buildings in the spring of 1801. Surely
some residents of the Inner Temple still remembered
them from ten years before: Randal Norris, who had diligently
advocated for John Lamb once he lost his capacity to work; Mrs.
Norris, his wife; and Samuel Lovel, who had worked in the Great
Hall alongside their father and was now the Temple pannierman,
or baker.[1] Old friends must have found ways to help the Lambs
slip back into the plenitude of Inner Temple life without suffering
the idle curiosity of those who did not know them from years
past. Besides, Mary and Charles returned as lessees, not as servants. They were rising into the middle class. "Nothing is so dis-
agreeabl[e] to me as the clamours and applauses of the mob,"
wrote Charles that summer. "For this reason I live in an *obscure* situation in one of the courts of the Temple."[2]

It was the upstairs properties that were rented out in the Inner
Temple; the barristers, benchers, and students tended to cluster
on the ground and first floors. Charles and Mary's room perched
on the top floor of a five-story building at the north end of the
King's Bench Walk. It was cold and small, but private, well lit, and
open. "I prefer the attic story for the air!" Charles wrote in his
first letter from their new home:

I have neither maid nor laundress, not caring to be troubled with them! . . . when you come to see me, mount up to the top of the stairs—I hope you are not asthmatical—and come in flannel, for it's pure airy up there. And bring your glass, and I will shew you the Surrey Hills. My bed faces the river so as by perking up upon my haunches, and supporting my carcase with my elbows, without much wrying my neck, I can see the white sails glide by the bottom of the King's Bench walks as I lie in my bed. An excellent tiptoe prospect in the best room: casement windows with small panes, to look more like a cottage.[3]

Charles may have hired "neither maid nor laundress," but he had his "old housekeeper," as he now called Mary.[4] While Charles left home every weekday, dutifully working at East India House from ten to four, Mary saw to the homely tasks of daily existence. She had to fetch water for drinking, cooking, and cleaning from courtyard pumps, carrying it bucket by bucket up the stairs. She probably shopped for food nearly every day, visiting the market a few blocks away. Occasionally Mr. Lovel or, once she befriended them, other kitchen workers might have slipped her surplus from the Inner Temple Hall. She must have roasted meat in the fireplace, boiled turnips and potatoes in a heavy pot set right on the coals, which she had also hauled upstairs that morning. Laundry was washed in large basins, then hung on lines stretching from one side of the room to the other. Candlelight extended productive hours past dark, and many a letter was written, many a game of whist played in the Lamb household by the flickering light of tallow tapers. As word went out, sewing and mending work likely began to come in, and Mary Lamb resumed her mantua-making trade, bringing a bit of money into the household. For both Mary and Charles, though, satisfaction came not from daytime obligations but from friends and ideas, literature and conversation—the stuff that filled their evenings.[5]

Surely some of those conversations revolved around current world events, which could not be ignored. Britain had been facing the threat of a French military invasion since 1793, and the French were advancing all around them. By 1799 Napoleon was rising to power. French ships were barricading paths of commerce on land and water, stifling Britain's economy. "I cannot forbear speaking a word or two on the situation of our own country," Thomas Robinson wrote in 1800, describing conditions at home to his brother, the barrister and diarist Henry Crabb Robinson, who was then traveling in Germany.

> You cannot be aware, I think to the extent in which it exists, of the distress of all orders of people among us on account of the high price of provisions. . . . High bounties are accordingly offered to encourage the importation of grain, and various plans of economy are recommended to diminish the consumption of bread. The causes of the distressed state of the country are a subject of controversy both within and out of Parliament. The Administration are, of course, very strenuous in maintaining that the *war* has no share in it, while the Opposition as loudly attempt to prove it is the principal cause.[6]

"The times continue excessively hard with us," Robinson wrote a year later, in January 1801. "Indeed the cloud of evil seems to threaten more and more every day. Corn rises every market-day, and indeed alarm is spreading in all directions, . . . Buonaparte seems as if he would make the assumed title of *great nation* a valid claim, and I fear it is as clear that the sun of England's glory is set. Indeed I am become quite an alarmist, which I believe is equally the case with the democrat and the aristocrat."[7]

Democrat and aristocrat—both faced hard times. "If I don't have a Legacy left me shortly, I must get into pay with some newspaper for small gains," Charles wrote wryly in the fall of

1801, knowing full well that no legacy lay in sight for him or his sister. "Mutton is twelve-pence a pound. I want some occupation, and I more want money."[8] But hard times did not keep Mary and Charles Lamb from developing a vigorous social life in their new setting. A circle of friends started growing. They met new acquaintances through old, and visitors often lodged with them while in London. Mary and Charles were always inviting people to the Temple for tea or supper.

IT WAS A ragtag bunch that climbed the stairs of the Mitre Court Buildings and spent their evenings with Mary and Charles Lamb. Writers, intellectuals, artists, philosophers—this fascinating group of people, the growing circle of friends that clustered around Mary and Charles Lamb, might be epitomized in the character of George Dyer.

Ten years older than Mary, Dyer had won honors at Christ's Hospital. From that point on he cobbled together an existence as a freethinking writer and educator. He moved to London, near the Inns of Court, in 1792, soon befriending Coleridge and, through him, Lamb. "The oftener I see him, the more deeply I admire him," Charles reflected. "He is goodness itself.—If I could but calculate the precise date of his death, I would write a novel on purpose to make George the *Hero*."[9]

"He was one of the best creatures morally that ever breathed," with "the kindest heart and simplest manners imaginable, . . . a scholar, but to the end of his days . . . a bookseller's drudge," recalled another contemporary.[10] Dyer made his living by proofreading, indexing, tutoring, and submitting occasional articles to popular magazines of the day.[11] His friends so cherished Dyer for his character that they tolerated his appearance and manners: "He was not sensible of any impropriety in wearing a dirty shirt or a ragged coat; and numerous are the tales told in illustration of his neglect of little every-day matters of comfort. . . . He has asked a friend to breakfast with him, and given him coarse black tea, stale bread, salt butter, sour milk, and has had to run out to buy sugar. Yet every one loved Dyer." Dyer worked briefly, tutoring the sons of the Earl of Stanhope, so engaging his loyalty that Lord Stanhope named him an executor of his estate. Dyer refused the task but still received an annuity for the rest of his eighty-five-year-long life.[12]

Dyer arrived one day at the Lambs' dressed in cotton pantaloons called "nankeens," named for Nanking, China, where the fashion originated. Meant to be worn stylishly tight to the leg, Dyer's were so big they flapped in the wind. He explained that they were brand-new, bought to impress a certain lady, but in fact they were "absolutely ingrained with the accumulated dirt of ages," according to Charles.

> And then he danced and capered, and fidgeted, and pulled up his pantaloons, and hugged his intolerable flannel vestment closer about his poetic Loins, . . . then he caught at a proof sheet, and catched up a Laundresse's bill instead . . . I could not bring him to one direct reply, he could not maintain his jumping mind in a right line for the tithe of a moment by Clifford's Inn Clock—he must go to the Printer's immediately—the most unlucky accident—he had struck off five hundred impressions of his Poems, which were ready for delivery to subscribers— . . . not till that morning had he discovered that in the very first page of said preface had he set out with a principle of criticism fundamentally wrong, which vitiated all his following reasoning—the preface must be expunged, altho' it cost him £30.

Charles and Mary compassionately diagnosed it as a case of "Midsummer madness."[13]

When Dyer's *Poems* came out six weeks later, Charles generously paid him two guineas for a copy, and he "skipped about like a
pea with its arse scorched, at the receipt of so much *Cash*." Charles
found the notes to the poems full of "beautiful absurdity," but he
was shocked to discover that "One of the Sonnets purports to have
been written in *Bedlam*! This for a man to *own.*——*!*——" Another,
titled "The Madman," was based on stories "collected by the author
from several madhouses."[14] Charles and Mary read these poems
together, and we can only imagine the conversations they
prompted between the two siblings, who assiduously avoided any
such public references to familiarity with a madhouse.

Charles passed the book on to Thomas Manning, a Cambridge
mathematician whom he had met through Charles Lloyd. Like
Dyer, Manning was more than a decade older than Charles, but
their friendship jelled quickly. He was a calming influence among
the poetical crazies. Charles valued his "steadiness & quiet which
used to infuse something like itself into our nervous minds." Mary
considered him the group's "ventilator."[15]

Soon after the Lambs befriended him, Manning followed his
passion and traveled to the Far East. In May 1806 he boarded the
Thames, a three-masted East Indiaman bound for Canton. East
India vessels carried letters back and forth between Lamb and
Manning for years. The traveler found work as a doctor and a
translator in China and India. He traveled through Tibet and, on
December 17, 1811, became the first Englishman to secure an
audience with the Dalai Lama.

> The Lama's beautiful and interesting face and manner
> engrossed almost all my attention. He was at that time about
> seven years old: had the simple and unaffected manners of a
> well-educated princely child. His face was, I thought, poeti-
> cally and affectingly beautiful. He was of a gay and cheerful
> disposition; his beautiful mouth perpetually unbending into a

graceful smile, which illuminated his whole countenance. Sometimes, particularly when he had looked at me, his smile almost approached to a gentle laugh.

They conversed through a Chinese interpreter, who translated the Lama's Tibetan into Latin for Manning.[16] Manning's adventures continued, as did his correspondence with Charles Lamb. In 1817 he was aboard a ship that foundered in the Java Sea. A rescue vessel took him to St. Helena, where he interviewed Napoleon, then two years into his final exile. Manning finally returned to England and wrote a brief narrative of his life abroad.

Through George Dyer, Mary and Charles met John Rickman, who had lived in the Southampton Buildings at the same time they did. Rickman ultimately found success as a government bureaucrat, managing Britain's first census and then securing a lucrative position as first clerk to the House of Commons. To Mary and Charles in 1801, though, Rickman was an aspiring poet and an amicable neighbor, whom Charles called "the clearest headed fellow," "fullest of matter with least verbosity," "hugely literate, oppressively full of information," and in general "the finest fellow to *drop* in a nights about nine or ten oClock, cold bread & cheese time, just in the *wishing* time of the night, when you *wish* for somebody to come in, without a distinct idea of a probable anybody."[17]

Rickman soon introduced the Lambs to James Burney, "a merry *natural* captain." An adventurer with a literary soul, Burney admired Shakespeare "because he was so *much of the Gentleman*" and greatly impressed Mary and Charles by making a pun in Tahitian.[18] He had sailed with Capt. James Cook on his last two South Sea voyages, and had taken command of the *Discovery* and brought it home safely after Cook was killed by Hawaiian natives in 1779.

Retired from the navy when he met Mary and Charles,

Captain Burney had set to writing histories of naval discovery. Others in his family had an artistic bent as well. His father, Charles, was a composer, music teacher, and music historian. His sister, Frances—best known as Fanny Burney—had left her post in the court of Charlotte and George III, married Alexandre d'Arblay, Lafayette's aide-de-camp, and become a novelist. Mary Lamb had certainly read her *Evelina, Cecilia,* and *Camilla,* sensitive renderings of domestic life and manners that influenced Jane Austen. Mme. d'Arblay did not become a personal acquaintance of the Lambs, but her nephew Martin Burney, son of the naval adventurer, remained a dear friend to the end of their days.

In and out of the scene wandered Samuel Taylor Coleridge, restlessly uncertain about matters of daily life—where he belonged, what his obligations ought to be—but imperially certain on matters of metaphysics. He would arrive in London unannounced, beg a room from friends, and soon become an overwhelming presence in the household. He was prone to "Coleridgizing," as Charles Lamb liked to say,[19] dominating all conversation with his fascinating, self-referential, transcendental monologues. Some were repulsed by his presence, but Mary and Charles welcomed him. Sometimes he stayed for weeks at a time. "The more I see of him in the quotidian undress and relaxation of his mind, the more cause I see to love him and believe him a *very good man,* and all those foolish impressions to the contrary fly off like morning slumbers," Charles told Manning.[20]

Mary's presence reliably enhanced the forming social circle. She was there whenever her brother brought his friends home, "oftener a listener than a talker," one visitor recalled,[21] but surely commenting now and then amid the spirited conversations. It was Mary's lot, as Charles later wrote in "Mackery End," "to have had for her associates and mine, free-thinkers—leaders, and disciples, of novel philosophies and systems; but she neither wrangles with, nor accepts, their opinions."

WHILE SHE HANDLED herself perfectly well in a smoky room full of argumentative males, Mary Lamb genuinely preferred female company. She was soon to meet the two women who would mean the most to her through the coming years: Sarah Stoddart and Dorothy Wordsworth.

Of the two women Sarah Stoddart was less like Mary. When they met, Mary was thirty-seven, Sarah in her twenties. She had grown up with her parents and her older brother, John, in Salisbury. Her father, a retired naval lieutenant, was aging quickly, so her brother, just receiving his second law degree from Oxford, took over the responsibility as Sarah's male elder. John Stoddart was focused and humorless, while his sister was inclined to be flighty. His paternalistic attitude annoyed her, but he took her future seriously. After all, he had left Oxford to assume a legal position in the College of Advocates, the Church of England's seminal court of marriage law.

Charles Lamb had known of John Stoddart for years. In a letter to Coleridge in the summer of 1796, he called him "a cold hearted well bred conceited disciple of Godwin."[22] How and when Mary met Sarah we do not know—most likely during a summer visit by Sarah to London in 1802, for by July of that year the two women had begun a lively correspondence. Or at least Sarah had begun writing Mary, gossiping about her string of suitors and complaining about the rules her brother imposed on her. He lived in London, while she still lived with her parents in Wiltshire. It made for a challenging guardianship.

For Mary to maintain this newfound friendship, she would have to write back. It was not easy for her. "I have often felt the disadvantage of my own wretched hand-writing," she told a friend.[23] Her alphabet came out large and unshapely, and she had difficulty lining up the words without ruled paper. She could not spell, and she knew it. Embarrassment hindered her expressive urge. But a new friendship and increased confidence encouraged Mary Lamb, having now enjoyed two years without any relapses into madness, to pick up a pen and write. "I am ashamed of having your kind letter so long by me unanswered," she wrote Sarah Stoddart on July 21, 1802. "It lies upon the table and reproaches me all day long—when I beged [sic] you would write to me, I forgot to inform you—I am much fonder of receiving letters, than writing them."[24] While Charles had already adopted the habit of signing letters with a phrase like "Mary sends her love," this letter to Sarah is the first we have in Mary's own hand.

The newness of writing combined with the newness of the friendship made Mary avowedly uneasy. Yet she kept putting words on paper, finding it a way to explore, explain, and grapple with those feelings. "I am always a miserable letter writer, and I feel the want, in writing to a new friend of being able to talk of the days 'O lang syne' [sic]: but this is a defect I trust time will remedy." After a paragraph of apologies, Mary relaxed and turned playful.

> I rejoice exceedingly to hear you have hopes of being in town again next winter—the evenings we spent together, were the pleasantest I have known for a *very* long time: yet I fear you have somehow procured a false character to obtain permission to return to us, I will with pleasure sign any paper of that kind you may have occasion for—I will protest you are the most amusing, good-humoured, good sister, and altogether excellent girl I know, or any other fibs you will please to dictate to me.[25]

When Sarah's prompt reply to this happy letter arrived, Mary was all in a dither. She and Charles were embarking on an impromptu journey, heading north to visit Samuel Coleridge. It was early August, and Mary found it "utterly impossible to write (what with the warm weather, which relaxes the thumbs, & what with a Journey into Cumberland, . . . which causes much speculation)."[26] The impending journey brought both joy and anxiety. Just two years before, Charles had traveled to Cambridge alone, feeling "something of dishonesty in any pleasures I take without *her*,"[27] yet both agreed that she would do better at home. In 1801, they had hazarded a trip to the beach in Margate, "to drink sea water and pick up shells,"[28] and Mary seemed the better for it. So now, in 1802, Charles took full advantage of his annual holiday from East India House.

They headed to Greta Hall in Keswick, the Lake District home to which, two years before, Samuel, Sara, and Hartley Coleridge had moved, in large part to be closer to the Wordsworths, who lived eleven or twelve miles away in little Dove Cottage in the village of Grasmere. Soon after the move, a second Coleridge son arrived, Derwent, born sickly but now becoming a beguiling toddler. Devoted to his children, Coleridge had little affection for his wife. "If my wife loved me, and I my wife, half as well as we both love our children, I should be the happiest man alive—but this is not—will not be!" he wrote a friend.[29] Stomach ailments plagued him—a modern diagnosis suggests it was neuralgia compounded by rheumatism[30]—and he was relying more heavily on laudanum for relief from pain. He had just spent the winter in London, leaving his family behind, and was obsessed with a woman named Sara Hutchinson, sister of the woman William Wordsworth would soon marry. Coleridge decided that Sara Hutchinson—or Asra, as he called her, to distinguish her from his wife—was the love of his life. He was reluctant to dissolve his marriage, though, which made Asra all the more intriguing.

Mary and Charles may not have known the full extent of the turmoil inside the soul of their dear friend Coleridge as they rode in a post chaise from London to Penrith, a journey of several days. They arrived "in the midst of a gorgeous sun shine, which transmuted all the mountains into colours, purple," Charles recalled for Manning. "We thought we had got into Fairy Land."[31] They stayed for three weeks with the Coleridges and came to dote on Derwent, nearly two, whom they fondly called "Pi-pos" after amusedly hearing him point out a "flying possum" in one of his favorite books. Charles told Coleridge that Derwent was "the only child (but one) I had ever an inclination to *steal* from its parents."[32] Mary promised to send him more books from London.

Mary and Charles had every good reason to believe that on this same journey they might spend time with the Wordsworths. They walked to Grasmere, only to find the sister and brother away from home, their house being tended by Catherine and Thomas Clarkson, with whom they "past a very pleasant little time,"[33] the start of another long friendship. Thomas Clarkson had dedicated years of his life to the abolition of the African slave trade. His relentless investigations of Britain's slave-trading ports provided the evidence used by William Wilberforce in his campaign to have Parliament abolish slavery in the 1780s and '90s. Bad health had forced Clarkson to retire from the effort, and it was during this period that he and his wife were staying at Dove Cottage. He later returned to the cause. In 1808 he published a triumphant *History of the Rise, Progress, and Accomplishment of the Abolition of the African Slave Trade,* and he worked for emancipation around the world through the rest of his life.

The Clarksons informed Mary and Charles that the Wordsworths were in Calais. The Treaty of Amiens, signed in March 1802, temporarily relaxed animosities between Britain and France, making cross-Channel travel possible. William Wordsworth took the opportunity to heal an old wound. Leaving behind Mary Hutchinson, the woman he intended to marry, he and his sister spent four weeks with Annette Vallon, his lover of ten years before. A fourth person joined them as they walked the seashore those August days: Caroline, the lovers' nine-year-old daughter.

Wordsworth had not seen the child since her baptism, and he would not see her again for another eighteen years.[34] In September, the foursome went their separate ways. Annette and Caroline returned home to Blois, southwest of Paris. Dorothy and William returned to Grasmere, and on October 4 Mary Hutchinson became Mrs. Wordsworth.

Mary Lamb may already have met the Wordsworths before 1802. Missing them that summer, she was disappointed not to get to know Dorothy better. The two women were similar in many ways. Their brothers were now friends, and a meaningful encounter between them must have seemed a likely possibility that would now have to wait for another time.

Dorothy and her brother William were younger than Mary, older than Charles. In a sense, they were even more a matched pair than the Lambs. Born only fifteen months apart, second and third of five children, they grew up in the little market town of Cockermouth, Cumberland, where their mother came from a well-regarded mercer's family and their father served as bailiff and coroner. While William attended grammar school, Dorothy learned to read and write at home. Their mother died when Dorothy was only six, and the household disbanded. William went away to school, and Dorothy went to live with a feisty, unmarried cousin whom she called "Aunt Threlkeld." Sewing was not Dorothy's pleasure. She would rather read a novel or a classic or, better yet, write. She wrote letters. She wrote diaries. Words flowed easily for her. Only the times kept Dorothy Wordsworth from being a published author like her brother.

In 1795 Dorothy and William Wordsworth reunited. Dorothy was twenty-four, William twenty-five, and like the Lambs, they chose to make a household together. They first moved into a country house, Alfoxden, which they discovered when they, along with Charles Lamb, visited the Coleridges in 1798. Then they found Dove Cottage in nearby Grasmere, where they lived for ten years. The new Mrs. Wordsworth joined the ménage in 1802.

During the Dove Cottage years, creative energies coursed between sister and brother, and most critics pay homage to Dorothy as part creator of many of Wordsworth's finest poems. They walked for hours together, communing with nature and the children and elders of the countryside. Coleridge commended Dorothy's keen eye and sensibility: "She is a woman indeed! in mind, I mean, and heart; . . . her manners are simple, ardent, impressive—. . . . Her information various—her eye watchful in minutest observation of nature—and her taste a perfect electrometer—it bends, protrudes, and draws in, at subtlest beauties & most recondite faults."[35] Dorothy kept lyrical notes of her observations of nature; William turned them into verse. In April 1802 Dorothy and William braved a raw spring wind to walk along the shore of Ullswater, an inland lake just north of Grasmere. In her journal Dorothy remembered the views this way:

> When we were in the woods beyond Gowbarrow Park we saw a few daffodils close to the water-side. . . . I never saw daffodils so beautiful. They grew among the mossy stones about and about them; some rested their heads upon these stones as on a pillow for weariness; and the rest tossed and reeled and danced, and seemed as if they verily laughed with the wind, that blew upon them over the lake; they looked so gay, ever glancing, ever changing.[36]

In 1804 William Wordsworth published his poem "Daffodils."

> *I wander'd lonely as a cloud*
> *That floats on high o'er vales and hills,*
> *When all at once I saw a crowd,*

A host, of golden daffodils;
Beside the lake, beneath the trees,
Fluttering and dancing in the breeze.

Like the bond between Mary and Charles Lamb, Dorothy and William Wordsworth's was an intense and interdependent relationship. It flowered into a poetic collaboration, set a bit off balance when the brother took a wife.

"On Monday, 4th October 1802, my brother William was married to Mary Hutchinson," Dorothy recorded in her journal:

> I slept a good deal of the night, and rose fresh and well in the morning. . . . I kept myself as quiet as I could, but when I saw the two men running up the walk, coming to tell us it was over, I could stand it no longer, and threw myself on the bed, where I lay in stillness, neither hearing or seeing anything till Sara [her new sister-in-law's sister] came upstairs to me, and said, "They are coming." This forced me from the bed where I lay, and I moved, I knew not how, straight forward, faster than my strength would carry me, till I met my beloved William, and fell upon his bosom.[37]

While Dorothy had no doubt she was welcome in Mr. and Mrs. Wordsworth's household, her relationship with her poetical brother changed forever. The entries in her journal dwindled, then stopped altogether three months later.

MARY AND CHARLES missed the Wordsworths, but Coleridge, his foot now healed, would not let them leave his Lake Country landscape without a climb up Mount Skiddaw, the three-thousand-foot peak that reigned on the horizon between Cockermouth and Keswick. "What was the great Parnassus' self to Thee, / Mount

Skiddaw?" Wordsworth had just written in a sonnet. They set out on foot to find answers to that question.

Mary was the first to tire, Charles later reported,

> when she got about half way up Skiddaw, but we came to a cold rill (than which nothing can be imagined more cold, running over cold stones) & with the reinforcemt. of a draught of cold water, she surmounted it most manfully.—O its fine black head & the bleak air a top of it, with a prospect of mountains all about & about, making you giddy, & then Scotland afar off & the border countries so famous in song & ballad.

For Mary and Charles, to be sure, it was "a day that will stand out, like a mountain," as he wrote Manning. On that day they breathed deeply of the landscape and the spirit, and Charles self-consciously labeled the experience with a word that would come to signify the era: "In fine I have satisfied myself, that there is such a thing as that, which tourists call *romantic,* which I very much suspected before: they make such a spluttering about it, and toss their splendid epithets around them, till they give as dim a light, as four oClock next morning the Lamps do after an illumination."[38]

That journey formed a touchstone in the memory of Charles Lamb, to be called up whenever the debate between city and country recurred. "I was born (as you have heard) bred, & have past most part of my time in a *crowd.* This has begot in me an entire affection for that way of life, amounting to an almost insurmountable aversion from solitude & rural scenes," Charles was fond of claiming.[39] Yet now a certain ambivalence crept in. Nature's serenity could put a rattled mind at ease. What's more, it was the spirit of the age, embodied in no one better than in the Lambs' friends, Coleridge and Wordsworth: to breathe deeply of country air and in that breath draw closer to the heart of what is good and true.

Mary Lamb connected with Dorothy Wordsworth sooner than

expected since, on their way home from Calais, the Wordsworths stopped in London. They stayed with a friend who lived in the Paper Buildings, also part of the Inner Temple, making them for the moment, as Charles put it, "near neighbors to us."[40] Their visit in early September 1802 coincided with Saint Bartholomew's Day. One imagines that Mary and Charles took great delight in guiding them through the spectacle of acrobats, musicians, puppeteers, freaks, and beggars crowding Smithfield Market during London's annual Bartholomew Fair.

DAILY LIFE assumed its routine, with Charles keeping books at the East India House and Mary tending to household matters at home. The evenings started early and stretched on into the night, full of friends and banter. A circle of lifelong friends was forming, the genial Lambs at its center. Spirits loosened their tongues; pipes elevated the mood. Friends knew to bring food, drink, or tobacco, but Mary and Charles were happy to share a bit of their own cheese or oysters, brandy or porter.

"Wine makes me hot, and brandy makes me drunk, but porter warms without intoxication; and elevates, yet not too much above the point of tranquillity," Charles wrote Coleridge, thanking him for a Christmas gift of porter. When John Rickman inquired what spirits Mary preferred, her brother answered outright, "[S]he prefers *Rum*."[41] It embarrassed her no end.

She probably occasionally shared a pipe with the men in the circle, filled with Virginia tobacco, if they could manage. "What do you think of smoking?" Charles asked Samuel Taylor Coleridge—by this point, in 1803, not the best adviser on the subject of intoxicants, but Charles probably didn't want advice anyway.

I want your sober, *average, noon opinion* of it.—I generally am eating my dinner about the time I should determine it.

Morning is a Girl, & c'ant smoke—she's no evidence one way or other.—& Night is so evidently *bought over,* that *he* ca'nt be a very upright Judge—. May be the truth is that *one* pipe is wholesome, *two* pipes toothsome, *three* pipes noisom, four *pipes* fulsom, *five* pipes quarrelsome, and thats the *sum* on't [*sic*].—But that is deciding rather upon rhime than reason. After all our instincts *may* be best.[42]

In the years to come the habits of smoking and drinking tormented Charles Lamb's health and conscience. Two of his well-remembered works are the poem "A Farewell to Tobacco" and the essay "Confessions of a Drunkard." "Liquor and Company and wicked Tobacco a' nights, have quite dispericraniated me," he wrote Thomas Manning.[43] Mary shared his predilection for tobacco but used it in a different form: "She took snuff liberally," wrote Mary Cowden Clarke in her retrospective portrait. "She had a small, white, and delicately-formed hand" which "hovered above the tortoise-shell box containing the powder so strongly approved by them both," sister and brother.[44] At the same time, Mary recognized the harm that smoking could do to her brother.

She stood as a guardian and model, but not a disciplinarian. She tolerated his excesses. "Charles was drunk last night, and drunk the night before," Mary once reported to Sarah Stoddart. Heading home one evening, "brimfull of Gin & water & snuff," Charles brought a new friend. "There was much gin & water drunk albeit only one of the party partook of it," Mary reported to Sarah. The guest "professed himself highly indebted to Charles for the useful information he gave him on sundry matters of taste and imagination, even after Charles could not speak plain for tipsyness."

The next evening "was to be a night of temperance," Mary wrote. Perhaps Charles had voiced a morning-after pledge. They and the Rickmans dined at the home of the Martin Burneys. "Ms Burney brought forth, first rum, then a single bottle of champaine, long kept in her secret hoard," Mary reported to Sarah, "then two bottles of her best current wine which she keeps for Mrs Rickman came out & Charles partook liberally of all these beverages."[45] Clearly she was watching out.

Their life together became a balancing act of mutual care and alternating excesses. While Charles stood fast by his promise to care for his sister if uncontrollable feelings overtook her, Mary was just as significantly Charles's "daily & hourly prop," as he recognized.[46] They seesawed back and forth, sharing weaknesses, offering solace, recognizing quietly between themselves that they both flirted with madness now and then. Sometimes the balance tipped one way, sometimes the other. One's hold on sanity allowed the other to slide. "When I am pretty well his low spirits, throws me back again," Mary told Sarah Stoddart, "& when he begins to get a little chearful then I do the same kind office for him——."[47]

Sometimes they sank into depressions simultaneously, but even those were moments of togetherness. "Do not say any thing when you write of our low spirits it will vex Charles," she whispered to Sarah in writing.

> You would laugh, or you would cry, perhaps both, to see us sit together looking at each other with long and rueful faces, & saying how do you do? & how do you do? & then we fall a crying & say we will be better on the morrow—he says we are like tooth ach & his friend gum bile, which though a kind of ease, is but an uneasy kind of ease, a comfort of rather an uncomfortable sort.[48]

Together they laughed, together they cried, together they read and, more and more during these early years of the nineteenth century, together they wrote. In 1802 Charles Lamb scraped together enough money to publish *John Woodvil,* a tragedy he had written about the era of Charles I. With it he included a short

poem called "High-Born Helen"—the first published work written by Mary Lamb.

> *High-born Helen, round your dwelling*
> *These twenty years I've paced in vain:*
> *Haughty beauty, thy lover's duty*
> *Hath been to glory in his pain.*
>
> *High-born Helen, proudly telling*
> *Stories of thy cold disdain;*
> *I starve, I die, now you comply,*
> *And I no longer can complain.*
>
> *These twenty years I've lived on tears,*
> *Dwelling for ever on a frown;*
> *On sighs I've fed, your scorn my bread;*
> *I perish now you kind are grown.*
>
> *Can I, who loved my beloved*
> *But for the scorn "was in her eye,"*
> *Can I be moved for my beloved,*
> *When she "returns me sigh for sigh"?*
>
> *In stately pride, by my bed-side*
> *High-born Helen's portrait's hung;*
> *Deaf to my praise, my mournful lays*
> *Are nightly to the portrait sung.*
>
> *To that I weep, nor ever sleep,*
> *Complaining all night long to her—*
> *Helen, grown old, no longer cold,*
> *Said, "You to all men I prefer."*

The poem sits at many removes from its author. It is written in
the voice of a man. It addresses, as one realizes by the end, a

painting. And in the end, in a curious twist of animation, it grants the painting a voice and a character. After twenty years of receiving admiration, the painting warms up and returns the favor.

Mary allowed Charles to publish her poem in his volume, but she wanted to keep its authorship a secret, even from their best friends. "Mary always desires to be most kindly remembered by you," Charles wrote Rickman. Then, as if in brotherly pride he could not contain himself, he continued, "She bids me *not* tell you, that an Epigram called *Helen* in my little Book, is of her writing. But it is, every tittle of it."[49] Mary herself remained silent about her first experience of being seen in print, but she must have felt the thrill and pride, as well as the anxiety, of authorship.

In these feelings Mary Lamb joined many female authors, her contemporaries and even those a generation after her. The Brontë sisters hid their identities in male names: Currer, Ellis, and Acton Bell were pseudonyms for Charlotte, Emily, and Anne Brontë. *Frankenstein* was not attributed to Mary Shelley in its first edition. Closer to Mary Lamb's time, the novelist Mary Brunton colorfully explained the anxieties of female authorship in an 1810 letter to a friend:

> I would rather, as you well know, glide through the world unknown, than have (I will not call it *enjoy*) fame, however, brilliant, to be pointed at,—to be noticed and commented upon—to be suspected of literary airs—to be shunned, as literary women are, by the more unpretending of my own sex; and abhorred as literary women are, by the pretending of the other!—my dear, I would sooner exhibit as a rope-dancer.[50]

To become recognized as a woman writer, one took significant social risks—risks Mary Lamb was not willing to add to her burden.

———

MARY LAMB entered the spring of 1803 with reason for confidence. In the six and a half years since the act that so marked her and made the memory that would never go away, she had spent only a fraction of her time in confinement: for six months after the matricide, then for two winter months in 1797–98 and one summer month in 1800—not one day in twelve, and none in nearly three years. She was running a household, fulfilling an occasional request for sewing or mending, visiting and corresponding with friends she held dear. She had even published a poem.

Then something happened, and it is difficult to say what.

Maybe it was that Samuel Coleridge, in London since mid-March, was living with the Lambs. He was by this point addicted to medicinal opiates. His marriage had deteriorated beyond recovery since the December 1802 birth of a daughter, their fourth child but the third to survive. Frequent nightmares woke him up and terrified him in the middle of the night. "While I am awake, by patience, employment, effort of mind, and walking I can keep the fiend at Arm's length," he wrote at this time, "but the Night is my Hell, Sleep my tormenting Angel. Three nights out of four I fall asleep, struggling to lie awake—and my frequent Night-screams have almost made me a nuisance in my own House."[51] Those screams, and concern over her friend's health, could have been disturbing Mary's sleep for nights on end.

Maybe it was that Charles, wound up with friends and poetry, whist and gin, needed too much from her. Maybe their life was becoming so routine that he was neglecting to thank her for her attention and her work. Or maybe, on the other hand, sensing her growing capabilities, Charles was pressing Mary for her own sake: *Write more poems! Visit more people! Engage!*

Maybe it was organic—a biological cycle with a rhythm all its own that no one, not even the mind within which it turned, could discern.

Or maybe it really was triggered by the circumstance to which

Coleridge attributed it: a chance conversation that brought back too vividly to Mary's mind the memory of her mother. In early April, Coleridge wrote home about the incident:

> I had purposed not to speak of Mary Lamb—but I had better write it than tell it. The Thursday before last [March 24, 1803] she met at Rickman's a Mr Babb, an old old Friend & Admirer of her Mother
>
> the next day she *smiled* in an ominous way—on Sunday she told her Brother that she was getting bad, with great agony—on Tuesday morning she layed hold of me with violent agitation, & talked wildly about George Dyer
>
> I told Charles, there was not a moment to lose
>
> and I did not lose a moment—but went for a Hackney Coach, & took her to the private Madhouse at Hogsden [Hoxton]
>
> She was quite calm, & said—it was best to do so—but she wept bitterly two of three times, yet all in a calm way. Charles is cut to the Heart[52]

Charles, Mary, and companions, very likely Coleridge, had gone to the Southampton Buildings, home of John and Susannah Rickman, for a pleasant evening—dinner, drinks, a smoke, a rousing conversation. In and out of these evening socials passed many a Londoner, to be sure, and that evening John Rickman introduced Mr. Babb, a personage known to the historical record only by this appearance. When Mr. Babb heard that he was in the presence of the grown children of a woman whom he had known and admired, he may have expatiated on her virtues and the loss he felt now that she was gone. He may even have asked questions, ignorant of how they cut to a tender quick, about events surrounding her death. Whatever happened that evening, Coleridge watched with trepidation as Mary's madness returned.

The sequence of Mary's symptoms, as reported in Coleridge's letter to his wife, is significant. The first day she shows an ominous smile. The third day she expresses an awareness that the illness is approaching. Then, on the fifth day, she erupts, grabbing Coleridge "with violent agitation" and "talking wildly." The outburst appears to have been brief, passing, and innocent, but there is a similarity of pattern here consistent with what was recorded about the days leading up to the act of matricide, particularly in that Mary seemed to have been self-aware as the symptoms overtook her.

Coupled closely with the outburst was Mary's deep sense of sorrow and dejection, displayed as she was delivered to the madhouse. Coleridge twice describes her as "calm" and resigned to the situation. She agreed, he grants, that it "was the best to do so," but on the way "she wept bitterly two or three times," devastated to find herself once again plunging into severe mental illness. This time Mary resided in Hoxton House—for what reasons we cannot be sure. It was located conveniently close to East India House headquarters, and despite their hundreds of inmates, the Hoxton House superintendents already knew the Lambs.

MARY WENT INTO Hoxton House in early April and returned home to her brother in early July, much distraught that "I have been a sad trouble to him." Depression continued to weigh on her, even after she came home. "I continued so long so very weak & dejected I began to fear I should never be at all comfortable again," she wrote Dorothy Wordsworth. "I strive against low spirits all I can, but it is a very hard thing to get the better of."[53]

Later that month the Lambs escaped the city and journeyed to the Isle of Wight. Their host, James Burney, was much amused by their ignorance of sailing. "We went by water," Burney wrote Rickman, "and friend Lamb (to give a specimen of his Seamanship) very ingeniously and unconsciously cast loose the fastenings of the mast, so that Mast, sprit, sails, and all the rest tumbled overboard with a crash." Once safely on the island, the group settled into such pleasant routines that Mary began to regain her spirits. "We do every thing that is idle, such as reading books from a circulating library, sauntering, hunting little crabs among the rocks, reading Church Yard poetry," reported Captain Burney. "Miss Lamb is the only person among us who is not idle. All the care she takes into her keeping. At Night however we do a little business in the smoking line. . . . Such is the edifying life we lead at the Isle of Wight."[54]

Charles Lamb added to the same letter, telling Rickman that Burney had written a "pretty good outline of our doings," but that he liked best the hours after supper, when "a gentle circumambience of the weed serves to shut out Isle of Wight impertinent scenery and brings us back in fancy to Mutton Lane and the romantic alleys . . . of nether Holborn."[55] Thanks to this trip, Mary returned to London feeling "stout and lively."[56] At the same time, though, she must have been quietly, privately, desperately adjusting to the knowledge that her life might always include an occasional visit to the madhouse.

8

CHILDREN'S BOOKS

As THEY HAD promised the Coleridge children, Mary and Charles Lamb did go shopping for books for them, and where else would they have gone but Newbery's, at the east end of Saint Paul's Churchyard? It was London's favorite place for books written for children, shelves amply stocked with all the hornbooks and chapbooks, alphabets and lessons, histories, fables, and miscellanies that English children of the day were reading. The publishing and bookselling business had been founded by the great John Newbery more than fifty years before. Newbery was far from the first creator of children's books, but his vision expanded the possibilities of the field and established it as a bonafide arm of the book business at a time when London was the publishing capital of the world. It is for him that the annual Newbery Award for distinguished American children's literature was named. John Newbery died in 1767, but his son Francis managed the business for decades thereafter.

Mary and Charles came away outraged at current tastes in children's literature. "Goody Two Shoes is almost out of print," Charles ranted to Samuel Coleridge.

Mrs. Barbauld's stuff has banished all the old classics of the nursery; & the Shopman at Newbery's hardly deign'd to reach them off an old exploded corner of a shelf, when Mary ask'd for them. Mrs. B's & Mrs. Trimmer's nonsense lay in piles about. Knowledge insignificant & vapid as Mrs. B's books convey, it seems, must come to a child in the *shape* of *knowledge,* & his empty noddle must be turned with conceit of his own powers, when he has learnt, that a Horse is an Animal, & Billy is better than a Horse, & such like: instead of that beautiful Interest in wild tales, which made the child a man, while all the time he suspected himself to be no bigger than a child. Science has succeeded to Poetry no less in the little walks of Children than with Men.[1]

They had wanted to send Hartley and Derwent *The History of Goody Two-Shoes,* published by Newbery in 1765 and reputed to have been written by Oliver Goldsmith. Mary had read the book as a child, and she probably had read it aloud to Charles as well. It tells the quaint and sentimental story of a sister and brother who fall on hard times:

> After their mother was dead, it would have done any one's heart good to have seen how fond these two little one's [*sic*] were of each other, and how, hand in hand, they trotted about. Pray see them, for they loved each other, though they were very poor, and for want of parents or friends to provide for them, they were both very ragged; as for Tommy, he had two shoes, but Margery had but one.

Circumstances force the siblings to separate. When kind benefactors purchase Margery a new pair of shoes, she takes great joy in them, crying out, "Two Shoes, ma'am, see, two shoes," from which moment she "obtained the name of Goody Two-Shoes."

Margery Meanwell comes through abandonment, abuse, loneliness, and adoption to become a learned and generous young woman. Recognizing how important reading was to her salvation, Margaret invents tiny wooden alphabet blocks and carries them from village to village, using them to instruct children in reading. Eventually she becomes the president of the "A, B, C, college."[2]

Antiquated to our eyes, in the mid–eighteenth century *Goody Two-Shoes* was a revelation, daringly different from existing children's reading material. "Do you intend this for children, Mr. Newbery?" the introduction to an 1813 edition asks rhetorically.[3] The story's simple narrative, with neither religious nor pedagogical principles forcefully shaping its content, represented a new type of reading material for children.

In eighteenth-century grammar schools such as William Byrd's Academy, which both Mary and Charles attended, children learned reading from hornbooks—stiff placards with handles to which a single sheet was attached, displaying the alphabet, simple letter combinations *(ab, eb, ib, ob, ub)*, and often a traditional religious passage, like the Doxology or the Lord's Prayer. From those, children graduated to an ABC, which matched alphabet letters, words or phrases, and pictures. Having mastered an ABC, a child was ready to read whole sentences.

It had been customary for children next to read texts with religious, or at least moral, content. John Bunyan's *Pilgrim's Progress* (1678) engaged young readers by turning a standard religious message into an interesting tale. In Isaac Watts's *Divine Songs Attempted in Easy Language for the Use of Children* (1715), sweet, simple poems captured the lyricism without the didacticism of Protestant virtue:

> *Hush! my dear, lie still, and slumber,*
> *Holy angels guard thy bed!*
> *Heavenly blessings without number*
> *Gently falling on thy head.*[4]

At about the same time, adventure classics still read today were written for adults but enjoyed by older children, such as Daniel Defoe's *The Life and Strange Surprising Adventures of Robinson Crusoe* (1719) and Jonathan Swift's *Gulliver's Travels* (1726).

In *Goody Two-Shoes,* though, published in 1765, Newbery introduced an entirely new genre of children's reading: a secular, domestic story with a narrative that entertains first and foremost and subtly teaches as well. Newbery published others along the same lines: *The Renowned History of Giles Gingerbread* (1764), for example, a series of adventures ending with a couplet admonishing every child, rich or poor, to learn to read:

> Giles Gingerbread, *he lov'd Cream, Custard, and Curds,*
> *And good Books so well that he eat up his Words.*[5]

At least one historian of children's literature calls *Goody Two-Shoes* and *Giles Gingerbread* the first trade books for children.[6]

But when Mary and Charles visited Newbery's in 1802, they found these favorites of theirs shoved into a corner along with "all the old classics of the nursery," while new "nonsense" was more prominently displayed: books written for children by Mrs. Barbauld and Mrs. Trimmer, two prolific authors whose principles carried writing for children in directions that did not win the Lambs' approval.

Anna Laetitia Aikin Barbauld, recently rescued from the shadows by feminist literary scholars, was a distinguished poet and essayist, highly respected in the days when Samuel Taylor Coleridge and Charles Lamb were just finding their way onto the printed page. In 1798 the editor of the *Lady's Monthly Museum* wrote that Barbauld's poems "are now in the possession of every person who has any pretensions to taste."[7] Coleridge so revered her work that he walked forty miles to meet her and soon wrote, "The more I see of Mrs Barbauld the more I admire her—. . . . She has great *acute-*

ness, very great—yet how steadily she keeps it within the bounds of practical Reason. This I almost envy as well as admire."[8]

Coleridge admired her poetry and her political and historical prose, in which she praised the French Revolution, argued against slavery, advocated for the poor and the working class, and attacked the government for continuing to wage war on France. But those were not the works displayed in Newbery's bookshop. In 1802 her *Lessons for Children* (1778–79) were selling like crazy: tiny books that offered a new, scientific way to teach reading. Barbauld's method represents the precursor to today's scaffolded approach to teaching reading, by which a child progresses through a sequence of texts, each using words and syntax chosen to match a certain level of ability.

For a three- or four-year-old reader, Barbauld believed, the medium was more important than the message. The time to convey moral and religious content came only after the child mastered the mechanics of reading words on the page.

Dark dismal November is come. No more flowers! no more pleasant sun-shine! no more hay-making! The sky is very black: the rain pours down. Well, never mind it. We will sit by the fire, and read, and tell stories, and look at pictures. Where is Billy and Harry, and little Betsey? Now, tell me who can spell best. Good boy! There is a clever fellow! Now you shall have some cake.[9]

Occasionally a moral message crept in, but always extolling reason and learning:

Do you know why you are better than puss? Puss can play as well as you; and Puss can drink milk, and lie upon the carpet; and she can run as fast as you, and faster, too, a great deal; and she can climb trees better; and she can catch mice, which you cannot do. But can Puss talk? No. Can Puss read? No. Then that is the reason why you are better than Puss—because you can talk and read. . . . If you do not learn, Charles, you are not good for half as much as puss. You had better be drowned.[10]

Sarah Trimmer took on a more vigorously Christian and Tory mission. Her books for children, as well as her short-lived *Family Magazine,* told stories intended to preserve the status quo. Wealthy landowners and aristocrats are wise and benevolent heroes; the poor risk ruin, sucked in by revolutionary rhetoric. In *The Servant's Friend* (1797), a new cook brings novels and ballads into Reverend Brown's household, threatening the morals of the young maidservant, Kitty, who is saved in the end by prayer.[11]

"Good Girls make their own clothes," children read in Sarah Trimmer's *Charity School Spelling Book* (1790), certainly one item among the "piles of nonsense" that so upset Mary and Charles at Newbery's shop. Remarkably long lived, this tiny volume (five and a half by three and a half inches) had gone into a seventh edition by 1802. The book taught reading in an orderly sequence, from the alphabet through phonemically arranged syllables to simple sentences, each with a moral slant: "It is a sad sight to see dirt on the skin" and "No one likes rude Boys and Girls, they get beat and chid."[12]

Two editions of *The Charity School Spelling Book* were published, one for boys and one for girls. Elementary reading lessons were identical in both books, but more advanced stories differed. Each gender read vignettes of moral character. Boys read of Dick Grange, who tormented his dog by tying bones to its tail; and of Jack Paine, who was "one of those boys that love to tease and vex the rest"; and of Ned Jenks, who would fight with others over nothing until "at last one gave him a blow that was the death of him." Girls read of Betty Clarke, who "had a sad trick, she would play with fire"; and Beckey Bond, a twelve-year-old who "would not make a bed, or sweep a room, or scrub a shelf." When Beckey was asked to care for a baby, she "would not take it up and feed it" and, responding to any crossness in the infant, "would give it a great slap, or stuff its mouth with trash to keep it quiet." Beckey is the epitome of the bad girl: "To romp with bad boys in the streets was the great joy of Beckey Bond's life, so she learnt of them to be bold, to swear, and to call names; and at last she learnt to steal, and came to a bad end, you may be sure." To offset the effect of Beckey's story, girls also read about Ann Stove, who did all she could to make her friends love her.[13]

Barbauld's and Trimmer's agendas differed, but Mary and Charles Lamb lumped them together, since neither satisfied their hunger for imagination and lyricism, for "wild tales" and poetry. Charles pounced on the issue: "Is there no possibility of averting this sore evil?" he asked Coleridge rhetorically. "Think what you would have been now, if instead of being fed with Tales and old wives fables in childhood, you had been crammed with Geography & Natural History.? *Damn them.* I mean the cursed Barbauld Crew, those *Blights & Blasts* of all that is *Human* in man & child."[14] Fueled by this passion for imaginative children's literature—and seeking ways to earn more money—Mary and Charles soon embarked on a project that would earn them their own place on the shelves of Newbery's bookshop.

Children's literature had also come to interest a friend of theirs, William Godwin. Godwin's life had taken significant turns since the days when he first socialized with the Lambs. He wrote continually, but he could not regain the readership he had won in the early 1790s with *Political Justice* and *Caleb Williams*. Watching friends suffer the slings and arrows of government repression, he adjusted his vision of what sort of writing he should attempt. He never departed from his deeply held beliefs in democracy and the perfectibility of human society, though, which subtly infuse all he wrote and published through the rest of his career.

Godwin first published a novel, *St. Leon: A Tale of the Sixteenth Century,* then a melodrama of the same era, *Antonio,* set in Spain, to which Charles Lamb contributed a prologue and epilogue. After much campaigning on Godwin's part, *Antonio* was performed at the Theatre Royal—once. Mary and Charles attended the disaster. Charles scribbled on his playbill, "Damned with Universal Consent."[15] Godwin revised *Antonio,* then wrote another play about Abbas, a sixteenth-century Persian shah, but neither the revision nor the new work saw the light of day.

In the meantime Godwin's publisher, Richard Phillips, suggested he write a biography of Geoffrey Chaucer, the author of *The Canterbury Tales.* Three years later, in 1803, Godwin's two-volume *Life of Chaucer* was issued. Seeing the growing market for children's readers, Phillips also asked Godwin to write a book of Bible stories. It came out in 1802, its authorship hidden behind the pseudonym William Scolfield. It proved Godwin's most successful book in years, remained in print for thirty years, and found its way to the United States in at least two pirated editions.[16]

Godwin, the notorious atheist, may have seemed an unlikely author for a book of Bible stories, but he considered Old Testament stories no different from fairy tales and fables. They stimulated children's imaginations, a need left unfilled by contemporary children's books like those by Mrs. Barbauld. The new wave in children's literature made youth "excellent geographers, natural historians and mechanics," but left them "exactly informed about all those things, which if a man or a woman were to live or die without knowing, neither man nor woman would be an atom the worse." Works of imagination, on the other hand, genuinely strengthened the moral fiber. "It is the heart which most deserves to be cultivated," Godwin wrote, "the pulses which beat with sympathy, and qualify us for the habits of charity, reverence, and attachment."[17]

While Godwin's theories of children's literature closely paralleled those of the Lambs, the three did not often socialize in those days. Godwin had too much to do in his own household, now that Mary was six and Fanny nearly ten. He was deep into his own experiment of turning principles into parenting. "Democracy restores to man a consciousness of his value, teaches him by the removal of authority and oppression to listen only to the dictates of reason, gives him confidence to treat all other men as his fellow beings, and induces him to regard them no longer as enemies against whom to be upon his guard, but as brethren whom it becomes him to assist."[18] Godwin had stated this principle in his most important work, and now he was trying to follow it as he raised his two daughters, teaching by inspiration rather than dogma, by discovery rather than rote memorizing.

In some ways Godwin's educational philosophy sounded facile: "The road to the improvement of mankind is in the utmost degree simple, to speak and act the truth."[19] In other ways it challenged the elders of society to slice through convention and call forth the genius intrinsic in every human being. Children enter the world "trailing clouds of glory," wrote Wordsworth in 1804, uttering one of the essential tenets of Romanticism. For Godwin education was to discover those inlying truths, not impose principles or practices that obscure them. It is an age-old argument—inspire versus instruct—which persists to the present day. Believing in inspiration as he did, Godwin placed himself in contradistinction to Barbauld and began to consider children's literature a promising arena, especially once prodded by his enterprising new wife.

As the story has it, Mary Jane Clairmont, calling herself a widow but more likely an unmarried mother, began the flirtation in 1801. According to a late-nineteenth-century biographer, Mrs. Clairmont saw the opportunity one day and leaned out of her window and cried, "Is it possible that I behold the immortal Godwin?"[20] Apparently the tactic worked.

The Lambs watched the courtship with some amusement. "I know no more news from here, except that the *professor* (Godwin) is *Courting*," Charles wrote Rickman.

> The Lady is a Widow with green spectacles & one child, and the Professor is grown quite juvenile. He bows when he is spoke to, and smiles without occasion, and wriggles as fantastically as Malvolio [the foppish suitor in Shakespeare's *Twelfth Night*], and has more affectation than a canary bird pluming his feathers when he thinks somebody looks at him. He lays down his spectacles, as if in scorn, & takes 'em up again from necessity, and winks that she may'nt see he gets sleepy about eleven oClock. You never saw such a philosophic coxcomb, nor any one play the Romeo so unnaturally.[21]

Playfulness was one thing, but when word came that Godwin intended to marry Mrs. Clairmont, Charles Lamb believed that he was "about to commit a folly."[22] She would add not one, as Charles had supposed, but two more children to the Godwin household: five-year-old Charles and three-year-old Jane (who later, using the name Claire, would become a major character in the dramas involving her stepsister Mary, Shelley, and Byron). Charles worried that Mrs. Clairmont brought "no fortune" to the marriage, and it was questionable whether she could earn money, although she had translated Voltaire and Rousseau.[23]

Despite Mrs. Clairmont's shortcomings William Godwin decided to marry her, persuaded even more vigorously by her pregnancy. On December 21, 1801, they became man and wife, the wedding witnessed by James Marshall, one of Godwin's oldest and most stalwart friends. The two parents set up one household at 29 the Polygon, south of the Thames in Somers Town. Mary Jane suffered a miscarriage; the couple's son, William, was born on March 28, 1803.

Friends began to notice a change in Godwin's lifestyle even before the bond became legal. "The Professor's Rib has come out to be a damn'd disagreeable woman, so much as to drive me & some more old *Cronies* from his House," Lamb wrote Manning in February 1802. "If a man will keep *Snakes* in his House, he must not wonder if People are shy of coming to see him *because of the Snakes*."[24] Things did not improve with time, at least in Charles's estimation. "Godwin (with a pitiful artificial Wife) continues a steady friend: tho' the same facility does not remain of visiting him often," Charles reported in September 1802. "That Bitch has detached Marshall from his house": James Marshall—"the old steady, unalterable, friend of the Professor," as Charles had called him.[25]

The new Mrs. Godwin infected relationships with other old friends as well, including the Lambs. When Coleridge didn't care to review Godwin's *Life of Chaucer*, Lamb took on the task, but try as he might, he could not complete it. "I have been sitting down for three or four days successively to the review which I so much wished to do well & to your satisfaction," he apologized to Godwin. "But I can produce nothing but absolute flatness and nonsense. My health and spirits are so bad, and my nerves so irritable, that I am sure, if I persist, I shall teaze myself into a fever."[26]

Enter Mrs. Godwin. She pried out of Charles Lamb his one objection to Godwin's book, which was the author's "filling out the picture by supposing what Chaucer did and how he felt, where the materials are scanty." Mary Jane Godwin told her husband, who came to believe that Charles flat-out disliked the book. "If Mrs. G. has been the cause of your misconstruction, I am very angry, tell her," wrote Charles to Godwin, extending "a peace offering of sweet incense between us."[27]

Mary Jane Godwin did inspire her husband in one salutary way. In partnership with her, he entered the business of writing, editing, printing, publishing, and selling children's books. In 1805 the Juvenile Library published its first volume:

FABLES
ANCIENT AND MODERN.
Adapted for the Use of Children from
Three to Eight Years of Age.
BY EDWARD BALDWIN, ESQ.

VOL. I.
ADORNED WITH THIRTY-SIX COPPER PLATES.

Published by Thos. Hodgkins Hanway Street, Octr. 6th. 1805.
LONDON: PRINTED FOR THOMAS HODGKINS,
AT THE JUVENILE LIBRARY, HANWAY STREET
(OPPOSITE SOHO SQUARE), OXFORD STREET;
AND TO BE HAD OF ALL BOOKSELLERS.

Nowhere was the risky name of Godwin to be seen. "Edward Baldwin" was a pseudonym, one of several Godwin assumed when writing for children. The volume was "adorned," as the title page promised, with thirty-six copperplate illustrations by William Mulready, an up-and-coming London illustrator. As "Baldwin" wrote in the preface, "If we would benefit a child . . . we must make our narrations pictures, and render the objects we discourse about, visible to the fancy of the learner."[28]

The City Juvenile Library shop opened on Hanway Street, north of the Thames, in March 1805, selling not only books but toys and puzzles, pens, paper, and ink.[29] The Godwins borrowed money to rent the entire building for forty pounds a year but planned to rent rooms above the shop for thirty-five. Thomas Hodgkins, hired as shopkeeper, lent his name to the title pages as printer. When Godwin discovered two years later that Hodgkins was embezzling from the firm, he fired him, and the books came to be published with the line, "Printed for M. J. Godwin and Co."[30] New titles poured forth from the Juvenile Library over the next few years: *History of England; History of Rome; History of Greece; Life of Lady Jane Grey; The Pantheon, or Ancient History of the Gods of Greece and Rome; A New and Improved Grammar of the English Tongue; The Junior Class Book, or Reading Lessons for Every Day in the Year.*

IT WOULD TAKE a year before the Lambs were brought into the fold of the Godwin enterprise. Meanwhile Mary and Charles worked together as much as they could, trying to find ways that his writing talents could increase their income. Earlier efforts had wasted time and spirit without earning a penny. In 1801 George Dyer had helped Charles get an assignment from the *Morning Chronicle,* but neither daily news nor daily deadlines suited his temperament. "I did something for them," Charles wrote John Rickman, "writing for the Lordly Editor of the Great Whig Paper," but "more than 3.4ths of what I [di]d was superciliously rejected."

In 1802 he agreed to write a column for the *Morning Post,* earning two guineas a week, well over one hundred pounds a year if he kept it up that long.[31] In his first essay he staked his claim to the column's title, "Londoner." "I love the very Smoke of London," he wrote, "because it has been the medium most familiar to my vision."[32] His editor scolded him, insisting he "take more pains about my paragraphs" and considering only one out of five printable.[33]

Charles analyzed the situation a different way. "The Routine has been drinking one night in noisy Company, & writing the next upon a head ach. My Spirits absolutely require freedom & leisure, & I think I shall never engage to do task work any more, for I am *sick.*"[34] The fact is that Charles Lamb was simply not a newswriter—he couldn't have cared less about the daily matters of government and economics. "I never could make any thing of his writings," wrote Dan Stuart, editor of the *Morning Post,* after Lamb's death. "Of politics he knew nothing; they were out of his line of reading and thought; and his drollery was vapid, when given in short paragraphs fit for a newspaper."[35] Quitting that assignment, Charles became "poorer but happier."[36] Mary was relieved: "Charles has lost the newspaper but what we dreaded as an evil has proved a great blessing," she wrote Sarah Stoddart, "for we have both strangely recovered our health and spirits since this has happened."[37]

Charles Lamb wrote for the theater, too, where he could let his imagination roam in days of yore. He never persuaded a theater to produce his tragedy *John Woodvil* but embarked on a farce, potentially more marketable to a London audience seeking escape in troubled times. The plot of *Mr. H* hung on the machinations of a character bent on keeping his family name, "Hogsflesh," a secret.

Through these months of literary effort, Mary did all she could to encourage and assist her brother. She probably listened to him recite new lines. Perhaps they read dialogue aloud together. While Charles was at work, Mary made fair copies of his drafted articles or scenes. She delivered manuscripts for him to newspaper editors and theater managers. But her brother's fluctuations between industry and despair exasperated her. "Charles often plans but never begins," she complained to Dorothy Wordsworth.[38]

SOMETHING HAD HAPPENED in Mary over the past few months. Self-doubt and dependency on her brother had silenced her through the months and even years after her act of murder. Now she was finding equilibrium, regaining the sense that she was an individual with observations and opinions that mattered. At the same time she was regaining the sense of herself as an equal— in fact, an elder—to Charles. He was a young man who could and did make mistakes. As her friendships with Dorothy Wordsworth and Sarah Stoddart solidified, she had strong female confidantes.

It seems quite clear, although it cannot be proved, that to each of these women she had divulged her secret. Having established a fundamental groundwork for honesty and trust, Mary Lamb became a more active participant in each of these two important friendships.

The relationship with Dorothy Wordsworth intensified over the tragic death of her younger brother, John. He was a ship's captain, sailing vessels to Asia for East India House. On February 1, 1805, under John Wordsworth's command, the *Earl of Abergavenny* sailed from Portsmouth in a convoy with four other trader ships, escorted by a military frigate. On board was two hundred thousand pounds' worth of goods and sterling, plus crew, soldiers, and passengers numbering at least four hundred. They were bound for India, where the vessel would offload cargo, load up with cotton, and carry it on to China.[39] On February 5 the ship ran aground in a rocky stretch called the Shambles Bank, off the Bill of Portland, damaging the hull so badly that, although Captain Wordsworth loosed it from the reef, the ship sank on its way back to shore, near Weymouth. More than one hundred people survived, including crew members, rescued by boats nearby, but Capt. John Wordsworth went down with his ship. His body washed ashore near Weymouth on March 20. Later that year, salvager John Braithwaite used a diving bell to recover about seventy-five thousand pounds' worth of silver and cargo.[40]

The loss of their brother was devastating to the Wordsworths. Both Dorothy and her sister, Mary, fell ill. Rumors insinuating drunkenness on the part of John Wordsworth crept into many of the public accounts. William wrote friends feverishly, seeking additional information. Charles, positioned at East India House, was in a prime position to find out more, but when he received the letter from William, he was struck with guilt, since neither he nor Mary had thought to convey their sympathy. "Mary is crying by me while I with difficulty write this," Charles responded, mentioning that he had been "wretchedly ill & low" for the past few weeks[41]—"a sad depression of spirits, a most unaccountable nervousness."[42] He promised to seek out Thomas Gilpin, a surviving crew member, to learn all he could. "Mary will write to Dorothy as soon as she thinks *she* will be able to bear it," he also promised. "It has been a sad tidings to us, & has affected us more than we could have believed."[43]

Charles not only spoke to Gilpin but also transcribed his testimony before the East India House Court of Directors. He transmitted all to Wordsworth with the reassurance that "It is perfectly understood at the E. I. House, that no blame whatever belongs to the Captn. or Officers."[44] Anxious to visualize the last hours of his brother's life even more clearly, Wordsworth sent Charles specific questions for both Gilpin and a midshipman named Benjamin Yates: Why didn't the boat make it to shore? Why weren't rescue boats aboard the *Earl* deployed? Where was John Wordsworth when the boat went down? What was the last thing he said? Why did the boat sink bow first? The sailors had answers for all these questions, summing up to an account that showed the captain "quite composd the whole time," in Yates's words,[45] and competent amid danger.

It took another month and another letter from Grasmere, this time from Dorothy, to prompt Mary to write. She, too, apologized profusely. "I thank you my kind friend for your most comfortable letter, till I saw your own hand-writing I could not persuade myself that I should do well to write to you, though I have often attempted it, but I always left off dissatisfied with what I had written, & feeling that I was doing an improper thing to intrude upon your sorrow."[46]

Mary Lamb seems to have realized that she, as much as any one, could console Dorothy authentically. Her words echoed the comfort she found in the vision of her mother she had experienced while in Fisher House nearly ten years before:

I wished to tell you, that you would one day feel the kind of peaceful state of mind, and sweet memory of the dead which you so happily describe as now almost begun, . . . That you would see every object with, & through your lost brother, & that that would at last become a real & everlasting source of comfort to you, I felt, & well knew from my own experience in sorrow, but till you yourself began to feel this I did not dare to tell you so.

With this letter, Mary enclosed a poem she had written. She ascribes her own thoughts to their mutual friend, Samuel Taylor Coleridge, who at the time was traveling in the Mediterranean, likely unaware of the Wordsworths' tragedy:

> *Why is he wandering o'er the sea?*
> *Coleridge should now with Wordsworth be.*
> *By slow degrees he'd steal away*
> *Their woe, and gently bring a ray*
> *(So happily he'd time relief)*
> *Of comfort from their very grief.—*
> *He'd tell them that their brother dead*
> *When years have passed o'er their head,*
> *Will be remember'd with such holy,*
> *True, & perfect melancholy,*
> *That ever this lost brother John*
> *Will be their hearts companion.*
> *His voice they'll always hear, his face they'll always see,*
> *There's nought in life so sweet as such a memory.*

No one—not even Mary Lamb herself—would consider this verse a literary triumph. "I know [these poor lines] are much worse than they ought to be," the poet admitted to Dorothy.[47] But in them, she identifies a state of mind becoming familiar to her:

"holy, / True, & perfect melancholy," colored irreversibly by sorrow and redeemed only because the memory of the departed is better than anything waking life can offer.

Poetry was becoming a more comfortable medium of communication for Mary Lamb.

IN THIS SAME YEAR, 1805, Mary also played the part of counselor to her other best friend. Sometime late in 1803, Sarah Stoddart had moved to the Mediterrean island of Malta to join her brother and his wife. As the French advanced by land and sea, claiming territories as they went, Malta had become a hot spot. Its position seventy miles south of Sicily made it strategic as a military outpost and a site for commercial blockades. Leading his fleet to Egypt, Napoleon had landed on Malta in 1798 and declared it a department of his French Republic. Admiral Nelson's forces seized the island in 1800, and officials such as John Stoddart, appointed king's and Admiralty advocate, were positioned on the island to maintain British control.

Sarah complained fiercely of having to live in Malta. How could she get on with her search for a husband on a tiny island? At least in England, instead of her brother's scrutiny, she had the female counsel of her friend Mary Lamb, who at nearly forty was neither parent nor competitor. Then, in the spring of 1805, word reached John Stoddart that his father had died. He did not want his mother to live on her own, so he finally agreed to send his sister home.

"Poor Miss Stoddart!" Charles wrote to William Wordsworth. "She is coming to England under the notion of passing her time between her mother & Mary, between London & Salisbury." It was "poor Miss Stoddart" because, as Charles put it, "her Mother is gone out of her mind." It was "poor Miss Stoddart" as well, Charles must have been thinking, because she had "not a woman-friend in London."[48] Not a woman friend, that is, but Mary—who was once again confined in a madhouse.

"Last Monday week was the day she left me," Charles wrote Dorothy in mid-June 1805, answering a letter intended for his sister. "Late hours" had taken their toll, Charles ventured. Certainly the nights since John Wordsworth's death, two months before, had been a strain. Charles's own illness and low spirits had demanded much of his sister. A diminishing cycle could start between the two of them. "When she begins to discover symptoms of approaching illness, it is not easy to say what is best to do," he admitted. "Being by ourselves is bad, & going out is bad. I get so irritable & wretched with *fear,* that I constantly hasten on the disorder. You cannot conceive the misery of such a foresight."[49]

Writing to Dorothy Wordsworth, something of a surrogate for his own sister, Charles allowed himself a few sincere moments of sentiment. He reflected on how his character interacted with—and depended on—that of his sister.

Meantime she is *dead* to me,—and I miss a prop. All my strength is gone, and I am like a fool, bereft of her co-operation. I dare not think, lest I should think wrong; so used am I to look up to her in the least & the biggest perplexity. To say *all that* I know of her would be more than I think any body could believe or even understand; and when I hope to have her well again with me it would be sinning against her feelings to go about to praise her: for I can conceal nothing that I do from her. She is older, & wiser, & better than me, and all my wretched imperfections I cover to myself by resolutely thinking on her goodness. She would share life & death, heaven & hell with me. She lives but for me. And I know I have been wasting & teazing her life for five years past incessantly with my cursed drinking & ways of going on. But even in this upbraiding of myself I am offending against her; for I know that she has cleaved to me *for better, for worse*; and if the balance has been against her hitherto, it was a *noble trade*.[50]

These are hardly the words of a saintly man who has sacrificed his life for the sake of his crazy sister. Apparently Charles Lamb, too, underwent a certain apotheosis of feeling at this juncture, recognizing his sister's strengths and chastising himself for having taken them for granted. One month later, though, the crisis behind him, Charles wrote more lightheartedly to Thomas Manning: "My old housekeeper has shewed signs of convalescence, and will shortly resume the power of the Keys."[51]

A NEW FEELING pervaded the household when Mary returned in August. As glib as he was inclined to be, Charles more clearly recognized the ways in which he depended on Mary. Meanwhile Mary was beginning to take the occasional madhouse visits in stride. These six weeks spent in a madhouse represented only the second time in five years. She flippantly called it her "banishment," a word that carries both acceptance and scorn. We do not know in which establishment she registered in 1805, but it likely was a place where she was already known and recognized for her generally mild demeanor and curability. She returned home charged with compassion for madhouse patients—and she conveyed those ideas bluntly to her friend, Sarah Stoddart, who was struggling with the question of how to care for her mother.

"It was perhaps so ordered by providence that you might return home to be a comfort to your poor Mother," Mary Lamb wrote Sarah in November. Returning home, Sarah Stoddart had found her widowed mother so disturbed that she required care beyond what her daughter could give her. Sarah placed her mother in a Salisbury madhouse, probably Laverstock House, run by the surgeon William Finch, whose family operated madhouses in both Wiltshire and in London.[52] Stoddart must have looked to her friend for guidance and consolation as she took this difficult step; she must have described to Mary how upsetting it was to see her mother's irrational behavior. Something untoward had happened—maybe she stole someone else's belongings or grabbed food off the plate of a fellow patient. Maybe, accused of the petty crime, she ranted in self-defense. Maybe she fought her madhouse keeper physically.

"Do not I conjure you let her unhappy malady afflict you too deeply," Mary advised her friend. "I speak from experience & from the opportunity I have had of much observation in such cases that insane people in the fancy's they take into their heads do not feel as one in a sane state of mind does under the real evil of poverty the perception of having done wrong or any such thing that runs in their heads."

As she writes words that venture into the risky area of life inside a madhouse, Mary Lamb seems to lose control of her writing style. She strings together phrases in an atypically wandering way, seeming almost to write from the confused state of mind that she associated with a madhouse confinement. Maybe she noticed it happening, because she ended this paragraph and started a new one, writing with more precision. With a clear sense of the message she wanted to convey to Sarah Stoddart about her mother, Mary Lamb made a wise and interesting plea for kindness over analysis:

> Think as little as you can, & let your whole care be to be certain that she is treated with *tenderness*. I lay a stress upon this, because it is a thing of which people in her state are uncommonly susceptible, & which hardly any one is at all aware of, a hired nurse *never,* even though in all other respects they are

good kind of people. I do not think your own presence necessary unless she *takes to you very much* except for the purpose of seeing with your own eyes that she is very kindly treated.

Here Mary goes even further in divulging insider knowledge: Those suffering from madness need, more urgently than anyone can understand, kind treatment. Seeping out from between these lines are the horrors that Mary Lamb herself witnessed, perhaps even experienced: harsh treatment by careless nurses, the cruelty of caretakers who ignored the human needs of their wards. When Mary advises that Sarah "think as little as you can," she is urging her to ignore irrational words or abnormal actions and simply empathize, human to human, with her mother.[53]

The morning after sending this advice, Mary Lamb awoke with an anxious sense of regret. She wrote Sarah immediately, explaining that the letter of the previous day was written "after a very feverish night." She apologized profusely for intruding and advising when Sarah probably did not need any advice. "That which gives me most concern is the way in which I talked about your Mothers illness," she wrote, "& which I have since feared you might construe into my having a doubt of your showing her proper attention without my impertinent interference. God knows nothing of this kind was ever in my thoughts."

Headed toward recanting, Mary Lamb does not, however. She repeats, even more pointedly, the lessons she has learned through her now twelve cumulative months of madhouse life:

I have entered very deeply into your affliction with regard to your Mother, & while I was writing, the many poor souls in the kind of desponding way she is in whom I have seen, came afresh into my mind, & all the mismanagement with which I have seen them treated was strong in my mind, & I wrote under a forcible impulse which I could not at that time resist,

but I have fretted so much about it since, that I think it is the
last time I will ever let my pen run away with me.

The letter is a fascinating combination of searing commentary
and retreating self-doubt. Mary turns her attention to herself in
the next paragraph and as much as says so:

> Your kind heart will I know even if you have been a little dis-
> pleased forgive me when I assure you my spirits have been so
> much hurt by my last illness that at times I hardly know what I
> do—I do not mean to alarm you about myself, or to plead in
> excuse that I am very much otherwise than you have always
> known me—I do not think any one perceives me altered, but I
> have lost all self confidence in my own actions, & one cause of
> my low spirits is that I never feel satisfied with any thing I
> do—a perception of not being in a sane state perpetually
> haunts me. I am ashamed to confess this weakness to you,
> which as I am so sensible of I ought to strive to conquer.[54]

Some modern-day observers believe that Mary Lamb underwent humiliating treatments during her madhouse stays.
Considering the treatments for mental illness then in vogue, it is a
reasonable hypothesis. Vomiting, purging, bloodletting, and binding
were still in practice, and new techniques were being explored, like
mechanical swings and electrical shocks. Mary Lamb likely saw, and
possibly experienced, many of the techniques, old and new.
Inquiries by the 1815 Lunacy Commission uncovered inhumane
practices going on in most of London's madhouses. At Hoxton
House many patients slept three to a bed. Elsewhere patients slept
on soiled straw in mass rooms that were unheated and infested with
vermin. Commissioners discovered that many madhouse patients
had lost front teeth due to the force with which keepers shoved a
teapot-shaped feeding instrument into their mouths.[55]

Evidence and logic suggest, however, that her madhouse stays did not wound Mary Lamb psychologically. Charles's descriptions of Mary's first, and so far longest, stay in a madhouse—the six months she spent at Fisher House after the murder of her mother—portray acts of kindness, feelings of respect, and even a modicum of free license given by the madhouse keepers to Mary Lamb within two weeks of her confinement. She may have been a victim of abuse then or later, but between her docile character and her growing understanding of how madhouses operate, Mary Lamb knew the kind of treatment a patient could, and should, receive in that setting. In short, she had likely seen worse than she had experienced. In a single madhouse, especially one as big as Hoxton House, patients might be treated in a variety of ways.

Without government regulation, caretakers could use gentle treatment and cleanliness—or the opposite—to control behavior. Mary Lamb had already learned in her youth to behave not just meekly but generously. The same generosity, an inborn empathic nature, led her to watch the madhouse treatment of others with horror, and to convey those horrors, even if in a muffled way, to Sarah Stoddart. Among all the possibilities, Mary urged Sarah, her mother must receive the kindest treatment possible in the madhouse.

THE YEAR 1805 had been momentous for Britain in its war with France. Napoleon, now France's self-crowned emperor, made mockery of the Amiens treaty with his naval maneuvers. His moves to conquer Britain by sea were foiled by the glorious Lord Nelson, whose bravery and genius in the Battle of Trafalgar, on October 21, had ended with eighteen battleships sunk or seized, twenty thousand enemy soldiers taken prisoner, the menacing Franco-Spanish naval fleet decimated, and France's Adm. Pierre de Villeneuve captured. Shot by a sniper at the battle's end, Adm. Lord Nelson died in glory, aware that the British had landed a decisive victory. Even Charles Lamb, the man who ignored current events, could not help from feeling excitement and grief over what had happened. "Was'nt you sorry for Lord Nelson?" he wrote two weeks after the admiral's death. "I have followed him in fancy ever since I saw him walking in Pall Mall (I was prejudiced against him before) looking just as a *Hero* should look: and I have been very much cut about it indeed. He was the only pretence of a Great Man we had."[56]

While the nation combined victory celebrations with mourning, Mary Lamb wrote Catherine Clarkson a letter on Christmas Day, calling 1805 "a sad, and dreary year."[57] One friend's brother had drowned, another's mother had gone mad. Charles struggled with ill health and depression. She had once again needed madhouse care. One spark of hope glimmered by the end of the year, though. William and Mary Jane Godwin hired Charles to write a book for the Juvenile Library.

No records remain of the genesis of *The King and Queen of Hearts*. Its title page says it was "Printed for Tho[s]. Hodgkins. Hanway Street. Nov[r]. 18. 1805" and explains that the book intends "Showing how notably the Queen made her Tarts, and how scurvily the Knave stole them away, and other particulars belonging thereunto." The traditional two-stanza jingle of theft and confession appears on the book's first page. Charles Lamb added fourteen six-line jingles, spiced with his own idiosyncratic wit and illustrated with cartoons by William Mulready.

Lamb and Mulready introduce into the story three black pages to the queen. Pambo, the knave of hearts, is fingered as the tart thief by one of the pages, a twist that infuses race and class into the simple plot. Both illustrator and versifier take liberties on the last page: Mulready shows the king and queen pouring themselves more wine, while Pambo attacks his accuser in the background:

Their Majesties so well have fed,
The tarts have got up in their head:
"Or maybe 'twas the wine!"—hush gipsey
Great Kings & Queens indeed get tipsey!
Now, Pambo, is the time for you:
Beat little Tell-Tale black & blue

These last-page twists certainly muddy the moral of the original nursery rhyme, but neither Mr. nor Mrs. Godwin seems to have editorialized. They left a wry tale that would have rankled both Mrs. Barbauld and Mrs. Trimmer. Thus began a satisfactory relationship between authors and publishers of this new line of children's literature.

The next Lamb contribution to the Juvenile Library would make history.

9

TALES FROM SHAKESPEARE

Relations warmed between the Lamb and the Godwin households as work brought them together. Mary and Charles presented the Godwins with a fine gift of salted salmon—a good way to salute Charles's new publishers. "Having observed with some concern that Mr. Godwin is a little fastidious in what he eats for supper," Charles wrote in the accompanying note, clearly drafted in collaboration with his cook and house-keeper, Mary,

> I herewith beg to present his palate with a piece of dried Salmon. I am assured it is the best that swims in Trent. If you do not know how to dress it, allow me to add, that it should be cut in thin Slices and broil'd in Paper *previously prepared in Butter.* Some add *Mash'd Potatoes.* Wishing it exquisite, I remain,
>
> much as before,
> Yours Sincy
>
> C Lamb[1]

Apparently the Lambs could abide Mrs. Godwin as long as she was advancing Charles's writing career.

The children's book complete, it was time to finish the farce, which was taking far too long. Charles chalked it up to his social life and, intent to have a script he could peddle to theaters, he rented a room—perhaps right in the Inner Temple—as an after-dinner study: "Have taken a room at 3/—a week to be in between 5 and 8 at night," he wrote, "to avoid my *nocturnal* alias *knock-eternal* visitors."[2]

That left Mary more time to herself. "Charles has just left me for the first time alone to go to his lodging, and I am holding a solitary consultation with myself, as to the how I shall employ myself," she wrote her friend Sarah. "Writing plays, novels, poems, and all manner of such-like vapouring and vapourish schemes are floating in my head." Without Charles to guide and critique her, her pen flowed freely—but her conscience also pulled her back to the mundane tasks of life, the work a woman was supposed to do. "Then I think I will make my new gown, & now I consider the white peticoat will be better candle-light work, and then I look at the fire and think if the irons was but down I would iron my Gowns. . . . So much for an account of my own confused head."[3] Confused she may call herself, but the glimmering self-concept as *author* was growing inside Mary Lamb.

Too soon Charles finished his play, and Mary's attention turned back to him. "I am to hear it read this night," she wrote two nights after he had sequestered himself in his study. "I am so uneasy between my hopes, & fears of how I shall like it, that I do not know what I am doing." If she voiced any misgivings, they did not worry her brother, because the very next day—after she had copied the script over into something that could be shown to others—Mary carried a copy of *Mr. H* to Drury Lane Theatre, knocking on door after door before she finally found the theater manager's. "He was very civil to me," she reported to Sarah, "said it did not depend upon himself, but that he would put it into the Proprietors hand, and that we should certainly [*sic*] have an answer from them." That very night, Charles declared a writing holiday, "to rest himself after his labour."[4]

Three weeks later Charles still considered himself on holiday from writing. He had relinquished his study and was back at home, which was "the reason why I have not had any time to spare," Mary complained to Sarah Stoddart:

> I wish he may happen to hit upon some new plan to *his* mind for another farce—when once begun I do not fear his perseverance, but the hollidays he has allowed himself I fear will unsettle him. I look forward to next week with the same kind of anxiety I did to the first entrance at the new lodging. We have had as you know so many teazing anxieties of late, that I have got a kind of habit of foreboding that we shall never be comfortable, & that he will never settle to work which I know is wrong, and which I will try with all my might to overcome—for certainly if I could but see things as they really are, our prospects are considerably improved.[5]

At about this time, in the spring of 1806, the Godwins asked Mary Lamb to write a book for the Juvenile Library. It was to be a children's Shakespeare, a storybook collection, prose versions of the best of his plays, intended to be read to children when young and by children once they were able. It is significant that it was Mary, not Charles, whom they hired to fulfill the assignment.

As a correspondent Mary Lamb fell silent. All her writing energy went into her book, but Charles spoke for her. "She is doing for Godwins Bookseller 20 of Shakespears plays to be made into Childrens tales," Charles wrote Thomas Manning on May 10, 1806. "Six are already done by her to wit The Tempest, Winters Tale, Midsummer Night, Much ado, Two Gentlemen of Verona & Cymbeline: & the Merchant of Venice is in forwardness. . . . I think it will be popular among the little people. Mary has done them capitally, I think you'd think." In the same letter Charles revealed that he was helping her write some of the stories: "I have done Othello & Macbeth and mean to do all the Tragedies."[6] He still clearly considered it Mary's book. No doubt one commented on the writing of the other, back and forth, a sort of two-heads-are-better-than-one mutual authorship that resulted in a book authentically written by the two of them together. That had very likely been the case before, with *Mr. H*, *The King and Queen of Hearts,* and even the newspaper pieces Charles had written. This time, though, there was the prospect that Mary Lamb might share the limelight.

At times she took the lead in the partnership. "Charles has written Macbeth & Othello, King Lear & has begun Hamlet," she wrote Sarah Stoddart in early June. "You would like to see us as we often sit writing on one table (but not on one cushion sitting) like Hermia & Helena in the Midsummer's Nights Dream, or rather like an old literary Darby and Joan. I taking snuff & he groaning all the while & saying he can make nothing of it, which he always says till he has finished and then he finds out he has made something of it."[7]

At other times she needed the encouragement. "Mary is just stuck fast in All's Well that Ends Well," he wrote William Wordsworth in late June:

> She complains of having to set forth so many female characters in boy's clothes. She begins to think Shakspear must have wanted Imagination.——I to encourage her, for she often faints in the prosecution of her great work, flatter her with telling her how well such a play & such a play is done. But she is stuck fast & I have been obliged to promise to assist her. To do this it will be necessary to leave off Tobacco. But I had some thoughts of doing that before."[8]

The Godwins promised sixty guineas upon publication, planned for the end of the year. Midway through the project,

Mary realized that she could keep doing this sort of writing and bring in a tidy income. "I go on very well," she wrote Sarah Stoddart as the summer began, "& have no doubt but I shall always be able to hit upon some such kind of job to keep going on."[9] She cautiously estimated she might be able to add fifty pounds a year to the family coffers.

The final product was a two-volume collection, 520 pages total, a little duodecimo (twelve pages printed together on one large sheet of paper). The title page read:

TALES

FROM

SHAKESPEAR.

DESIGNED

FOR THE USE OF YOUNG PERSONS.

— * —

By CHARLES LAMB.

EMBELLISHED WITH COPPER-PLATES.

=======

IN TWO VOLUMES.

VOL. I.

=======

PRINTED FOR THOMAS HODGKINS, AT THE JUVENILE LI-BRARY, HANWAY-STREET (OPPOSITE SOHO-SQUARE), OXFORD-STREET; AND TO BE HAD OF ALL BOOKSELLERS.

———

1807.

The self-explanatory title has worked to sell the book ever since. The spelling of the playwright's name was never codified in his lifetime, and in fact not until well into the twentieth century did "Shakespeare" become the standard. "Shakespear" was a common variation, but the Lambs—neither one a stickler for spelling—alternated it with the spelling used today. By the end of the nineteenth century, publishers were using the standard spelling of "Shakespeare" in the title of the new editions of the Lambs' *Tales*.

The subtitle was crafted carefully, like those of so many other children's readers of the time, to promise utilitarian value. Somewhere along the way, it was decided that Charles would be listed as sole author. Publication details convey that the book was to be sold not only at the Juvenile Library shop but at others, such as Newbery's. The book sold well from the very beginning, going into a second edition in its second year. *Tales from Shakespear* has been in print ever since.

The Lambs carried out the original plan, writing stories corresponding to twenty of Shakespeare's plays: fourteen comedies and six tragedies. If brother and sister divided labor between the two genres, still Mary wrote more than two-thirds of the text. If instead, as suggested earlier, every story was a collaboration—drafts shared, reworked, and edited back and forth—then the project might be better called a partnership. Neither scenario supports the listing of Charles as sole author, however, but the Godwins knew the market, and, as significantly, Mary may have shied from public view.

In writing *Tales from Shakespear,* Mary tackled a complex assignment whose result would be tested against the great plays themselves, known more in her day as theatrical events than literary texts (and certainly not as the groan-inducing textbook obligations they have become for too many today). To turn a play by Shakespeare into a story for a young reader, Mary had to find graceful ways to evoke foreign contexts, explain underlying moral values, turn action into narrative, and maintain diverse characters. Stories work differently from plays, and stories for children work differently from those intended for adults. Her decisions involved not only what to include but what to exclude, for length, propriety, and simplicity. In essence she had to transform a three-hour stage experience into an hour-long verbal event, holding children's interest as she kept true to the original. That she agreed to the assignment reflects the state of her mental health and self-confidence.

Shakespeare's plays open with dialogue, often between minor characters, to set the scene and propel the plot. Mary Lamb sifted through those lines and determined the most critical information needed for the "once upon a time" for every story.

Katharine the Shrew was the eldest daughter of Baptista, a rich gentleman of Padua. She was a lady of such an ungovernable spirit and fiery temper, such a loud-tongued scold, that she was known in Padua by no other name than Katharine the Shrew. It seemed very unlikely, indeed impossible, that any gentleman would ever be found who would venture to marry this lady, and therefor Baptista was much blamed for deferring his consent to many excellent offers that were made to her gentle sister Bianca, putting off all Bianca's suitors with this excuse, that when the eldest sister was fairly off his hands, they should have free leave to address young Bianca.

For her young audience Mary explained the title right away. In the play Shakespeare slid in the word "shrewd" four times before Katharine's suitor, Petruchio, ever speaks of taming "the curstest shrew," and not until Act IV does any character call Katharine a shrew.[10] Mary Lamb may have made the subtle obvious, but she was remembering her audience of children.

Sometimes the forward movement of a plot forced her to summarize and simplify, but at other times she paused in her narrative to dwell in the complex grace of Shakespeare's imagination—as when she introduced Puck, the mercurial servant to Titania, queen of the fairies, in *A Midsummer Night's Dream:*

Puck (or, as he was sometimes called, Robin Goodfellow) was a shrewd and knavish sprite, that used to play comical pranks in the neighbouring villages—sometimes getting into the dairies and skimming the milk, sometimes plunging his light and fairy form into the butter-churn, and while he was danc- ing his fantastic shape in the churn, in vain the dairymaid would labour to change her cream into butter; nor had the vil- lage swains any better success; whenever Puck chose to play his freaks in the brewing copper, the ale was sure to be spoiled. When a few good neighbours were met to drink some comfortable ale together, Puck would jump into the bowl of ale in the likeness of a roasted crab, and when some old goody was going to drink he would bob against her lips, and spill the ale over her withered chin; and presently after, when the same old dame was gravely seating herself to tell her neighbours a sad and melancholy story, Puck would slip her three-legged stool from under her, and down toppled the poor old woman, and then the old gossips would hold their sides and laugh at her, and swear they never wasted a merrier hour.

These colorful pranks Mary found at the opening of Act II, in dia- logue Shakespeare used between Puck and the fairy to tell of Titania and Oberon's arguments over a changeling child—critical in his play but streamlined out of Lamb's story. Yet Mary valued how these lines evoked the character of Puck, liaison between the human and fairy worlds—not to mention how much sheer slap- stick they added, to the delight of every puckish child hearing or reading her tale.

Mary Lamb considered it her responsibility to familiarize young readers with Shakespearean vocabulary. When Prospero frees Ariel at the end of *The Tempest,* for instance, the fairy still sings his famous song, introduced by this passage:

Before Prospero left the island, he dismissed Ariel from his service, to the great joy of that lively little spirit, who, though he had been a faithful servant to his master, was always longing to enjoy his free liberty—to wander uncontrolled in the air like a wild bird, under green trees, among pleasant fruits and sweet-smelling flowers. . . .

"Thank you, my dear master," said Ariel; "but give me leave to attend your ship home with prosperous gales, before you bid farewell to the assistance of your faithful spirit; and then, master, when I am free, how merrily I shall live!"

Here Ariel sang this pretty song:—

> *Where the bee sucks, there suck I:*
> *In a cowslip's bell I lie;*
> *There I couch when owls do cry.*
> *On the bat's back I do fly*
> *After summer merrily.*
> *Merrily, merrily, shall I live now*
> *Under the blossom that hangs on the bough.*

The song was Ariel's own, taken word for word from Shakespeare, but the narrative that preceded it was an amalgam of language from throughout the play, plucked from speeches of both Ariel and Prospero.

The Lambs deftly feathered many familiar Shakespearean quotations into their *Tales*. When Juliet appears at the window, she says, "O Romeo, Romeo! wherefore art thou Romeo?" As Macbeth murders Duncan, a voice cries out, "Sleep no more! Macbeth doth murder sleep." Lady Macbeth never says "Out, damned spot," but her speech urging her husband to murder is collapsed into a paragraph, in which "she threw contempt on his change of purpose, and accused him of fickleness and cowardice;

and declared that she had given suck, and knew how tender it was to love the babe that milked her, but she would, while it was smiling in her face, have plucked it from her breast and dashed its brains out, if she had so sworn to do it as he had sworn to perform that murder." On the other hand, "To be or not to be" must have seemed too cerebral to the Lambs for a preadolescent audience, for it comes through simply as a declaration of Hamlet's "irresoluteness and wavering of purpose, which kept him from proceeding to extremities."

The witches' "Double, double, toil and trouble" is missing from *Macbeth*, but the contents of their kettle are not. When Macbeth returns for more wisdom from the ugly hags, he finds them "engaged in preparing their dreadful charms":

> Their horrid ingredients were toads, bats, and serpents, the eye of a newt and the tongue of a dog, the leg of a lizard and the wing of the night owl, the scale of a dragon, the tooth of a wolf, the maw of the ravenous salt-sea shark, the mummy of a witch, the root of the poisonous hemlock (this to have effect must be digged in the dark), the gall of a goat, and the liver of a Jew, with slips of the yew-tree that roots itself in graves, and the finger of a dead child: all these were set on to boil in a great kettle or caldron, which, as fast as it grew too hot, was cooled with a baboon's blood: to these they poured in the blood of a sow that had eaten her young, and they threw into the flame the grease that had sweaten from a murderer's gibbet. By these charms they bound the infernal spirits to answer their questions.

As offensive as this list might be to readers today, the authors actually edited the original for their audience. The Jew is not described as "blaspheming"; the yew-tree is explained as a shrub known for roots that disturb graveyards; the finger comes from a

child, not a "birth-strangled babe / Ditch-deliver'd by a drab."
"Nose of Turk and Tartar's lips" are missing from the recipe. The
concoction remains, nonetheless, brimful of icky ingredients sure
to entertain young readers. No moral lessons here.

Simplifying language and plot, Mary Lamb had to make some
decisions. Often she left out Shakespeare's comic counterpoint.
The lovable mechanics do not appear in *A Midsummer Night's
Dream*, so the story lacks the bumptious rehearsals and raucous
performance of *Pyramus and Thisbe*. Only Bottom remains, and he
is nothing but an unnamed clown "who had lost his way in the
wood," falling asleep conveniently near Titania so Puck can clap
an ass's head on him to fool the fairy queen. Malvolio, the cloying
steward in *Twelfth Night,* so sure that yellow stockings will win
Olivia's affection, disappears in Mary Lamb's version. Hamlet
does not expatiate on the skull of Yorick with the gravedigger, but
King Lear does brave the storm on the heath in the company of a
fool, who uses "his merry conceits . . . to outjest misfortune."

ALL THESE ADAPTATIONS of the original Shakespeare served literary and educational purposes, as the Lambs clearly laid out in a
preface to the first edition:

> The following Tales are meant to be submitted to the young
> reader as an introduction to the study of Shakespeare, for
> which purpose his words are used whenever it seemed possi-
> ble to bring them in; and in whatever has been added to give
> them the regular form of a connected story, diligent care has
> been taken to select such words as might least interrupt the
> effect of the beautiful English tongue in which he wrote:
> therefore, words introduced into our language since his time
> have been as far as possible avoided.

The preface indicates the care taken by Mary and Charles in deciding, word by word and phrase by phrase, whether language ought to be borrowed or paraphrased. Mary's comedic assignment posed the more difficult challenge along these lines, since plot drives tragedy but is often secondary in comedy to puns and pratfalls, so much harder to simplify into a story. *All's Well That Ends Well* "teazed me more than all the rest put together," she told Sarah, but she scribbled good news at the end of her letter just before mailing it: "I am in good spirits just this present time, for Charles has been reading over the *Tale* I told you plagued me so much and he thinks it one of the very best."[11] She regretted having to write so much dialogue—rarely found in children's books of the time—but explained in the preface that "in those [Tales] made from the Comedies the writers found themselves scarcely ever able to turn [Shakespeare's] words into the narrative form: therefore it is feared that, in them, dialogue has been made use of too frequently for young people not accustomed to the dramatic form of writing."

Mary and Charles Lamb recognized that their version defused the power of Shakespearean language. Their *Tales* offered "faint and imperfect images" of the plays' original language, "transplanted from its own natural soil and wild poetic garden," which perforce "must want much of its native beauty." Not only diction but content presented a challenge. "It has been wished to make these Tales easy reading for very young children . . . but the subjects of most of them made this a very difficult task."

Aside from these endearing apologies, Mary and Charles Lamb's preface positioned their book boldly among feminist efforts like *A Vindication of the Rights of Woman*. Girls, just as much as boys, and at just as young an age, should read and enjoy Shakespeare, they asserted. "For young ladies," reads the preface, "it has been the intention chiefly to write; because boys being generally permitted the use of their fathers' libraries at a much earlier age than girls are, they frequently have the best scenes of Shakespeare by heart, before their sisters are permitted to look into this manly book."

It is to Mary Lamb, more than to Charles, that this feminist purpose for their *Tales* can be attributed. Charles clearly distanced himself from this aspect of their work. Writing a note to William Wordsworth, alerting him that a copy of the *Tales* would soon arrive in Grasmere by coach, Charles refused to claim authorship of this portion of the preface, which he described as having "a more *feminine* turn and does hold me up something as an instructor to young Ladies: but upon my modesty's honour I wrote it not."[12]

The Lambs do not insist on absolute equality of the genders, though—that would be to leap too far beyond social realities. They accept that the better-educated brother will read Shakespeare in the original at an earlier age, and they hope that his sister, primed by "having some notion of the general story from one of these imperfect abridgments," will more fully enjoy hearing him read his favorite scenes aloud. They think of their *Tales* not as substitutes but rather as enticements to the later reading, by girls and boys, of Shakespeare's originals:

> What these Tales shall have been to the YOUNG readers, that and much more it is the writers' wish that the true Plays of Shakespeare may prove to them in older years—enrichers of the fancy, strengtheners of virtue, a withdrawing from all selfish and mercenary thoughts, a lesson of all sweet and honorable thoughts and actions, to teach courtesy, benignity, generosity, humanity: for of examples, teaching these virtues, his pages are full.

Charles may not have wanted to take credit for addressing the book to "young Ladies," but the strategy proved to make good business sense. *Tales from Shakespear* went on sale in January 1806. The Godwins issued a second edition of the collected tales in 1809, adding an "Advertisement" before the preface, in essence confirming Mary's sense of audience:

> The Proprietors of this work willingly pay obedience to the voice of the public. It has been the general sentiment, that the style in which these Tales are written, is not so precisely adapted for the amusement of mere children, as for an acceptable and improving present to young ladies advancing to the state of womanhood. They therefore now offer to the public an education prepared with suitable elegance.

In short, the Juvenile Library had found a market niche among preadolescent female readers.

For illustrations the Godwins again hired William Mulready. Admitted to the prestigious Royal Academy at the age of fourteen, Mulready was only twenty when he began creating copperplate engravings to illustrate the Godwins' books. So impressed with him were they that they devoted an entire Juvenile Library book to his early career: *The Looking-Glass: A True History of the Early Years of an Artist; Calculated to awaken the Emulation of YOUNG PERSONS of both Sexes, in the Pursuit of every laudable Attainment: particularly in the Cultivation of the Fine Arts.* Mulready's paintings would earn him acclaim into the Victorian era, but his book illustrations earned him his keep.[13]

Copperplate engraving was a two-step process: first the image was drawn, then it was etched onto the metal plate for printing. Often different artists performed the two steps. Indeed, many engravers just copied existing drawings, paintings, or sculptures for their illustrations. Such a division of labor probably occurred in the creation of *Tales from Shakespear,* and for some of the work, the Godwins hired another London artist: William Blake.

Blake was not, like Mulready, an up-and-coming young star. Nearly fifty years old, he had been making a living as a printer and engraver since 1784. His acquaintance with William Godwin went back years, through the radical publisher Joseph Johnson: Blake illustrated Mary Wollstonecraft's *Original Stories from Real Life* when Johnson reissued it in 1791. In 1806, when he worked on the Lambs' *Tales,* William Blake had already conceived many of the masterpieces for which he is revered today—*The Marriage of Heaven and Hell, Songs of Innocence and Experience,* and his two great visionary works, *Milton* and *Jerusalem.* He composed the poetry as he engraved the art, so his larger works were years in the making, still in progress when the Godwins hired him.[14]

Nowhere in the first edition of *Tales from Shakespear* does one read the name of William Blake, but the frontispiece—an image of Prospero commanding the seas to swell, with Miranda, hair flowing, standing at his side—as well as the illustrations for three other comedies and one tragedy, all have earmarks of Blake's style: sculptured and sinewy limbs, gracefully sorrowful eyes, flowing lines of draped clothing, elongated figures, and a dynamic of movement not found in the book's other engravings.[15]

While a modern viewer may delight in the Blake illustrations, Charles Lamb did not. He complained more of content than of style and blamed all the mistakes on "the baby"—his code name for Mary Jane Godwin. "You will forgive the plates," he wrote Wordsworth,

> when I tell you that they were left to the direction of Godwin, who left the choice of subjects to the *bad baby,* who from mis-chief—(I suppose) has chosen one from damn'd beastly vul-garity (vide Merch. Venice) where no atom of authority was in the tale to justify it—to another has given a name which exists not in the tale, *Nic. Bottom,* & which she thought would be funny, though in this I suspect *his* hand, for I guess her reading

does not reach far enough to know Bottom's Xtian name— —
& one of Hamlet, & Grave diggg [*sic*: "digging"], a scene which
is not hinted at in the story.[16]

In short, several illustrations or captions conveyed details consciously omitted in the Lambs' versions—a stupid oversight, in
Charles's opinion. Whether because of his objections or for financial reasons, the second edition of *Tales* included only an engraving of a bust of Shakespeare.

Reviewers generally favored *Tales from Shakespear*. The *Critical
Review,* in its May 1807 issue, included this laudatory comment,
referring to the edition created as multiple volumes, one per play:

> We have compared these little volumes with the numerous
> systems which have been devised for riveting attention at an
> early age, and conquering the distaste for knowledge and
> learning which so frequently opposes itself to the instruction
> of children; and we do not scruple to say, that unless perhaps
> we except Robinson Crusoe, they claim the very first place,
> and stand unique, without rival or competitor.

The Godwins reprinted this blurb in the second edition.

With *Tales from Shakespear,* Mary Lamb proved that when put to
the task, she wrote swiftly. "I shall soon have done my work and
know not what to begin next," she wrote Sarah Stoddart at the
end of June. It took her fewer than six months to finish the project. Instead of taking their customary three- to four-week summer holiday, the Lambs stayed in London and finished their book.
"We thought if we were any where and left them undone, they
would lay upon our minds, and that when we returned we should
feel unsettled, and our money all spent besides," Mary explained.
"Next summer we are to be very rich and then we can afford a
long journey somewhere, I will not say to Salisbury because I

really think it is better for you to come to us, but of that we will talk another time."

But the prospect of finishing made Mary Lamb nervous. "My mind is so *dry* after poring over my work all day," she wrote Sarah. She was less worried about getting another assignment than about finding a new subject on which to write. "Set your brains to work and invent a story either for a short childs story or a long one that would make a kind of Novel or a Story that would make a play," she asked Sarah. Charles favored a play, but Mary was more interested in fiction. "Seriously," she insisted to Sarah, "will you draw me out a skeleton of a story either from memory of any thing that you have read or from your own invention and I will fill it up in some way or other."[17]

Finished with her own labors, Mary found her mind filled with worries over others. After two years of wandering, Samuel Taylor Coleridge had returned to London. He stayed with the Lambs in August 1806. They found him fascinating, as always, yet his dependence on laudanum was taking a physical and emotional toll. Coleridge tempted Charles back into smoking (again) by offering him a big "Segar." Mary held back from complaining, for she had a higher goal in mind. She must have sensed that he was avoiding contact with his wife, and she plotted out steps to force Coleridge to face that problem. "You must positively write to Mrs Coleridge this day," she told him authoritatively in a letter delivered to him while he was still in London, "and you must write here that I may know you write or you must come and dictate a letter for me to write to her. I know all that you would say in defence of not writing . . . yet a letter from me or you *shall go today.*"[18]

Mr. and Mrs. Coleridge did correspond in September and October. "Be assured, that to leave London is the strongest wish, of which a mind and body so enfeebled as mine, is capable," Samuel wrote Sara.[19] He finally arrived in Keswick in November. Meanwhile, friends recognized that, as Wordsworth put it, "he recoils so much from the thought of domesticating with Mrs. Coleridge, with whom, though on many accounts he much respects her, he is so miserable that he dare not encounter it."[20]

At the same time, Mary Lamb was advising Sarah Stoddart, still considering suitors right and left. Her immediate prospect was a farmer named Mr. Dowling, whom Sarah's eldest brother, John, asked Mary to meet and judge. "I have received a long letter from your brother on the subject of your intended marriage," Mary wrote Sarah in October 1806:

> He says that if Mr D. is a worthy man he shall have no objection to become the brother of a farmer, and he makes an odd request to me that I shall set out to Salisbury to look at & examine into the merits of the said Mr D—& speaks very confidently as if you would abide by my determination. . . . The objects he starts are only such as you & I have already talked over such as the difference in age, education, habit of life &c.[21]

Mary preferred not to travel to Salisbury. She suggested that Sarah bring her intended to London at Christmas and promised she would not be harsh in her judgment.

As the courtship continued and a proposal seemed imminent, John Stoddart even asked Mary Lamb to draw up the marriage contract. He told her exactly how it should be done: Sarah should keep separate interests from her husband, to protect the wealth that her brother feared would be drained by farm and farmer. Mary reported these commands to her friend, adding her own hunch as to what the future might hold:

> . . . as to settlements, which are matters of which I never having had a penny in my own disposal I never in my life thought of, and if I had been blessed with a good fortune, & that marvellous blessing to boot a husband I verily believe I should have

crammed it all uncounted into his pocket——. But thou hast a cooler head of thy own & I dare say will do exactly what is expedient & proper . . . yet perhaps an offer of your own money to take a farm may make *uncle* do less for his nephew & in that case Mr D might be a loser by your generosity——. [W]eigh all these things well & if you can so contrive it let your brother *settle* the *settlements* himself.[22]

These are not the idealistic words of a feminist—no Mary Wollstonecraft insisting on female rights to property—but rather the practical words of a realist, advising on likely consequences.

Nudge to Coleridge, aide to John Stoddart, adviser to his sister, Sarah—Mary Lamb continued at the same time to be counselor and caretaker for Charles. In his eyes the completion of *Tales from Shakespear* did not matter half so much as the performance of *Mr. H*, which opened at Covent Garden on December 10. Mary and Charles attended the opening with Henry Crabb Robinson, whom they had just met and who—at thirty-one, just Charles's age—aspired to write professionally as well. "The prologue was very well received," Robinson wrote about *Mr. H* in his diary. "But on the disclosure of the name, the squeamishness of the vulgar taste in the pit showed itself by hisses. Lamb joined and was probably the loudest hisser in the house."[23]

Hisses! Despite his bravado, they struck Charles to the quick. "Mr. H.——came out last night & failed," Lamb wrote William Wordsworth the day after. "The quantity of friends we had in the house my brother & I being in Public Offices &c. was astonishing—but they yielded at length to a few hissers——. A hundred hisses—damn the word, I write it like *kisses*—how different—a hundred hisses outweigh a 1000 *Claps*. The former come more directly from the Heart."[24] Fourteen months later those hisses were still ringing in his ears.[25]

But Charles Lamb had developed his own set of psychological

defenses, chief among them his easy slides into irony, humor, and self-deprecation, which masked deep feelings of defeat and despair. "We bear our mortification pretty well," he concluded to Wordsworth, but he would not let his sister add any of her own words to the letter. Later that day Mary tried to write the news to Sarah Stoddart, but (as she said soon after) she "found myself utterly incapable of writing one connected sentence, so stout was the phylosophy I wished to boast of."[26] Charles took over. "Mary is by no means unwell, but I made her let me write," he explained. He called her "a little cut at the ill success of Mr. H. which came out last night and *failed*," but, he assured Mary's friend, "We are determin'd not to be cast down."[27]

Mutual determination seems to have kept both siblings from sliding into debilitating states of mind, for by December 23, Mary proudly reported, Charles had resolved to write one more farce, having learned from his mistakes. If that one failed he would give up drama entirely. He already had a new interest, Mary reported: by combing through rare books at the British Museum and in private collections, he would salvage forgotten poetry from centuries past. The plan resulted in Charles Lamb's most significant work of literary criticism, *Specimens of English Dramatic Poets, Who Lived About the Time of Shakespeare: With Notes,* published by Longman in 1808.

Despite the disappointment over *Mr. H,* 1806 proved a year of triumph for Mary Lamb. She had completed a book, soon to be published, and looked forward to writing the next. Her health had stayed steady. Friends looked to her for wisdom and guidance. She had moved through the stress of writing and the blast of her brother's failed play without any significant recurrence of mania or depression. She continued to cook and sew, but she also created and counseled. Self-doubt had not disappeared altogether, but it was counterbalanced by pride, accomplishment, confidence, and authority. Mary Lamb was grasping for, and attaining, all that society could offer her.

Then something snapped—again.

IN THE ABSENCE of correspondence from January to July 1807, it is difficult to piece together the circumstances. Charles Lamb blamed it on summer travel. As they had planned, Mary and Charles set off in June for a three-week holiday to visit Thomas and Catherine Clarkson, the couple they had first encountered at Dove Cottage in 1802. The Clarksons lived in Bury St. Edmunds, an ancient Suffolk town northeast of London, renowned for its quiet and its wholesome air. The household atmosphere must have been charged with enthusiasm, considering that just months before, Parliament had finally voted overwhelmingly to abolish the slave trade, consummating Thomas Clarkson's efforts over decades.

Despite the genial setting Mary began to feel those uncomfortably familiar symptoms. She tried to ignore them; in what may have been simply an impulsive act of generosity, she gave Charles's new coat to the Clarksons' manservant. She confided in Charles, and her symptoms grew undeniable. The Lambs departed so hastily that they left Mary's books and papers behind.

Once back in London, Charles wrote the Clarksons. "You will wish to know how we performed our journey," he said. "My sister was tolerably quiet until we got to Chelmsford, where she began to be very bad indeed." It was Charles's good fortune that he found William Knight, a Quaker grocer and friend of the Clarksons, whom he asked for help in handling Mary. Somehow the Knight family located a straitjacket for them, into which Charles fastened his sister "to confine her arms" for the journey home. Bound physically, Mary still thrashed mentally. "I am so fatigued," Charles wrote, "for she talked in the most wretched desponding way conceivable, particularly the last three stages, she talked all the way." Mary herself was "sadly tired and miserably depressed" by the time they reached London.[28]

They did not even go home first; they traveled straight to Hoxton. "I have great satisfaction that she is among people who have been used to her," Charles wrote, but it frustrated him to learn that the Hoxton caretakers would not let him visit until she was "getting pretty well." He estimated that her stay would last a few weeks, but knew it could be longer. "She has been confined 5. 6. 7. & even 10 weeks at a time," he wrote Catherine Clarkson.[29]

No record remains of how long this confinement lasted, but it appears not to have been much longer than a month. A letter from Charles Lamb to John Rickman, inviting him to a game of cribbage on a Wednesday evening, can be dated to late July 1807, and it includes the note that "Mary desires her compliments to Mrs. R. & joins in the invitation." So apparently she was home and well enough to receive company before the end of the summer. No further details remain to explain this episode in Mary Lamb's mental health history, not even letters from Charles bemoaning his solitude. Perhaps that very silence demonstrates that in 1807 both brother and sister were facing the truth. At the very same time that Mary Lamb was discovering her strength and creativity, those uncontrollable cycles into, through, and back out of insanity were becoming a regular feature of her life.

10

SCHOOLGIRL TALES

On May 1, 1808, Sarah Stoddart finally married, with Mary Lamb as her bridesmaid. The courtship had begun two years before with a simple line in a letter from Mary to Sarah: "William Hazlitt the brother of him you know is in town, I believe you have heard us say we like him."[1]

The Hazlitt brothers, John and William, were sons of a Unitarian minister from Wem, Shropshire, just north of Shrewsbury. Even those who loved and admired William considered him somewhat strange. He was the sort of person whose insistence on honesty made him so defiant of social custom that his behavior was often awkward and always unexpected. P. G. Patmore, a journalist of the time, recalled that he first met Hazlitt when the young man applied to him, offering to present literary lectures:

> I saw a pale anatomy of a man, sitting uneasily, half on half off a chair, with his legs tucked awkwardly underneath the rail, his hands folded listlessly on his knees, his head drooping on one side, and one of his elbows leaning (not resting) on the edge of the table by which he sat, as if in fear of its having no right to be there. His hat had taken an odd position on the floor beside him, as if that, too, felt itself as much out of its element as the owner.[2]

He was not a striking figure. "His bashfulness, want of words, slovenliness of dress, &c., made him sometimes the object of ridicule," wrote Henry Crabb Robinson. Girls especially loved to tease him.[3] Patmore found him "loose, unstrung, inanimate," with an "anxious and highly-intellectual face" animated by a "love of truth," which was, he soon discovered, both "the leading feature of his mind" and "the key to all its weaknesses, errors, and inconsistencies." Hazlitt rarely held his tongue, always finding something critical to say about anyone he met. He was "by nature," so Patmore came to recognize, "*a lone man,* living, moving, and having his being, for and to himself exclusively; as utterly cut off from fulfilling and exercising the ordinary pursuits and affections of his kind, and of his nature, as if he had been bound hand and foot in a dungeon, or banished to a desert"[4]—not, from the sound of it, a particularly good catch as a husband.

Hazlitt had spent four formative years, aged five to nine, in Boston, Massachusetts, where his father sought acceptance as a Unitarian minister. He had considered the same path and attended Hackney Unitarian College. His older brother, John, found good work in London as a painter of miniature portraits, and the artist's life lured William from the ministry. Although he did do some painting, William Hazlitt ultimately turned to writing. In the long run his career paralleled that of his friend, Charles Lamb, and the two of them stand out as the finest essayists of the period. Unlike Lamb, though, Hazlitt was passionately interested in government and politics, hence better suited to write for London's newspapers. The political ethic implicit in his Unitarian upbringing—championing the people, defying the elite—came through in much of what he wrote. He was a child of the Enlightenment. "It is reason, not the will of another, that gives the law," he once wrote. He held everyone and everything up to rational scrutiny.[5]

Social graces meant little compared with intellect and artistry to Mary and Charles Lamb, and those strengths drew them to William Hazlitt. The three first met in 1803 at William Godwin's, at a dinner on March 22, attended as well by Coleridge, the Holcrofts, and Mary Wollstonecraft's younger brother, James.[6] As usual, philosophical debate punctuated the evening. "They were disputing fiercely which was the best—*Man as he was, or man as he is to be,*" recalled Hazlitt. Charles Lamb—always "with a *bon-mot* in his mouth," said Hazlitt—came through with the transcendent answer to the debate: "Give me man as he is *not* to be," he quipped.[7] The two iconoclasts connected.

The friendship between the Lambs and Hazlitt deepened. He lived at 34 Southampton Buildings, just up Chancery Lane from them, the very buildling in which they had lived before moving back to the Inner Temple. "William Hazlitt is painting my brothers picture," Mary wrote Sara Coleridge in October 1804, "which has brought us acquainted with the whole family. I like William Hazlitt & his sister very much indeed, & I think Mrs Haslitt [Mrs. John Hazlitt] a pretty goodhumoured woman. She has a nice little girl of the Pypos kind [like Coleridge's "Pi-pos," or Derwent], who is so fond of my brother that she stops strangers in the street to tell them when *Mr Lamb is coming to see her.*"[8] Hazlitt's painting is no doubt the finest of all the extant images of either Mary or Charles: an exquisitely rendered oil portrait, with the subject dressed to match his antiquarian interests, wearing the stiff neck ruffle of a Renaissance lord.

During the summer of 1807 Sarah Stoddart and William Hazlitt fell in love. Mary could not have been Sarah's close adviser through the twists and turns of the courtship, since it proceeded through the two months she spent in Hoxton House. By November, though, Mary was back at home, fascinated to learn how the odd fellow Hazlitt played suitor to her flirtatious friend. She asked Sarah for more information about their "comical love affair."

Letters had been whizzing back and forth between London and

Salisbury, with Sarah's expectations running hot and cold. Hazlitt's embarrassed behavior confused her. Sarah reported it all to Mary, who now eagerly counseled her friend. When Sarah complained of a "strange letter" from Hazlitt, Mary urged her to "preserve the said letter, that I may one day have the pleasure of seeing how Mr Hazlitt treats of love."[9]

It would be an understatement to say that Mary encouraged Sarah in the courtship. She joked that since both the women whom Sarah would soon call sister-in-law—Mrs. John Stoddart and Mrs. John Hazlitt—had lately either given birth or announced pregnancies, "you are likely to have plenty of Nephews and neices [sic]." She tempered her eagerness as she closed her letter: "Determine as wisely as you can in regard to Hazlett [sic], and if your determination be to have him, Heaven send you many happy years together." Yet she could not keep from revealing a smile: "I confess I should like to see Hazlitt and you come together if (as Charles observes) it were only for the joke sake. . . . Write instantly to me."[10]

To Mary's distress Sarah kept her courtship with Hazlitt a secret from her brother, recently returned to London from Malta. Mary Lamb stood ready to negotiate, but she insisted that Sarah—or, even better, William Hazlitt himself—first tell John Stoddart what was up.

Hazlitt I know is shy of speaking first but I think it of such great importance to you to have your brother friendly in the business that if you can overcome his reluctance it would be a great point gained: for you must begin the world with ready money—at least an hundred pound; for if you once go into furnished lodgings you will never be able to lay by money to buy furniture.

If you obtain your brothers approbation he might assist you, either by lending or otherwise—I have a great opinion of his generosity, where he thinks it will be useful.[11]

Mary assured Sarah that the brother on the other side of the courtship, John Hazlitt, knew of the discussions of marriage and had even offered some furniture.

While Mary Lamb was busily advising Sarah Stoddart on the steps to secure marriage, Charles Lamb was concocting an extended hoax, somehow oddly connected to the courtship. It was a three-way joke among himself, Hazlitt, and Joseph Hume, a mutual friend. "I suppose you know what has happen'd to our poor friend Hazlitt," Lamb wrote Hume, and he quoted what appeared to be a newspaper item:

Last night Mr. H., a portrait painter in Southampton Buildings, Holborn, put an end to his existence by cutting his throat in a shocking manner. It is supposed that he must have committed his purpose with a pallet-knife, as the edges of the cicatrice or wound were found besmeared with a yellow consistence, but the knife could not be found. The reasons of this rash act are not assigned; an unfortunate passion has been mentioned; but nothing certain is known. The deceased was subject to hypochondria, low spirits, but he had lately seemed better, having paid more than usual attention to his dress and person.

Hazlitt responded with a hilarious "petition & remonstrance" proving that "he is not dead, as has been pretended by some malicious persons, calling themselves his *friends* (the better to conceal their base purposes)." He enumerated eight reasons to prove that he was not dead, beginning with: "he, the said W. Hazlitt, has regularly for the last month rang the bell at eleven at night, which was considered as a sign for the girl to warm his bed, & this being done, he has gone to bed, & slept soundly for the next twelve to fourteen hours" and including: "Fifthly, that growing tired of his sedentary posture, he has occasionally got up from his chair & walked across the room. . . . Also, that he has twice attempted to read some of his own works, but has fallen asleep over them." All points proved, argued Hazlitt, that he was still alive.[12]

The repartee went on for two weeks, each man trumping the other. It was a private escapade of wit among three friends, a sort of bachelor party in writing, spiked with a touch of latent animosity and more than a little dose of the humiliation males sometimes subject each other to when they sense in one of their kind that excess of embarrassing emotion called love.

Despite Charles's teasing, both he and his sister were genuinely pleased to think that their two dear friends would be married. They invited Sarah to come live with them in London, to be closer to her betrothed as they planned their life together— Charles's idea roundly seconded by Mary and approved by William Hazlitt. John Stoddart, however, insisted that his sister act with due propriety and stay nowhere but at his home in London before the wedding. Even though Sarah had stayed without censure at the Lambs' many times before, to do so on the eve of her wedding would "have a very strange appearance," John Stoddart told Mary Lamb.[13] The trouble was, his in-laws were visiting through April, so Sarah would have to put off her move to London, hence her wedding, until May. He may have had other reasons, too—"something about settlements," Charles reported to Manning, was slowing the progress toward marriage. John Stoddart needed confirmation that William Hazlitt could support his sister as she deserved. Charles Lamb suspected otherwise. *"Pauper est Cinna, sed amat,"* he quipped to Manning—"Cinna [a character in Martial's Latin epigrams] is poor, but he loves."[14]

Both women sewed furiously as the wedding approached. Sarah Stoddart embroidered a band of cloth for her bridesmaid's dress, but Mary wanted to make herself a gown of off-white Chinese silk sent to her by Thomas Manning. "Manning would like to hear I wore it for the first time at your wedding," Mary told Sarah. As a final touch Mary planned to wear the lovely brooch John Stoddart had given her—especially dear to her because, "having never had any presents from gentlemen in my young days, I highly prize all they now give me."[15]

Mary's communiques to Sarah as they prepared for the wedding show giddy anticipation over the coming ritual coupled with an easy intimacy between the two women. "I shall have no present to give you on your marriage," Mary warned Sarah in March,

> nor do I expect I shall be rich enough to give anything to baby at the first christening, but at the second, or third child's I hope to have a coral or so to spare out of my own earnings. Do not ask me to be Godmother for I have an objection to that— but there is I believe no serious duties attached to a bride's maid, therefore I come with a willing mind, bringing nothing with me but many wishes, and not a few hopes, and a very lit- tle of fears—of happy years to come.

Only half in jest, Mary attaches a postscript to the letter: "What has Charles done that nobody invites him to the wedding?"[16]

Of course Charles attended the wedding. Mary gracefully accompanied the bride, and Sarah Stoddart became Mrs. William Hazlitt on May 1, 1808. We know that Mr. and Mrs. John Stoddart witnessed the marriage, and we can assume that several Hazlitts attended as well. The ceremony took place in Saint Andrews Church, Holborn, in whose graveyard lay the remains of Elizabeth Lamb.

The ceremony sent Charles into hysterics. Years later he recalled that "I was at Hazlitts marriage & had like to have been turned out several times during the ceremony."[17] Inappropriate behavior at solemn occasions was a personality trait he could not shake. Charles later confessed the sin in "The Wedding," an essay that described a different ceremony but revealed his inability to keep a straight face during any matrimonial event. "Ceremony and I have long shaken hands," he wrote, but it seemed that every time, "something ludicrous occured to me at this most serious of all moments." During the wedding he wrote about, he claimed to be "betrayed to some lightness, for the awful eye of the parson— and the rector's eye of Saint Mildred's in the Poultry is no trifle of a rebuke—was upon me in an instant, souring my incipient jest to the tristful severities of a funeral."

Sarah and William Hazlitt embarked on a marriage that would produce one son, William, born in September 1811, during the period when his father was finding a new calling as a journalist. The marriage lasted ten years longer, not too happily. Both partners had their dalliances, as they admitted when they met in Scotland for an easy divorce.[18] "There was a sheer want of cordial sympathy from the first set-out," their grandson, William Carew Hazlitt, wrote decades later. "They married after studying each other's characters very little, and observing very little how far their tempers were likely to harmonize."[19] All that lay in the unknowable future, of course. For the moment Sarah and William were eager newlyweds, and Mary and Charles were glad to see them so.

AT THE TIME of the Stoddart-Hazlitt wedding, two Juvenile Library projects were under way in the Lamb household. Charles was writing a life of Ulysses, retelling the great adventure stories of the *Odyssey*. Mary was writing another book for young ladies: a collection of stories, each told in a different girl's voice, titled *Mrs. Leicester's School*.

The book takes place as a group of ten girls arrive at Amwell

School, a fictitious charity school for girls, a female version of Christ's Hospital—the school of Mary Lamb's dreams, in other words. On the first evening there, the girls' teacher draws them into a circle in front of the fireplace. After offering the girls many words of comfort and encouragement, the teacher asks, "Let me prevail upon you to relate some little anecdotes of your own lives." *Mrs. Leicester's School* is, then, a collection of the stories each of those ten girls told.

The concept was original. It was not, like *Tales from Shakespear* or *The Adventures of Ulysses,* a retold classic. Nor was it an overtly moral tale. Only in the introduction does an adult voice dominate, as "M. B.," the teacher, explains how she undertook to copy down the stories. Like Newbery's innovative books before it, *Mrs. Leicester's School* fits the modern concept of a trade book for children, conceived for the ten-to-twelve-year-old set, whose comfort with reading allowed them to move to a higher level of plot and idea.

M. B. warrants that she tried to be as transparent a transcriber as possible, letting the girls' voices show through—a fiction, of course, but also a resolution on the part of the author to anchor her imagination in the lives and consciousnesses of schoolgirls aged eight, nine, and ten:

> If in my report of her story [that of Miss Villiers, the first to speak], or in any which follow, I shall appear to make her or you speak an older language than it seems probable that you should use, speaking in your own words, it must be remembered that what is very proper and becoming when spoken, requires to be arranged with some little difference before it can be set down in writing. Little inaccuracies must be pared away, and the whole must assume a more formal and correct appearance. My own way of thinking, I am sensible, will too often intrude itself; but I have endeavoured to

preserve, as exactly as I could, your own words and your own peculiarities of style and manner, and to approve myself.

Your faithful historiographer,
as well as true friend,

M. B.

The plan was to evoke the state of mind of ten different pre-adolescent girls, shunning the voice of the adult who speaks from principle, higher knowledge, or moral superiority. So different was this strategy from any other followed in the books of the Juvenile Library that it is tempting to believe that it was the invention of Mary Lamb.

She had long recognized her special ability to empathize: to see deeply into other people's characters, to put aside her own identity and to see with and to be in another's. It was her deep and sympathetic feeling, coupled with her intellect, that brought her admiration from men of such high standards as Coleridge, who said her mind was "elegantly stored—her Heart feeling,"[20] and Hazlitt, who said that "he never met with a woman who could reason, and had met with one only thoroughly reasonable—the sole exception being Mary Lamb."[21]

The same traits characterized her relationship with her brother. Empathy meant tolerance, intellect meant honesty. Their bond became more flexible, strong, and enduring than those in many a marriage. Mary once told Sarah Stoddart that the foundation of any friendship must be honesty: "telling each other at the moment everything that happens,—where you go—and what you do—that free communication of letters and opinions, just as they arise, as Charles and I do."[22]

Mary Lamb once claimed that for her well of empathy, she had counterexamples in her family to thank. In a revealing letter to Sarah, written in 1803, she intimates that her mother and her aunt "made each other miserable for full twenty years of their lives." The letter offers a glimpse of the tense family dynamics in which she lived as a child. "In some degree theirs is the secret history I believe of all sisters-in-law," wrote Mary:

> —and you will smile when I tell you I think myself the only woman in the world, who could live with a brothers wife, and make a real friend of her. partly from early observation of the unhappy example I have just given you, and partly from a knack I know I have of looking into peoples real characters, and never expecting them to act out of it—never expecting another to do as I would do in the same case.[23]

We also have Charles's comment to Coleridge that his mother responded to Mary's expressions of love "with coldness & repulse." In a turn of events recognized by psychologists, the girl child protected herself against the ambient negativities around her by developing an exquisitely refined instinct for the feelings of others.[24]

Mary Lamb plied that empathy as she wrote *Mrs. Leicester's School*. The girls in her book share a cluster of concerns: the reality of death, the promise of reading, the inequity of the social classes, and the mysteries of identity, particularly between a daughter and her mother—concerns resoundingly significant to Mary Lamb. In the first story we hear from Elizabeth Villiers, whose earliest memory is "my father teaching me the alphabet from the letters on a tombstone that stood at the head of my mother's grave." Issues of motherhood and identity infuse the story told by Ann Withers, born a servant, switched at birth, and raised in aristocratic luxury. Ultimately the truth is found out, and not only her highborn would-be mother but also her serving-class mother forsake her. Having worked closely with Shakespeare's classics of switched identities, Mary Lamb wrote one of her own, exploring the influence, or absence, of a mother on a daughter.

City-born Louisa Manners shares her memory of a visit to her grandmother in the country. "I had never in all my life been out of London; no, nor had I ever seen a bit of green grass," she exclaims, and recounts her favorite country pleasures: picking laps full of wildflowers, delighting in lambs and chicks and ducklings, watching the bees make honey, and hearing simple country lore from her beloved "Grandmamma." Very likely Louisa Manners's memories echo those of Mary Lamb on visits to her grandmother, a servingwoman at Blakesware estate in Hertfordshire, or to her great aunt, the mistress at Mackery End, the country home recalled in Charles's essay.

Emily Barton's "Visit to the Cousins" tells another story about life in the country, this time in a minor key. Sent from London at a young age to live with country relatives, Emily finds herself shunned by cousins and aunt alike. She runs away, distraught, but is rescued by her parents. Mary Lamb must have smiled as she added a whimsical detail when the reunited family considers where to shop for books:

> As we were returning home down Cheapside, papa said, "Emily shall take home some little books. Shall we order the coachman to the corner of St. Paul's Churchyard, or shall we go to the Juvenile Library in Skinner Street?" Mamma said she would go to Skinner Street, for she wanted to look at the new buildings there. Papa bought me seven new books, and the lady in the shop persuaded him to take more, but mamma said that was quite enough at present.

Mary Lamb's other two schoolgirl stories were those of Margaret Green (the "young Mahometan" who declares her sympathies with Islam) and Charlotte Wilmot, "The Merchant's

Daughter," who tells a reversal-of-fortune story. Charlotte's father was a merchant; their family enjoyed "very opulent circumstances," and she "assumed airs of superiority over Maria Hartley, whose father was a clerk in my father's counting-house." When Mr. Wilmot's business flounders and his property is possessed, who should take in Charlotte but the Hartley family? From Maria she learns all the "useful works and employments," and one presumes—although Mary Lamb does not outright moralize here—that she is the better for it.

As with *Tales from Shakespear*, Charles Lamb contributed to *Mrs. Leicester's School.* "My Sister's part in the Leicester School (about two thirds) was purely her own; as it was (to the same quantity) in the Shakspeare Tales which bear my name," he told a friend years later. Even more than in the *Tales,* his three in *Mrs. Leicester's School* stand out as different from the rest. The sentences are longer, phrases and clauses woven together into a complex whole, as compared with Mary's short, direct sentences, better suited to a juvenile reader. Every story begins, to suit the plan, with the narrator introducing her origins and situation. But in Charles's three stories, the narrative quickly dives into matters of motive and interpretation. His style in these stories hints at the intricate, intertwining associations of thought so admired in his later essays. Mary's stories remain simple description of facts, through which we discern a richer psychological tapestry underlying them. Mary writes as a child, while Charles writes to one.

Charles contributed a few curiosities, but at the heart of this little book of short stories stand the seven written by Mary Lamb. It is possible, as assumed by the few literary historians who have considered *Mrs. Leicester's School*, that Mary lost steam and turned to her brother for help in finishing. Yet it is equally possible that Charles, intrigued, joined her in the intellectual challenge and conceptualized three more characters sitting in front of the Amwell School fireplace. Perhaps they collaborated as intimately as they did on *Tales from Shakespear*. We will never know, but it is fair to say that in concept and execution, *Mrs. Leicester's School* is the closest we have to a book solely by Mary Lamb.

The Godwins published the book without any author's name on the title page. Between 1809 and 1825 *Mrs. Leicester's School* went through nine editions. It was popular, and it was unique. It offered thought-provoking stories written in simple prose. It raised moral issues without moralizing. Even more than *Tales from Shakespear*, it was a book for girls. The anonymous reviewer in the *Critical Review*, who had praised the Lambs' *Shakespear*, waxed even more enthusiastic about *Mrs. Leicester's School*:

> With much satisfaction do we express our unqualified praise of these elegant and most instructive Tales. They are delightfully simple, and exquisitely told. The child or parent who reads the little history of Elizabeth Villiers will, in spite of any resolution to the contrary, be touched to the heart, if not melted into tears. Morose and crabbed censors as we are represented to be, we closed the volume, wishing there had been another, and lamenting that we had got to the end.[25]

The Godwins used these comments to great advantage, reprinting them in subsequent editions.

While his praise never found its way into print, Samuel Taylor Coleridge likewise greatly admired *Mrs. Leicester's School*. "It at once soothes and amuses me to think," wrote Coleridge, "—nay, to know, that the time will come when this little volume of my dear, and well nigh oldest friend, dear Mary Lamb, will be not only enjoyed but acknowledged as a rich jewel in the treasury of our permanent English Literature."[26] In fact British and American publishers kept the book in print through the nineteenth century, but after that it became a scholarly curiosity.

1. This portrait of Mary and Charles Lamb represents the one known image of Mary taken from life. Painted in 1834, it conveys a brother and sister failing in health. Charles, fifty-nine, would die within the year; Mary, seventy, would live more than a decade longer.

2. Only fashions, not landscape, changed between this 1720s view of the Inner Temple and those childhood memories carried by Mary Lamb from the 1760s and '70s. Looking south down King's Bench Walk, one could see boats sailing by on the Thames.

NEW MORALITY;— or _The promis'd Installment of the High-Priest of the THEOPHILANTHROPES._

3. Thanks to the patronage of Samuel Salt, the Lamb family shared his Inner Temple quarters at 2 Crown Office Row, shown here. Mary and Charles's childhood household was probably at the back of the building at center. The crenellated Temple Church rises up behind.

4. James Gillray's cartoon, "New Morality," was published in the Tory *Anti-Jacobin Review* in January 1798. It satirizes Charles Lamb and Charles Lloyd as a toad and frog reading their book, *Blank Verse,* amid a throng of other reprobate intellectuals.

5. This 1770 engraving after John Collet's illustration of *The Rival Milleners* clearly suggests the lascivious reputation of mantua makers and milliners in late-eighteenth-century London.

6. In 1903 Herbert Railton sketched the house at 7 Little Queen Street into which the Lamb family had moved after leaving the Inner Temple in 1792. It was here that Mary Lamb killed her mother in September 1796.

7. William Godwin was a bereaved widower and a fallen hero in 1802, the date of this portrait.

8. Mary Wollstonecraft was pregnant and newly married to William Godwin in 1797, when John Opie painted this portrait.

9. Young Samuel Taylor Coleridge, here twenty-three, rekindled his schoolboy friendship with Charles Lamb in London.

10. Charles Lamb had known William Wordsworth for about a year at the time of this portrait, in 1798.

11. William Hazlitt, essayist and eccentric, was introduced to his future wife, Sarah Stoddart, by Mary and Charles Lamb.

12. Dorothy Wordsworth, William's sister, shown here in her sixties, was one of Mary Lamb's closest friends.

13. Despite occasional estrangements, Samuel Taylor Coleridge, shown here late in life, remained one of Charles and Mary Lamb's dearest friends.

14. Here sixty years old in 1830, William Wordsworth maintained a lifelong friendship with the Lambs and his Lake Country neighbor, Samuel Taylor Coleridge.

15. Grandiose when it was built in 1676, the so-called New Bethlem Hospital had sunk into disrepair by 1796. Mary Lamb might have been placed here had it not been for her brother Charles.

16. Seventeenth-century sculptor Caius Gabriel Cibber created these two larger-than-life figures for the massive gateposts at New Bethlem's entryway, representing the opposing states of a disturbed mind, melancholy and mania.

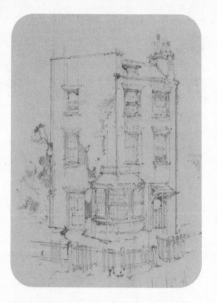

17. In 1903 Herbert Railton sketched the corner building at 45 Chapel Street, Pentonville, where Charles Lamb lived with his father and aunt. Mary moved in after their father's death in 1799.

18. In 1802 Mary and Charles Lamb walked from Coleridge's Lake Country home in Nether Stowey to the Wordsworths' Dove Cottage, above, in the village of Grasmere.

19. Mary Lamb enjoyed many fond memories from childhood days here at Mackery End, the Hertfordshire country house where she often stayed with her great-aunt, who was the housekeeper. She and Charles visited in 1815, an occasion he later memorialized in an essay named for the house.

20. Charles Lamb had a "head worthy of Aristotle" atop a puny body, said one friend. He always wore black stockings, high black garters, and black shoes, recalled another.

21. Mary Lamb wrote this letter to Sarah Stoddart Hazlitt in December 1808. Earlier pages had discussed a plan of William Godwin's to erect a monument to great men of history, hence the reference to "the dead men." The Lambs had recently met dramatist James Sheridan Knowles ("Noales") through the Hazlitts. Both women were concerned about the mental state of John Hazlitt, Sarah's brother-in-law.

22. One woman remembered Charles Lamb's face to be "the gravest I ever saw, but indicating great intellect." Many, including Lamb himself, noted that his nose was, as one friend put it, "of the Jewish cut."

23. This image of Mary Lamb, sketched after her death, was certainly taken from the 1834 portrait. One cannot be sure how accurately it displays her features, but it does portray, as one young admirer put it, "a countenance of singular sweetness, with intelligence," as well as her ever-present mobcap.

24. Leaving the Inner Temple in 1817, Mary and Charles moved to this busy street corner of London, 20 Russell Street, between Drury Lane and Covent Garden.

25. A barrister trained in the Inner Temple, Thomas Talfourd met the Lambs there in 1815 and became a close friend. He wrote the first Lamb biography, published in 1837 and revised in 1848.

26. London artist Daniel Maclise drew this cartoon of William Godwin in the 1830s. No longer a revolutionary political hero, Godwin haunted London bookstalls and wrote an occasional book of his own.

27. After years of Mary's occasional stays in London madhouses, in 1833 she and Charles moved into this cottage in Edmonton, the home of Mr. and Mrs. Walden.

Prospero and Miranda

28. This illustration, the frontispiece for Mary and Charles Lamb's *Tales from Shakespear*, portrays Prospero and Miranda in an early scene of *The Tempest*. It was drawn by William Mulready and very likely engraved for printing by William Blake.

Nic Bottom & the Queen of the Fairies.

29. This illustration, portraying a scene from *A Midsummer Night's Dream*, irritated Charles. Its emphasis on the ass-headed Bottom showed an ignorance of Mary's retelling of the play. The fairies' midair poses strongly suggest William Blake's hand in the engraving of the image.

W. Hopwood. del.   J. Hopwood. sculp.

In this manner, the epitaph on my mother's tomb being my primer and my spelling-book, I learned to read. —— Page 9.

30. As a frontispiece for *Mrs. Leicester's School*, this illustration portrays Elizabeth Villiers, the first girl to tell her story in the book. Young Elizabeth learned to read by tracing the letters on her mother's tombstone.

——— *He fear'd the little bird.*
That singing in the air he heard,
Was telling his transgression.

p. 7.

31. The poem chosen as a frontispiece illustration for the second volume of Mary and Charles Lamb's *Poetry for Children* was "The Boy and the Skylark: A Fable," which explores the psychology of wrongdoings kept secret.

MRS. LEICESTER'S SCHOOL was written in 1808 and printed with the date 1809. Although an absence of correspondence two centuries later may reflect lost letters rather than smooth author-editor relations, we have no evidence that the Godwins had to coach or cajole Mary as she wrote her book. Charles's *Adventures of Ulysses* was published at the same time, but only after heated disagreements between author and editor.

The Adventures of Ulysses told the wild tales and fantastical adventures of Ulysses and his mates, returning to Greece after the war with Troy. Charles told Thomas Manning that he took the stories "not from the Greek—I would not mislead you—nor yet from Pope's Odyssey, but from an older translation of one Chapman," referring to the 1611 translation of Homer's *Iliad* and *Odyssey*—the same translation that Keats would memorialize in his 1816 sonnet, "On First Looking into Chapman's Homer."

But the sensibilities for which Homer—and even Chapman—wrote differed from those of Godwin's young readers. He may have allowed the King of Hearts to become tipsy and Maria Howe, a character in *Mrs. Leicester's School*, to become witch-obsessed, but he was not about to allow the Cyclops to vomit all over the page. Godwin the anarchist now played the censor and reined in his radical author. He laid forth the logic behind his editorial changes. "It is strange with what different feelings an author & a bookseller looks at the same manuscript," he diplomatically began. "I know this by experience: I was an author—I am a bookseller. The author thinks what will conduce to his honour: the bookseller what will cause his commodities to sell." From there he proceeded to the truism that publishers of children's books have always followed: "It is children that read children's books (when they are read); but it is parents that choose them. The critical thought of the tradesman puts itself therefore into the place of the parent, & enquires what will please the parent, & what the parent will condemn."

Then he got to the heart of the matter:

> We live in squeamish days. Amidst the beauties of your manu-script, of which no man can think more highly than I do, what will the squeamish say to such expressions as these? "devoured their limbs, yet warm & trembling, lapping the blood." p. 10, or to the giant's vomit, p. 14, or to the minute & shocking description of the extinguishing the giant's eye, in the page fol-lowing. You I dare say have no formed plan of excluding the female sex from among your readers, & I, as a bookseller, must consider that, if you have, you exclude one half of the human species.

He made one other request, likewise grounded in the character of his audience: "I should also like a preface," he asked of Lamb. "Half our customers know not Homer, or know him only as you & I know the lost authors of antiquity."[27]

Charles Lamb answered contentiously. He agreed that the giant's vomit was "perfectly nauseous" and would delete it, but the other passages he considered "lively images of *shocking* things," intrinsic to the story in spirit and fact, in keeping with gothic hor-ror novels all the rage in those days. "I assure you I will not alter one more word," he declared.[28]

In the end Lamb and Godwin compromised. The giant does not vomit, but Ulysses's men do manage a gory mess as they plunge a red-hot stake into the Cyclops's eye: "Ulysses helped to thrust it in with all his might, still further and further, with effort, as men bore with an auger, till the scalded blood gushed out, and the eye-ball smoked, and the strings of the eye cracked, as the burning rafter broke in it, and the eye hissed, as hot iron hisses when it is plunged into water."

The Adventures of Ulysses brought a little more money into the Lamb household, but it was not the work that most engaged Charles Lamb's imagination that year. His inquiries into the forgotten poets of the English Renaissance were shaping up into a book.

"Specimens are becoming fashionable," he wrote Manning. Scientists indeed were collecting specimens—of bones, of feathers, of insects, of flowers, even of air from all corners of the world. Lamb borrowed a word from the physical sciences and applied it to his literary pursuits. We would probably call the result an anthology today. "Longman is to print it & be at all the expence and risk, & I am to share the profits after all deductions i.e. a year or two hence I must pocket what they please to tell me is due to me. But the Book is such as I am glad there should be. It is done out of old plays at the Museum & out of Dodsley's collection &c. It is to have Notes."[29] The new enterprise thrilled Charles Lamb. It was a serious literary research project, a book for adults from a respectable London publisher, and a work for royalties, not task work for hire. It marked a new era in the Lamb household, the start of Charles's career as an author to be taken seriously.

It had been a notably positive year. Mary Lamb had stayed in good mental health all through 1808, no spells, no madhouse confinements since the summer before. Once again she and her brother enjoyed their life of double singleness. They saw the publication of one children's book and completed manuscripts for two others. Charles's scholarly studies were coming to fruition. Friends filled their evenings with conversation and whist so routinely that the Lambs now announced that they received guests on Wednesdays. As Charles coyly wrote to Thomas Manning, "All great men have public days."[30]

In his cleverness he omits a mention of the great woman essential to his "public days." But she was there. "As, amongst certain classes of birds, if you have one you are sure of the other," wrote Thomas De Quincey, "so, with respect to the Lambs . . . seeing or hearing the brother, you knew that the sister could not be far off. If she *were,* you sighed, knew what that meant, and asked no questions."[31]

11

POETRY FOR CHILDREN

On April 3, 1809, Robert Lloyd, who had now known Mary and Charles Lamb for more than ten years, wrote to his wife after visiting them:

> I spent yesterday with Lamb and his sister—it is sweetly grati-
> fying to see them. They were not up when I went. Mary (his
> sister) the moment I entered the Room, calling from her
> chamber, said—"Robert, I am coming." They appear to sleep
> in Rooms by each other.
>
> If we use the expression, their Union of affection is what we
> conceive of marriage in Heaven. They are the World *one* to the
> *other.*[1]

By this time in their lives, Mary at forty-four and Charles at thirty-four had reached a modicum of comfort on many different levels. War with France continued, but in some sense their Britain had found ways to settle into that routine, too, even making the most of it.

Two years before, despite Nelson's victory at Trafalgar, Napoleon's land forces had appeared unstoppable, moving north into the Low Countries, east into Austria and Prussia, south into Italy. But France's alliances with Spain and Portugal had weakened, and now the countries of the Iberian Peninsula were joining with Britain to fight French expansion. Britain's naval strength allowed it to blockade trade to all the French-dominated regions of Europe, which improved commerce and boosted the economy.

The Lambs, too, were enjoying a financial upturn. The steady stream of writing that Mary and Charles had been producing, combined with the salary the East India House paid its reliable accountant, meant that they no longer had to scrimp and worry over what they could afford to offer friends on Wednesday evenings. "We have bought some very fine chairs & window curtains and we intend almost to ruin ourselves, in various other articles of expensive furniture," Mary and Charles wrote in a joint letter to Thomas Holcroft's daughter, who enjoyed paying them visits when she was in London. "And we have hired a maid too, you will find strange alterations at your next hollidays."[2]

Economic stability paralleled personal equilibrium. Mary Lamb had enjoyed another full year without a madhouse visit. She and her brother enjoyed a routine and a symbiotic relationship, as Charles memorialized in his essay, "Mackery End, in Hertfordshire." He calls his sister by the pseudonym he coined for her, Bridget Elia:

> Bridget Elia has been my housekeeper for many a long year. I have obligations to Bridget, extending beyond the period of memory. We house together, old bachelor and maid, in a sort of double singleness; with such tolerable comfort, upon the whole, that I, for one, find in myself no sort of disposition to go out upon the mountains, with the rash king's offspring, to bewail my celibacy. We agree pretty well in our tastes and habits—yet so, as "with a difference." We are generally in harmony, with occasional bickerings—as it should be among near relations. Our sympathies are rather understood than expressed; and once, upon my dissembling a tone in my voice more kind

than ordinary, my cousin burst into tears, and complained that
I was altered.

Mary Lamb time and again asserted that she was happier in their
state of "double singleness" than she ever would have been married. Call it rationalization, call it resignation: It was the code by
which she lived. When Sarah Stoddart Hazlitt sent her the sad
news of a miscarriage, Mary replied with the equally sad news
that Susannah Rickman's infant had died. "I am glad I am an old
maid," she wrote Sarah, "for you see there is nothing but misfortunes in the marriage state."[3]

Love of literature held the sister and brother together. "We are
both great readers in different directions," Charles grants in
"Mackery End," with his taste running to antique literature and hers
to modern: "She must have a story." Charles attributes Mary's taste
in reading to her education, or lack thereof—one area in which the
brother far exceeded the sister, as both well knew.

> Her education in youth was not much attended to; and she
> happily missed all that train of female garniture which passeth
> by the name of accomplishments. She was tumbled early, by
> accident or design, into a spacious closet of good old English
> reading, without much selection or prohibition, and browsed
> at will upon that fair and wholesome pasturage.

Wryly congratulating his sister for her obliviousness to traditional female ways, he also blames her spinsterly fate on those
eccentricities. She is all the better for it, he states in this essay:
"Had I twenty girls, they should be brought up exactly in this
fashion. I know not whether their chance in wedlock might not
be diminished by it; but I can answer for it, that it makes (if the
worst come to the worst) most incomparable old maids."

———

MARY AND CHARLES LAMB enjoyed a delicate balance of reciprocal power, not the hierarchical order of husband over wife. A
wonderful episode of apartment redecoration illustrates the relationship. "We still live in Temple Lane, but I am now sitting in a
room you never saw," Mary informed a recent visitor:

> Soon after you left us we were distressed by the cries of a cat
> which seemed to proceed from the garrets adjoining to ours,
> and only separated from ours by a locked door on the farther
> side of my brother's bedroom, which you know was the little
> room at the top of the kitchen stairs. We had the lock forced
> and let the poor puss out from behind a pannel of the wain-
> scot, and she lived with us from that time, for we were in grat-
> itute [*sic*] bound to keep her as she had introduced us to four
> untenanted, unowned rooms, and by degrees we have taken
> possession of these unclaimed apartments.[4]

First she used the new space to dry laundry. Then they moved
Charles's bed, then a table and chair, into one of the rooms. It was
one way to shield Charles from his "knock-eternal" friends. "I persuaded him that he might write at his ease in one of these rooms,"
Mary said, "as he could not ere hear the door knock, or hear himself
denied to be at home, which was sure to make him call out and
convict the poor maid in a fib. Here I said he might be almost really
not at home." Mary made him a fire and "bid him write away."

That very evening he came down the stairs "with a sadly dismal
face. He could do nothing he said with those bare white-washed
walls before his eyes. He could not write in that dull unfurnished
prison." After Charles set out for work the next day, Mary laid old
carpeting on the floor, took prints down from the kitchen walls
and hung them in Charles's new study, and "after dinner, with

great boast of what an improvement I had made I took Charles once more into his new study."[5]

Thus began a shared project in which Charles participated with "innocent delight," recalled Henry Crabb Robinson.[6] Mary energetically described the transformation to her friends:

A week of busy labours followed. . . . My brother & I almost covered the walls with prints, for which purpose he cut out every print from every book in his old library, coming in every now and then to ask my leave to strip a fresh poor author, which he might not do you know without my permission as I am elder sister. There was such pasting—such pasting—such consultation where their portraits and where the series of pictures from Ovid, Milton & Shakespear would show to most advantage and in what obscure corner authors of humbler note might be allowed to tell their stories. . . . —To conclude this long story about nothing, the poor despised garret is now called the print room and is become our most favorite sitting room.[7]

"I am elder sister," Mary comfortably asserted—and her brother likewise regarded her to have primacy, not just because she was older but because she was wiser, too, as he elaborated in "Mackery End":

That which was good and venerable to her, when a child, retains its authority over her mind still. She never juggles or plays tricks with her understanding.

We are both of us inclined to be a little too positive; and I have observed the result of our disputes to be almost uniformly this—that in matters of fact, dates, and circumstances, it turns out, that I was in the right, and my cousin in the wrong. But where we have differed upon moral points; upon something proper to be done, or let alone; whatever heat of opposition, or steadiness of conviction, I set out with, I am sure always, in the long-run, to be brought over to her way of thinking.

In an atmosphere of mutual respect and reciprocal authority, each sibling rarely feared the judgment of the other, but there were some tender areas, as we have already seen. Charles was smitten with guilt when he overdid his drinking or smoking. Mary fretted when she overstepped the bounds of gentlewomanly behavior. She wanted to assure Charles that she could maintain self-control, because those same bounds defined the limits beyond which a woman's behavior might be called mad.

Charles's cameo in "Mackery End" does not whitewash Bridget Elia. He cites two weaknesses that relate to her state of mind. "I must touch upon the foibles of my kinswoman with a gentle hand, for Bridget does not like to be told of her faults," he begins gingerly:

> She hath an awkward trick (to say no worse of it) of reading in company: at which times she will answer *yes* or *no* to a question, without fully understanding its purport—which is provoking, and derogatory in the highest degree to the dignity of the putter of said question. Her presence of mind is equal to the most pressing trials of life, but will sometimes desert her upon trifling occasions. When the purpose requires it, and is a thing of moment, she can speak to it greatly; but in matters which are not the stuff of the conscience, she hath been known sometimes to let slip a word less seasonably.

This characteristic, to be found in many a preoccupied intellectual, seems to contradict the other trait with which Charles faults his sister. She occasionally tends to be a busybody: "In a season of distress, she is the truest comforter," Charles avows, "but in the teasing accidents, and minor perplexities, which do not call out the *will* to meet them, she sometimes maketh matters worse by an excess of participation"—written like a man who wished his older sister would stop bothering him about his intemperances.

ON THE OCCASION of Robert Lloyd's visit in April 1809, Mary and Charles proudly shared news of their next writing project. "They are writing a Book of Poetry for children together," Lloyd wrote his wife. "It is *task* work to them, they are writing for money, and a Book of Poetry for Children being likely to sell has induced them to compose one."[8]

Poetry for Children was to be Mary Lamb's third contribution to the Juvenile Library. As Robert Lloyd indicated, poetry collections already represented a standard genre of children's literature, in those days sure to sell. The models already existed, from Watts's classic *Cradle Hymns* to newer books, like *Original Poems for Infant Minds* (1804), written by the sisters Ann and Jane Taylor, who continued to publish poems for children into the Victorian era. Jane Taylor's name may not be remembered, but her verse certainly is: She wrote "Twinkle, Twinkle, Little Star."

A crowded playing field signified a popular genre. "Poetry for Children, entirely original. By the author of 'Mrs. Leicester's School,'" read the title page of the new book, "Printed for M. J. Godwin, at the Juvenile Library, No. 41, Skinner Street. 1809." The two bound volumes were tiny, five and a half by three and three-eighths inches, just slightly bigger than index cards today, with eighty-four poems printed on "paper of the thinnest imaginable texture," as one Victorian book collector described it.[9] Priced at just one shilling sixpence, the first printing sold out in less than three years. Instead of reprinting the book, though, the Godwins included the Lamb poems they thought best in an 1811 anthology, *The First Book of Poetry*, edited by W. F. Mylius, headmaster at a Catholic boys' school in Chelsea. It became one of their mainstay titles and stayed in print for more than fifteen years.

Copies of the first and only edition of *Poetry for Children* became so scarce that in 1827 Charles Lamb was asking his friends if they had one. "One likes to have one copy of every thing one does," he wrote. "I neglected to keep one of 'Poetry for Children,' the joint production of Mary and me, and it is not to be had for love or money."[10] Late-nineteenth-century antiquarians could not lay hands on a single copy until a book collector found two in Australia, purchased at an estate sale in Plymouth, England, in 1866.[11] Fewer than ten copies of the title are known to exist in collections today. In fact more copies exist of early-nineteenth-century American reprints—truncated, probably pirated, and printed in Boston or New Haven—than of the Godwin original.

Charles was eager that certain of the poems be recognized as his. In June 1809 he sent the entire collection to Robert Lloyd, marking with a check each one he claimed as his own.[12] That checklist has since been lost, and the annotations were never recorded. Only the slightest hints remain. Lamb occasionally packed up books and sent them on East India House schooners to Thomas Manning in the Far East. On the second of January, 1810, he sent *Poetry for Children*. "There comes with this [letter] two volumes . . . of minor poetry, a sequel to 'Mrs. Leicester'; the best you may suppose mine; the next best are my coadjutor's; you may amuse yourself in guessing them out; but I must tell you mine are but one-third in quantity of the whole. So much for a very delicate subject."[13] Uncomfortable with, yet certain of, his superior skills as a poet, Charles Lamb initiated the game that continues to this day among the few readers interested enough to distinguish his from Mary's among all eighty-four poems.

There are some external clues—three of the poems were included in an 1818 volume of Charles's *Works,* and another poem was quoted by Charles at the end of an essay, attributed to "a quaint poetess of our day."[14] Scholars have tended to assume that those with tighter rhythm and wittier rhyme are Charles's, and that on the other hand, as one critic puts it, "Mary would some-times put a word a little out of its right place in order to get her rhyme—and her rhyme, sometimes, was such as betrayed her to be native-born of the metropolis of England."[15] What is forgotten amid all this divvying up, from prideful Charles on, is the way in which brother and sister wrote together.

One of the poems in *Poetry for Children* epitomizes their collaboration. Maybe it began as a word game between them. Maybe Mary (or Charles) wrote a parody of a real conversation. The result is no masterpiece, but it is an amusing invention on the theme of dual authorship, titled "What is Fancy?"

SISTER.

I am to write three lines, and you
Three others that will rhyme.
There—now I've done my task.

BROTHER.

Three stupid lines as e'er I knew.
When you've the pen next time,
Some question of me ask.

SISTER.

Then tell me, brother, and pray mind,
Brother, you tell me true:
What sort of thing is fancy?

BROTHER.

By all that I can ever find,
'Tis something that is very new,
And what no dunces can see.

While few, if any, of the poems (maybe not even this one) may have been written as Mary and Charles passed the paper back and forth, each writing a few lines, the collaboration was likely complicated and intimate, with edits, critiques, responses, and rewrites all influencing the final product, as appears to have happened when the sister and brother coauthored before.

Many of the poems are written in the voice of a child, often about nine or ten years old. Some assume the point of view of an even younger child, four to six, allowing the poet to play upon childish innocence or misunderstandings. Situations in most poems arise out of children's everyday lives. A handful retell classics—Moses in the bulrushes, David and Goliath, Jesus's admonition to "suffer little children"—and even those are about children. Many contain a moral message, always subtly implanted in the story line. In the main these poems teach more by example than by rule.

A cluster of themes predominates, some echoing those of *Mrs. Leicester's School*. Family attachments, parent to child and sibling to sibling, form the substance of more than half the poems. Birds and insects abound, fragile and symbolic, sometimes as natural creatures and sometimes as fabular characters. Charity, tolerance, and generosity triumph over envy and social superiority, temperance and plain dress over greed and vanity. As in *Mrs. Leicester's School,* books and reading, writing, and education matter to these children.

Fundamental to all the poems is a belief in the security of home and family. A parent lovingly calls his child a "straggler into loving arms, / Young climber up of knees." A youngster delights that "I have got a new-born sister; I was nigh the first that kiss'd her." A child in a large family spins a verse beginning, "Brothers and sisters I have many: / Though I know there is not any / Of them but I love." Through twenty-eight lines of rhymed couplets, the child recites their names, deciding which is the favorite, then concluding:

> *I've nam'd them all, there's only seven;*
> *I find my love to all so even,*
> *To every sister, every brother,*
> *I love not one more than another.*

Sibling relationships are not so uniformly saccharine, though. "Discontent and Quarrelling" pits sister against brother in a conversation that begins with Jane's complaints that her friend Lydia has finer clothing and dolls than she does. Robert tattletales:

> *O mother, hear my sister Jane,*
> *How foolishly she does complain,*
>   *And tease herself for nought.*
> *But 'tis the way of all her sex,*
> *Thus foolishly themselves to vex.*
>   *Envy's a female fault.*

Jane snaps back, defending her gender and reminding her brother of an instance of his own envy when a friend seemed to have a happier lot. At that, Robert stammers:

> *Let's see, what were the words I spoke?*
> *Why, may be I was half in joke—*
>   *May be I just might say—*
> *Besides that was not half so bad;*
> *For, Jane, I only said he had*
>   *More time than I to play.*

"May be, may be," Jane taunts, "And may be, brother, I don't tell / Tales to mamma like you." The patient mother's voice intrudes, exhorting her children to "cease your wrangling, cease, my dears."

As in the life of the adult Lambs, so in the households of some children in these poems, when loving parents are absent, sibling love holds fast the ties.

> *My parents sleep both in one grave;*
> *My only friend's a brother.*
> *The dearest things upon the earth*
> *We are to one another.*

Illness and death loom in the world of *Poetry for Children*. In "Nurse Green," events unfold through the conversation of a sleepless child and a comforting mother. "What cause is there yet keeps my darling awake?" asks the mother, and the child replies, "O mother, there's reason—for Susan has told me, / A dead body lies in the room next to ours." The mother concurs, apologizing that "but for forgetfulness" she would have shown her child the coffin "of your poor old Nurse Green." Thoughts of the nearby remains terrify the child. To comfort her the mother picks up her worried child and holds her, saying, "Come, bury your fears in the arms of your mother; / My darling, cling close to me, I am alive."

Few during Mary Lamb's lifetime would have responded to this poem as we do today, aware of what had happened in the Lamb household thirteen years before. But Charles knew, and Mary knew—and if one or two of their closest friends read the poem, they knew, too—that in it, sister and brother together were unraveling details laden with pain and horror from their own memories, then reweaving them into scenarios with happy endings.

Gender-driven disparities in education propel a lighthearted pair of poems about sibling rivalry, "The Sister's Expostulation on the Brother's Learning Latin" and "The Brother's Reply." "Shut these odious books up, brother," begins the first, as a sister complains that her brother, now studying Latin, has abandoned her and is "so conceited grown / With your Latin, you'll scarce look

/ Upon any English book." She reminds him of the pleasures they shared, reading Shakespeare and Milton together, which "alas! now you are gone, / I must puzzle out alone." The poem ends with her direct plea that he come "back to English and to me."

"Sister, fie, for shame, no more, / Give this ignorant babble o'er," begins "The Brother's Reply." He explains the learning process, from vocabulary, grammar, and syntax to the classic authors "in the tongue they us'd when living" and compares it to the steps his sister took, first learning to form letters and moving on to her "fine text-hand at last." Furthermore he promises that studying Latin will not result in his abandoning English literature: "Them when next I take in hand, / I shall better understand." The punch line comes, though, with his promise to his sister to even out disparities: "(If our parents will agree) / You shall Latin learn with me."

At about the time of writing *Poetry for Children,* Mary Lamb did embark on learning Latin. Her brother had learned the ancient language at Christ's Hospital. He knew it well enough to dash off letters to friends in Latin just for fun. Together Mary and Charles read Tasso, Catullus, and Juvenal. She became so proficient that by 1820 she had Latin students of her own. "I employ my time in writing Latin exercises during the whole of the morning," she wrote a young student, "and my brother is so kind as to correct and growl over them in the evening." All her students appear to have been young women, but she intended, as she wrote to one of them, "to make a scholar instead of a scholaress of you."[16]

At the same time that *Poetry for Children* encourages children in reading and writing, it discourages materialism and class pride. It is amusing to think that Mary Lamb, who had spent so many hours making and mending clothing, would write "Time Spent in Dress."

> *Without some calculation, youth*
> *May live to age and never guess,*

That no one study they pursue
    Takes half the time they give to dress.

. . . .

And ever when your silent thoughts
    Have on this subject been intent,
Set down as nearly as you can
    How long on dress your thoughts were bent.

If faithfully you should perform
    This task, 'twould teach you to repair
Lost hours, by giving unto dress
    Not more of time than its due share.

The moral lesson most frequently conveyed in *Poetry for Children* is tolerance, charity, and concern for the weak and lowly. Two poems treat racial prejudice. Others make pleas for the underdog, from "The Butterfly," in which a sister persuades her brother not to mutilate an insect, to "The Reproof," in which a mother scolds her daughter for scorning "a wretched beggar-boy." "The Beggar-Man," harmonious with this theme, is a poetic reiteration of the truism that despite his "abject, stooping, old, and wan" appearance, the beggar was once someone's beloved child.

CURIOUSLY "THE BEGGAR-MAN" was written by neither Mary nor Charles Lamb, but by their brother, John. Judging from Mary and Charles's letters, John Lamb figured little in their everyday lives. He worked his whole life as an accountant with the South Sea Company and married a widow whose children joined their household. They never had children of their own. Over the years relations between the siblings must have warmed, for John Lamb did occasionally join Mary and Charles for a few rounds of whist on a Wednesday evening.

Where Charles Lamb was diminutive, his brother was imposing. "The broad, burly, jovial bulk of John Lamb"—so called by a frequenter of the Lambs' Wednesday evening soirées—would bring with him "the slender clerks of the old South Sea House, whom he sometimes introduces to the rooms of his younger brother, surprised to learn from them that he [Charles] is growing famous."[17] After one such evening Henry Crabb Robinson declared John Lamb "grossly rude and vulgar so that I am resolved never to play with him again."[18] In fact John Lamb did not get along with many of his sister and brother's friends. He had never trusted Coleridge. He had become a devoted art collector, and once he and William Hazlitt argued so viciously about the Dutch masters, John Lamb punched Hazlitt and knocked him to the ground. A painting from John Lamb's collection, a dour portrait of John Milton, now hangs in the New York Public Library.

While Mary and Charles were composing poems for children, their brother had his own writing project, a treatise against cruelty to animals. It was a cause promoted avidly by the Scottish Whig statesman Thomas, Lord Erskine, who had brilliantly defended Horne Tooke and Thelwall in 1794 and briefly served as Lord Chancellor in 1806 and 1807. In 1809 Baron Erskine championed a "Bill for preventing Malicious and Wanton Cruelty to Animals," primarily designed to protect horses. His concern was abuse against work animals, but John Lamb wanted the bill to protect all living creatures, and in particular those killed for human food. In effect he advocated that the law enforce vegetarianism, and he singled out the eel as an animal deserving of the government's protection. He was outraged, for example, that cooks skewered and grilled eels live, a practice contrary to the inborn sense of what is right. "If an eel had the wisdom of Solomon," he argued, and were told, that it was necessary for our subsistence that he should be eaten, that he must be skinned first, and then broiled; . . . he would conclude that the cook would so far use her reason as to cut off his head first, which is not fit for food, . . . for however the other parts of his body might be convulsed during the culinary operations, there could be no feeling or consciousness therein, the communication with the brain being cut off.[19]

But instead cooks all over Britain stewed eels head and all——an insult to human decency and the animal kingdom. John Lamb wrote with such passion and singlemindedness that he must have been oblivious to the oddness of his arguments, the convolutions of his sentences. He leaned on his literary brother to promote the tract. He asked Charles to send it out to journalists he knew, among them Henry Crabb Robinson, who then wrote regularly for the *Times*. Charles may have been unaware of Robinson's low opinion of his brother, for he dutifully sent him a copy of the book. With a hint of a smile, though, he requested that Robinson not let his housekeeper read it, "for I remember she makes excellent Eel soup."[20]

While Charles Lamb humored his older brother, no evidence remains to help characterize the relationship between Mary and John Lamb. He may still have treated her with supercilious skepticism, in which case she would most likely have responded with distant politeness. That polite affability so typical of Mary Lamb is the topic of one of her poems. "The Confidant" portrays a girl richly endowed with that particularly female virtue, selfless regard for others.

> *Anna was always full of thought*
> *As if she'd many sorrows known,*
> *Yet mostly her full heart was fraught*

With troubles that were not her own;
For the whole school to Anna us'd to tell
Whatever small misfortunes unto them befell.

While other poets might have congratulated Anna for her generosity and compassion, Mary Lamb's poem portrays the dangers
inherent in her character. "Full of thought," bearing "troubles that
were not her own," Anna suffers a withdrawal akin to depression,
losing health, appetite, and affect. Once she is relieved of the burdens of others, however, she regains her energy.

It was an unusual take on a commonly valued virtue—but it
was a lesson Mary Lamb knew well. Her entire life had been one
of service. As the only daughter in a serving-class family, it was
the demeanor that her parents—and, for that matter, her grandmother—modeled toward others and expected from her. From
childhood on she tended home and family. In early adulthood she
was the caretaker in a house full of needy elders. Through her
adult life, while lovingly supported by her brother, she supported
him, too, physically and emotionally. In "The Confidant" Anna
moves through a period of retreat and detachment to a satisfactory end. In real life Mary Lamb cycled through the pattern over
and over: caring, finding herself overwhelmed, retreating and
detaching, recovering herself, and then returning to the situation
in which she must start caring again. So grateful was she to her
brother that she would never deny him. She could break out of
the cycle in a poem, though—or occasionally escape into a madhouse for a reprieve.

IN THE SUMMER of 1810, when *Poetry for Children* was published,
it had been fourteen years since the breakdown that resulted in
Elizabeth Lamb's murder, thirteen since Mary Lamb's initial
release from Fisher House in April 1797. In those years Mary

Lamb had made seven visits to the madhouse, each confinement lasting about six weeks. In all, her spells of irrationality averaged a month per year, but six years had been entirely madhouse-free: 1799, 1801, 1802, 1804, 1806, and 1808.

In 1809, when the Lambs moved from one Inner Temple address to another—"The Household Gods are slow to come in a new Mansion, . . . How I hate and dread *New Places!*" Charles wrote Coleridge—it seems that the strain sent Mary again to the madhouse. "I have been turned out of my Chambers in the Temple by a Landlord who wanted them for himself," Charles explained to Coleridge, "but I have got other at No. 4 Inner Temple Lane, far more commodious & roomy." The move occurred on a Saturday, and "on Monday following Mary was taken ill, with the fatigue of moving, and affected I believe by the novelty of the Home she could not sleep." The pattern was recurring and now, Charles simply reported, "she has a month or two's sad distraction to go through."

Charles, and likely Mary as well, had by 1809 become inured to a pattern of her plunges into irrationality every other year, requiring a six- to eight-week madhouse stay thereafter. Charles did not, however, take it lightly. "What sad large pieces it cuts . . . out of her life who is getting rather old," he reflected. Mary was now in her mid-forties, and he felt his age, too, partly through sympathy but also because of his own physical and mental condition. "We may not have many years to live together. I am weaker & bear it worse than I ever did. But I hope we shall be comfortable by & bye."[21]

After six weeks in the madhouse in 1809, Mary had returned home strong enough to travel with Charles to Winterslow, the Stoddart family home, where Sarah and William Hazlitt now lived. The Lambs balanced the uncertainties of travel with the pleasures of a visit to two of their closest friends. "The journey has been of infinite service to her," Charles reported to Coleridge on their return home late in October. "Her illness lasted but 6 weeks, it left her weak, but the Country has made us whole."[22]

12

THE POLITICS OF
NEEDLEWORK

ARY WROTE A thank-you note to Sarah Hazlitt a few
days after she and Charles returned home from their
visit to Winterslow. In it she expressed the sense of
comfort and easy emotion that prevailed in their household in
late 1809:

> The dear quiet lazy delicious month we spent with you is
> remembered by me with such regret that I feel quite discon-
> tented & Winterslow-sick. I assure you I never passed such a
> pleasant time in the countery [sic] in my life, both in the house
> & out of it—the card playing quarrels, and a few gaspings for
> breath, after your swift footsteps up the high hills excepted,
> and those drawbacks are not unpleasant in the recollection.

Sarah and William's country habits were different from Mary and
Charles's, right down to the food they put on the table. The
Lambs came home eating more meat and preferring salted butter,
"to make our toast seem like yours," but soon they slipped back
into old habits. "The dry loaf, which offended you, now comes in
at night unaccompanied, but, sorry am I to add, it is soon followed by the pipe and the gin bottle.—We smoked the very first
night of our arrival." Mary skipped through other news cheerily.
"Great News!" she wrote. "My beautiful green curtains were put

up yesterday." With other repairs and decorative touches, 4 Inner Temple Lane was becoming pleasantly livable.

Mary reported having completed the favor Sarah asked of her: The baby caps Sarah had made were delivered to her sister-in-law Mary Hazlitt for her newborn. As if in hushed tones, Mary added to the letter that John Hazlitt "has been very disorderly lately":

> I am going to tell you a secret for Mrs H says he would be very sorry to have it talked of. One night he came home from the Alehouse, bringing with him a great rough ill-looking fellow whom he introduced to Mrs Hazlitt as Mr Brown a gentleman he had hired as a mad keeper to take care of him at forty pounds a year, being ten pounds under the market price for keepers, which sum Mr Brown had agreed to remit out of pure friendship. It was with great difficulty, and by threatening to call in the aid of watchmen & constables that she could prevail on Mr Brown to leave the house.

It must have felt, among other emotions, uncannily affirming for Mary Lamb to find herself a rational observer outside such an episode.

Other significant news followed: "A man in the India House has resigned by which Charles will get twenty pounds a year," Mary wrote.[1] Charles's salary had been increasing steadily through his fifteen years at East India House. They were finally financially comfortable, but Mary found it difficult to adjust to such prosperity. "We intend almost to ruin ourselves," she wrote another friend, scolding herself when they bought new chairs and curtains.[2]

"We have almost worked ourselves out of Child's Work," Charles wrote Coleridge. "I dont know what to do, and I must do something for money." Charles, as used to scrimping as his sister, could rhapsodize about the evils of money, now that he had enough:

Not that I have immediate wants, but I have prospective ones. O money money how blindly thou has been worshipped, & how stupidly abused! Thou art health, & liberty, and strength and he that has thee may rattle his pockets at the Devil. Nevertheless do not understand by this that I have not quite enough for my occasions for a year or two to come.[3]

Mary and Charles Lamb were never wealthy, but they had successfully moved out of the servant class into which they were born and into the growing middle class of nineteenth-century Britain. They enjoyed financial security—something they had not experienced since Samuel Salt's death in 1792—but there was always an underlying tension, a sense that they had moved into a social stratum in which they did not belong. "I wish the good old times would come again, when we were not quite so rich," Charles has Bridget Elia say in one of his most famous essays, "Old China." "I do not mean, that I want to be poor; but there was a middle state in which I am sure we were a great deal happier."

Mary Lamb found the transition into the middle class difficult, in part because of the role it forced her to play. In a servant-class existence all worked: men and women, young and old. The goal of the rising middle-class family in pre-Victorian Britain was to attain a level of luxury so that the woman of the household could enjoy the fineries of life: dabble in art and music, see to the moral education of the children, and keep up appearances by attending to fashion in dress and interior design. By all accounts Mary Lamb should have been proud that she and her brother had attained that state. The needlework and the writing for children that she had once done to earn money could now be done in leisure, simply for the pleasure of it. Circumstances allowed her to take her place among the women of the comfortable middle class.

As manager of the household, she was now expected to hire, fire, and manage servants. She did not take kindly to the role. She was too empathetic. She made bad choices. She had no eye for the earmarks of a good maid. Instead she turned to her new fascination, phrenology—by which one reads a person's character through the shape of his or her skull—and used it to select the woman to hire.

"I have a new maid coming this evening," she wrote Dorothy Wordsworth. "I took a girl lately from the country, who was fetched away in a few days by her sister who took it into her head that the Temple was an improper place for a girl to live in. I wish the one that is coming may suit me. She is seven & twenty with a very plain person therefore I may hope she will be in little danger here."[4]

In ten days the new hire collapsed of illness and exhaustion. "My new maid is now sick in bed. Am I not unlucky?" Mary wrote, keeping Dorothy Wordsworth up to date. "She would have suited me very well if she had been healthy, but I must send her away if she is not better tomorrow." Charles added his own expansive version of the story to the letter:

> We are in a pickle. Mary from her affectation of physiognomy has hired a stupid big country wench who looked honest as she thought, and has been doing her work some days but without eating—eats no butter nor meat, but prefers cheese with her tea for breakfast—& now it comes out that she was ill when she came with lifting her mother about (who is now with God) when she was dying, and with riding up from Norfolk 4 days & nights in the Waggon. She got advice yesterday & took something which has made her bring up a quart of blood, and she now *lies* a dead weight upon our humanity in her bed incapable of getting up, refusing to go into an hospital, having no body in town but a poor asthmatic dying Uncle whose son lately married a drab who fills his house, and there is no where she can go, and she seems to have made up her mind to take her flight to heaven from *our bed*.[5]

From Charles we hear little blame—only a slight wagging of the finger at Mary's "affectation of physiognomy"—but it is clear that Mary had failed as a household employer.

Mary Lamb preferred climbing the class ladder by increasing her knowledge. She enjoyed the respect and sense of belonging she felt among Charles's literary friends, who were likewise moving up in the world. John Rickman had lately been elevated to clerk of the House of Commons, and Martin Burney had entered a law office. Charles's responsibilities at East India House grew, so much so that he found himself at times staying at the office into late evening.[6] He and his friends were rising to their deserved levels of authority and respect, but Mary Lamb never felt sure that she could, or wanted to, call herself a gentlewoman. The arguments between her roughhewn aunt and her upward-yearning mother now went on inside her own head. That anxiety—the sense of having left the servant class but not yet made it to the next rung up—comes through clearly in the essay "On Needle-work," Mary Lamb's next publication.

A NEW WOMEN'S MAGAZINE appeared on the London scene early in 1815, the *British Lady's Magazine*. The editor grandly stated his intentions in the opening article:

> With a certain reference to the portion of society, for whose perusal it is more immediately designed, the object of the magazine of the present day should be to exhibit the form and pressure of the times, by an easy and discursive attention, to the progressive march of science, literature, policy, morals, manners, religion, and, in short, to whatever may reasonably be expected to please or inform. . . . What the newspaper is to the political and daily world, the magazine should aim to be, respecting its literary, scientific, and social progress; . . . its movements should be calm, impartial, and dignified.

Such definitions pertained to all magazines, but this new one addressed an "especial appropriation," considering that at present "the female is partaking, to an unprecedented extent, in that taste for intellectual acquirement, so perceptible in every department of civilized life. . . . To shut up the avenues of literature to Woman, is peculiarly cruel; since to her, the harvest of tranquil and retired pursuit, is more certainly productive than even to the male."

With more leisure than ever, women were the most likely to learn by reading, proclaimed the editor of the new magazine. In fact women could be counted on to make more of the opportunity than men. The new magazine would not ignore fashion—"We have no objection to dress, decoration, and embellishment, in their proper places"—and yet "our higher views will not permit us to address our countrywomen through the medium of prints and patterns." The entire sensibility of the magazine would be dedicated to the refined and virtuous audience for whom it was named: "the BRITISH LADY, to whose service, [the editors] trust, their pages will be devoted, with integrity, consistency, and zeal."[7]

The *British Lady's Magazine* had a politely feminist slant. In April 1815, for example, its pages included a sketch of Miss Jane Porter, author of works on the Scottish kings and the aphorisms of Sir Philip Sidney; a character study of Madame Jacques Necker, wife of the French ambassador, translated from the French; a letter from a traveling threesome, Sarah, Susan, and Sophy, on the island of Madeira; and a meditation on "The French Revolution in Dress," pointedly political, culminating in praise of clothing "in the true English style of simple neatness."[8] April's "Retrospect of Politics" began by announcing that "Napoleon Bonaparte has recovered the throne of France." Although Napoleon had advanced in all directions through the Continent, Britain's allies had converged and overtaken Paris in March 1814. Louis XVIII had assumed the throne, and Napoleon had retreated in exile to Elba. But now, a year later, Bonaparte had reappeared on French soil, marching toward Paris, prompting Louis to flee to Belgium and allied forces to realign. Napoleon's resumption of the imperial throne, as announced to British ladies, came just three months before his final defeat by the Duke of Wellington at the Battle of Waterloo.

The magazine editors had no reason to foresee that triumph, but they did remind their readers that the momentous news from France ought not to turn British eyes from their own nation's concerns. The newly passed Corn Bill, preserving high prices for English-grown grain, favored rural landowners but incensed city dwellers, both middle class and poor, for it meant continuing high bread prices. The magazine's "London Intelligence" writer, while refraining from taking sides, reported two shooting deaths resulting from "riots in the metropolis" over the controversy.

"The king continues in good health," reported the magazine, deriving its information from a Windsor Castle bulletin, "and any deviation from a state of perfect composure, which had been observed in his majesty during the month of January, has entirely subsided for more than a fortnight past." Concern for the king's health was politic and patriotic. In April 1815, George III was a beloved figurehead but no longer a ruler.

George III's symptoms of mental and physical incapacity had once again surfaced on October 25, 1810, ironically the fiftieth anniversary of his accession to the throne. He swiftly suffered "great and increasing agitation of mind," unable to sleep, talking obsessively, then lapsing into gibberish, according to one court observer.[9] The royal family was already distraught over the ill health of the youngest of George and Charlotte's children, Amelia, who died on November 2. Her father did not comprehend the sad news until nine days later, in a moment when his delirium had somewhat abated.

The House of Lords was less willing to wait for the king's recovery this time than in 1788. On February 5 Spencer Perceval visited the royal chambers one last time to verify his right as prime minister, in the event of the regent's incapacity, to seal the commission assenting to the Regency Bill. In a moment of apparent lucidity George III himself assented to the bill. Starting on February 9, 1811, the Prince of Wales, now Prince Regent, ruled Britain. George III survived nearly another decade, still the beloved king in the eyes of his subjects, which is why the progress of his health, four years after he left the throne, would be news in a lady's magazine. He died on January 29, 1820, and his first son, the libertine Whig, became King George IV.

IN AMONG THIS CACOPHONY of news, gossip, entertainment, and advice, the April 1815 issue of the *British Lady's Magazine* included a letter submitted by a reader who signed her name "Sempronia" and titled her contribution "On Needle-work." It is undoubtedly the work of Mary Lamb.

"After reading at home from eight to ten I called on Miss Lamb, and chatted with her," Henry Crabb Robinson had noted in his diary on December 11, 1814. "She had undergone great fatigue from writing an article about needlework for the new *Ladies British Magazine* [*sic*]."[10] Word had traveled through the London writing community that a new magazine was forming and welcoming contributions. Mary saw it as an opportunity to speak out on behalf of mantua makers, those women still practicing the trade that she had left behind. It is an odd and ambiguous essay, at once adamant and conciliatory, with an argument that intertwines economic and class concerns, gender politics, and Mary Lamb's own personal history.

"Mr. Editor," the letter began, "In early life I passed eleven years in the exercise of my needle for a livelihood" —the years, in other words, from her coming of age at twenty, in 1785, to her matricidal outburst in 1796.[11] "Will you allow me to address your readers, among whom might perhaps be found some of the kind patronesses of my former humble labours, on a subject widely connected with female life—the state of needlework in this country."

From the start "Sempronia" straddled the class divide. By giving herself a Latinate name—a feminization of *semper,* the Latin for "always"—she revealed her erudition. "Among the present circle of my acquaintance," she wrote, "I am proud to rank many that may truly be called respectable." She distanced herself from British ladies, though, whom she identified with the "patronesses" of her past, but also set herself apart from the sisterhood of needleworkers, to which she years before belonged. By being of both classes, she was of neither, which secured her objectivity.

"Sempronia" set the groundwork for her argument:

> From books I had been informed of the fact, upon which "The British Lady's Magazine" chiefly founds its pretensions, namely, that women have of late been rapidly advancing in intellectual improvement. Much may have been gained in this way, indirectly, for that class of females for whom I wish to plead. Needlework and intellectual improvement are naturally in a state of warfare.

That last bold sentence echoed hollowly through the corridors of Mary Lamb's past, back to the days of her childhood, when her older brother gained entry to Christ's Hospital while she spent short afternoons at William Byrd's Academy, framed by longer mornings and evenings with a needle instead of a book in her hand.

Despite this bold statement, Mary Lamb knew it was a superficial judgment. Time spent sewing may take time away from books, but that did not mean that all needleworkers were simpletons. Skill in needlework did not preclude intelligence. That was one of the reasons she and Sarah Stoddart got along so well. "I have never half liked being at your brothers rooms since you left them," Mary once wrote Sarah of the evenings she spent with John Stoddart and Charles. "They sit and preach about learned matters, while I turn over an old book, and when I am weary look in the window in the corner where you and your work-bag used to be, and wish for you to rout them up and make us all alive."[12] The thought of the two women, sitting and sewing together, commenting cleverly on the male disquisition—or, more likely, carrying on a conversation of their own—delighted Mary.

The animosity between needlework and intellectual improvement would have been a provocative topic—echoes of Mary Wollstonecraft—but Sempronia shifted to a more timely issue: "Workwomen of every description were never in so much distress for want of employment." She attributed the problem to the intersection of increased leisure time and conscientious housewifely productivity in the lives of middle-class women. If only wives would use the time on their hands for mental improvement rather than household sewing, the condition of all women would improve. Sewing work—and the means to earn money—would revert to the seamstresses. Wives and mothers would improve themselves by using leisure time for study and conversation, not sewing and mending.

Is it too bold an attempt to persuade your readers that it would prove an incalculable addition to general happiness, and the domestic comfort of both sexes, if needle-work were never practised but for a remuneration in money? As nearly, however, as this desirable thing can be effected, so much more nearly will women be upon an equality with men, as respects the mere enjoyment of life. As far as that goes, I believe it is every woman's opinion that the condition of men is far superior to her own.

. . . many a lady who allows not herself one quarter of an

hour's positive leisure during her waking hours, considers her own husband as the most industrious of men, if he steadily pursue his occupation till the hour of dinner.

In some of Mary Lamb's arguments lie the seeds of a modern feminist consciousness—in arguments such as this one, impossible to read without a glance back to Mary Lamb's own upbringing:

If at the birth of girls it were possible to foresee in what cases it would be their fortune to pass a single life, we should soon find trades wrested from their present occupiers, and transferred to the exclusive possession of our sex. . . . The parents of female children . . . would feel it a duty incumbent on themselves to strengthen the minds, and even the bodily constitutions, of their girls, so circumstanced, by an education which, without affronting the preconceived habits of society, might enable them to follow some occupation now considered above the capacity or too robust for the constitution of our sex.

She turns her point around and asks the same question conversely:

Who, for instance, would lay by money to set up his sons in trade; give premiums, and in part maintain them through a long apprenticeship; or, which men of moderate incomes frequently do, strain every nerve in order to bring them up to a learned profession; if it were in a very high degree probable that, by the time they were twenty years of age, they would be taken from this trade or profession, and maintained during the remainder of their lives by the *person whom they should marry.* Yet this is precisely the situation in which every parent, whose income does not very much exceed the moderate, is placed with respect to his daughters.

Sempronia's arguments seem to be leading toward a larger feminist conclusion—a universal claim for the rights of education and professional identity for all women—but they fall short. They seem compromised to the modern reader, as if her logic reaches a midway point and stalls out through an acceptance of class and gender inequities. "I am no advocate for women, who do not depend on themselves for a subsistence, proposing to themselves to *earn money,*" writes Sempronia. She is instead arguing that the value found in domestic needlework does not equal the time and attention devoted to it in middle-class homes.

> It would be an excellent plan, attended with very little trouble, to calculate every evening how much money has been saved by needlework *done in the family,* and compare the result with the daily portion of the yearly income. Nor would it be amiss to make a memorandum of the time passed in this way, adding also a guess as to what share it has taken up in the thoughts and conversation. This would be an easy mode of forming a true notion, and getting at the exact worth of this species of *home* industry, and perhaps might place it in a different light from any in which it has hitherto been the fashion to consider it.

In short Sempronia argues the need to professionalize needlework: to regard it as the work of experts who have no other way to earn a living. Those middle-class women who genuinely enjoy needlework might take up "the good old contrivances in which our grand-dames were used to beguile and lose their time—knitting, knotting, netting." But, she pleads, leave the essentials to those who need the business:

> . . . if those works, more usually denominated useful, yield greater satisfaction, it might be a laudable scruple of conscience,

and no bad test to herself of her own motive, if a lady, who had no absolute need, were to give the money so saved to poor needle-women belonging to those branches of employment from which she has borrowed these shares of pleasurable labour.

The message is not what a modern reader expects to hear. Yet it was cleverly argued, knowingly informed, and personally meaningful. Mary Lamb's own history of work and wavering self-confidence drove the passion in this letter to British ladies, with whom she did not fully identify. In her own life she could see the shimmering goal of independence but never dared strive for it, fearful of the direction in which independence would lead her and hesitant to stray from her brother Charles. As in her revealing series of letters about treatment practices in the madhouse, written ten years before, Mary Lamb censored herself, setting limits to the reach of her intellect, frightened that once again untethered inclinations might cause her to destroy icons of the old familiar order.

As if to act out self-censure, Mary Lamb succumbed to a bout of madness soon after she completed "On Needle-work." At first she just felt exhausted. Henry Crabb Robinson noted that she was also flooded by feelings of unworthiness. "She spoke of writing as a most painful occupation, which only necessity could make her attempt," he noted. "She has been learning Latin merely to assist her in acquiring a correct style. Yet, while she speaks of inability to write, what grace and talent has she not manifested in 'Mrs. Leicester's School,' &c."[13]

It is from Robinson that we learn the most about this episode of withdrawal. On December 11, 1814, Mary told him of her "great fatigue" after writing. In the next few days she must have felt the signs of an oncoming outburst. By December 20 she had moved into a madhouse, leaving Charles alone at home. "Late in the evening" of that very day, Robinson recorded, "Lamb called, to ask me to sit with him while he smoked his pipe. I had called on him late last night, and he seemed absurdly grateful for the visit. He wanted society, being alone. I abstained from inquiring after his sister, and trust he will appreciate the motive."[14] As far as we can tell, Charles Lamb barely mentioned this 1814 madhouse episode in his letters. We know he was writing prodigiously during the winter—including, ironically, a short essay "On the Melancholy of Tailors."

More fillip than philosophy, the essay (attributed to a fictitious "Burton, Junior") identifies "a professional melancholy" among tailors. Referring often to Lamb's favorite, Robert Burton's Renaissance-era *Anatomy of Melancholy*, the essayist examines the "sullen incapacity for pleasure" among tailors and attributes it to two things: their sedentary work and the cabbage in their diets.

Writing this little piece at the same time Mary was writing "On Needle-work," Charles could have been emulating, competing with, mocking, or mirroring the work of his sister. Knowing his own inclination toward ironic self-deprecation, he could even have been mocking males in general, heightening the seriousness of his sister's concerns over female needleworkers by diminishing their male counterparts. No surrounding evidence helps one decide among the possibilities. Charles published the piece in a journal called *The Champion*. A week later a reply appeared. Some have attributed it to Lamb as well, and one shouldn't put it past him. Supposedly penned by a member of a large family of tailors, the letter earnestly argues their cheerfulness and defends a diet well supplied with "the wholesome plant," cabbage: "So far from feeling dull and stupid after it, we are all life and jollity, sing a pleasant song, and go comfortably to bed." The respondent signed his letter "J.D."—a pseudonym Lamb would use elsewhere.[15]

John Scott, the editor of *The Champion*, spotted Charles's talents and proposed that he write regularly for the weekly paper. Charles could not uphold the deal even one week. "I am sorry to seem to go off my agreement, but very particular circumstances have happened to hinder my fulfillment of it at present," he wrote Scott on December 12[16]—a muffled indication that his life had once again been thrown askew by his sister's sudden departure.

Mary was home again by spring. Robinson found her "pale and thin, but in no respect *alarmingly*."[17] Once again the Lambs were struggling to find the right housekeeper. They needed someone who could tolerate the relative emptiness of their household, as they learned by hiring someone who couldn't. "The fact is the poor girl is oppressed with a ladylike melancholy," Charles wrote to a friend who seems to have been helping them find a house-keeper, "and cannot bear to be so much alone, as she necessarily must be in our kitchen, which to say the truth is damn'd solitary, where she can see nothing and converse with nothing and not even look out of window. The consequence is she has been caught shedding tears all day long, and her own comfort has made it indispensable to send her home."[18] The Lambs certainly did not need a third person inclined toward melancholy. They rebounded by hiring someone just the opposite. "We have got an old woman coming," reported Charles, "who is too stupid to know when she is alone and when she is not."[19]

It was in this season, the spring of 1815, that Mary and Charles Lamb made the trip together to Mackery End in Hertfordshire, memorialized in his essay of that title. The farmhouse had once belonged to their mother's aunt, Anne Bruton Gladman. Family still lived in the house when they visited, and a cousin, Penelope Bruton, welcomed them. Mary told of their journey in a letter written on their return to London.

"I am very proud of having lately performed a thirty miles

journey and returned safe and well," she wrote in late May 1815.[20] Three of them had taken a coach north to Luton. Charles and his friend, Barron Field, rode in the open air and Mary rode inside. They intended to visit the home of the Earl of Bute, who had lately hung a Raphael and invited public viewings. "Inconsolable for our disappointment," they discovered the painting removed and Bute House closed to the public. Their loss is our gain, however, because they walked on toward their childhood haunt. This walk into the past provided an occasion for Lamb to record a deeper glimpse into the character of his sister—call her Bridget Elia, call her Mary Lamb.

"We walked two miles through the most beautiful park I ever saw by the side of a river," Mary wrote in her letter soon after,

> and when we left the park we followed its course five or six miles till it conducted us to a farm house where a *great* aunt of mine once dwelt and where I spent some portion of every year in my younger days: the last visit I made there I had the care and sole management of my little brother Charles then an urchin of three or four years, he then under my sole guidance.

Charles evoked that same moment of discovery in the essay, written years later: "The sight of the old farm-house, though every trace of it was effaced from my recollection, affected me with a pleasure which I had not experienced for many a year. For though *I* had forgotten it, *we* had never forgotten being there together, and we had been talking about Mackery End all our lives."

So often it was Charles who encouraged Mary to speak up or step out. This time Mary Lamb took the lead. Charles maintained that they should not venture onto the property. With a burst of obstinacy Mary "overcame his scruples," as she put it, and clambered over the orchard stile:

Three or four dogs barking at me enough to frighten me from any other farmhouse in England did not deter me from going in by myself. I found no soul of a large family I had left there. a granddaughter of my aunt's not then born received me in a most friendly manner, sent her husband to fetch in Charles and Field and immediately began to call us Charles & Mary with most cousin-like familiarity.[21]

"Bridget's was more a waking bliss than mine," Charles wrote in his essay. He describes her roaming the house and orchard and coming upon the site where she remembered a pigeon house "with a breathless impatience of recognition." He makes excuses for such behavior, "more pardonable perhaps than decorous at the age of fifty odd." (She had just turned fifty the previous December.) With affection and embarrassment, Charles added, "But Bridget in some things is behind her years."

Mary's report was unabashedly jubilant. "Charles says he never saw me look so happy in his life," she wrote. Even at such a moment she gauged her happiness through his eyes. Many take pleasure in returning to childhood haunts, but for Mary Lamb the visit to Mackery End meant a liberation from the burdens of memory and madness. As she did in her stories and poems, now she could on this spring afternoon travel back to the days before.

"When I saw [Charles] smoking his pipe with the farmer," she wrote days later, "I wished to realize a dream I have twice had lately that he was with me and he himself a little child also, for I seemed to feel as much loss of him as his cousin Sophy a little girl of his own age who is dead and who he well remembers playing with." The contrast between those times and these, starkly rendered as the smell of tobacco sifted through the air, evoked feelings of irrecoverable loss. Charles may have considered Mary "in some things behind her years," but she reached back to childish ways—in dream, fantasy, and writing, and now increasingly in daily thought and behavior—because she yearned to return to the simple innocence of childhood, those days of joy unclouded by a hovering memory, that time of life before her world had burst at the seams.

13

Elia Appears

If one were to name the things for which Mary and Charles Lamb are best remembered, they would be *Tales from Shakespear,* their literary circle of friends, and Charles Lamb's essays written under the pseudonym Elia. There were more than fifty, enough that by the end of his career he had published two collections of the *Essays of Elia.*

Adopting a persona worked for Charles Lamb. A precursor might be found in the essay on tailors he contributed to *The Champion.* He stepped outside himself and became more comfortable expressing serious, sometimes even sentimental, feelings. By the same token, assuming another's voice, he could point out the foibles of others without bearing the burden of blame. He could ridicule himself, whether it meant exaggerating Elia's quirks or conjuring up a Charles Lamb–like figure as an acquaintance of Elia's. Just as ceremony sent Charles into self-conscious hysterics, assuming an authentic writing voice did as well. It was easier to write as someone else. Once he discovered the technique, Charles Lamb was well on his way to achieving the success for which he is still renowned today as one of the most beguiling essayists of the English language.

"The South Sea House" appeared in August 1820 in the first issue of the new *London Magazine,* founded by John Scott, the editor who had so admired Charles's essay on tailors and melancholy. Writing this first essay by Elia, Charles realized that he was creating "a tissue of truth and fiction impossible to be extricated, the interlacings shall be so delicate, the partitions perfectly invisible."[1] The very puzzle of stitching together truth and fiction fascinated him. He adeptly met the magazine's monthly deadline.

Elia shared many characteristics and experiences with Charles Lamb, to be sure. Elia remembered his early days of working for the South Sea Company—where Charles Lamb had briefly worked, on his way to East India House, and which he knew for decades after through his brother. The South Sea clerks, so Elia wrote, "partook of the genius of the place!" and:

> They were mostly (for the establishment did not admit of superfluous salaries) bachelors. Generally (for they had not much to do) persons of a curious and speculative turn of mind. . . . Humourists, for they were of all descriptions; . . . for the most part, placed in this house in ripe or middle age, they necessarily carried into it their separate habits and oddities, unqualified, if I may so speak, as into a common stock. Hence they formed a sort of Noah's ark. Odd fishes. A lay-monastery. Domestic retainers in a great house, kept more for show than use. Yet pleasant fellows, full of chat—and not a few among them had arrived at considerable proficiency on the German flute.[2]

Elia reported that, like Charles Lamb, he "was born, and passed the first seven years of my life, in the Temple. Its church, its halls, its gardens, its fountain, its river, I had almost said—for in those young years, what was this king of rivers to me but a stream that watered our pleasant places?—these are of my oldest recollections."[3] From those days Elia remembered "the pensive gentility of Samuel Salt" in the essay "The Old Benchers of the Temple." "I suspect his knowledge did not amount to much," Elia dared to say. "It was incredible what repute for talents S. enjoyed by the mere trick of gravity." Salt depended mightily on "his man Lovel," a thinly veiled replica of the elder John Lamb:

> L. was the liveliest little fellow breathing, had a face as gay as Garrick's [David Garrick, a beloved actor], whom he was said to greatly resemble (I have a portrait of him which confirms it), possessed a fine turn for humorous poetry—next to [Jonathan] Swift and [Matthew] Prior—moulded heads in clay or plaster of Paris to admiration, by the dint of natural genius merely; turned cribbage boards, and such small cabinet toys, to perfection; took a hand at quadrille or bowls with equal facility; made punch better than any man of his degree in England; had the merriest quips and conceits; and was altogether as brimful of rogueries and inventions as you could desire.

It must have given Charles great pleasure to revive the memory of his father with such energy.

As Charles found his stride in essay writing, the evening gatherings he and Mary hosted grew in reputation. It had become a "moveable feast," Charles once said, for a while every Wednesday, then every Thursday, and occasionally a Tuesday when necessary. By the 1820s the Lambs' weekly get-togethers had become a literary and social phenomenon, an emblem of the times, a rising-middle-class English version of French salons of the Enlightenment.

"Early in the present century," wrote the author of an unsigned review of Charles Lamb's *Works,* published in 1848,

> there was, every Wednesday evening, in very humble quarters in the Temple, a snug little *réunion,* to which one would rather have been admitted than to any dozen brilliant conversaziones which London could offer. Nothing could be simpler than the entertainment; it had none of the attractions of wealth, of

fashion, or of celebrity. It was never chronicled in the *Morning Post*. . . . It was a very small room, dimly lighted, modest in its appearance, the walls graced with an engraving or two, and a famous head of Milton, the possessor's pride. A quiet rubber, the solemnity of which was from time to time relieved by quaint "quips, and cranks, and wanton wiles;" a plain clay pipe; a crust of bread and cheese—perhaps oysters; a foaming tankard of porter; a glass of ginger wine, and a glass or so of grog: these were all that hospitality could offer, but they were offered hospitably. The champagne was in the talk,—and to hear them was worth the sacrifice of any entertainment.[4]

William Hazlitt recalled with great affection the "many lively skirmishes" he and his cohorts had at the Lambs' "evening parties" in the second installment of his *London Magazine* essay, "On the Conversation of Authors":

There was L—himself, the most delightful, the most provoking, the most witty and sensible of men. He always made the best pun, and the best remark, in the course of the evening. His serious conversation, like his serious writing is his best. . . . His jests scald like tears: and he probes a question with a play upon words. What a keen, laughing, hair-brained vein of home-felt truth! What choice venom! How often did we cut into the haunch of letters, while we discussed the haunch of mutton on the table. How we skimmed the cream of criticism! How we got into the heart of controversy! How we picked out the marrow of authors!

Eating and talking—the things that Charles Lamb loved best, next only to sharing them with his friends.

Rarely mentioned but always present—and central to the success of these evenings—was the hostess, Mary Lamb. Thomas

Allsop, a friend of Coleridge's, recalled that she, more than the opinionated men of the circle, made him feel part of the conversation: "I have a clear recollection of Miss Lamb's addressing me in *a tone* acting *at once* as a solace and support, and after as a stimulus, to which I owe more perhaps than to the more extended *arguments* of all the others."[5] Mary Lamb was responsible for William Hazlitt's learning to be comfortable in public, wrote one observer. At the Lambs' "his struggles to express the fine conceptions with which his mind was filled, were encouraged by entire sympathy." As Hazlitt "began to stammer out" his ideas, "he was thoroughly understood, and dexterously cheered by Miss Lamb, whose nice discernment of his first efforts in conversation, were dwelt upon by him with affectionate gratitude, even when most out of humour with the world."[6]

The cast of characters evolved over the years. Old familiars walked on- and offstage as they happened to be in London. William Wordsworth visited often, his literary ascendancy giving him reason to do business there. Dorothy visited rarely. She tended to stay home with Mary Wordsworth and Sara Hutchinson, Mary's sister and Coleridge's elusive love, who had moved in with the Wordsworths years before. Dorothy doted on her nieces and nephews and found intellectual satisfaction in teaching them. An influenza epidemic in 1835 left Sara dead and Dorothy confined to a wheelchair, her mind ranging into realms of madness similar to those she had seen in her dear friend Mary Lamb.

Samuel Taylor Coleridge spent more time in London than anywhere else. When he was able, he delivered lectures on literature and philosophy. His dependence on laudanum remained inextricably interwoven with his physical debilities, causing mental anguish and professional instability. He often visited and sometimes stayed at the Lambs'. Their deep love for him never diminished—Charles Lamb poignantly called him "an Arch angel a little damaged"[7]—but it was hard to watch him ruin his life and mind.

There were times, Charles admitted, when he felt repulsed by Coleridge. He and Mary kept watch over him, his whereabouts and condition, doing what they could to bring him back to the track of health and productivity. "I know how zealously you feel for our friend," Charles wrote John Payne Collier, a literary impresario whom Charles hoped might champion Coleridge. "He is in bad health and worse mind: and unless something is done to lighten his mind he will soon be reduced to his extremities: . . . I am sure that you will do for him what you can."[8] Collier did arrange for Coleridge to lecture on Shakespeare, then kept notes of the whole series, leaving to history a record of Coleridge's oratorical genius.

When the marriage between Sarah and William Hazlitt ended so unfortunately, Mary and Charles both soured on Hazlitt for a time. He left Sarah with their ten-year-old son William; he published nasty comments about Coleridge and Wordsworth. "C——— is the only person who can talk to all sorts of people, on all sorts of subjects, without caring a farthing for their understanding one word he says—and *he* talks only for admiration and to be listened to, and accordingly the least interruption puts him out," wrote Hazlitt in the *London Magazine*.[9] Still Charles felt "something tough in my attachment to H——— which all these violent strainings cannot quite dislocate or sever asunder. I get no conversation in London that is absolutely worth attending to but his."[10] They maintained a rocky friendship for years, but the Lambs never warmed to William's second wife. Sarah Hazlitt never remarried. She remained a steady friend but rarely joined their evening socials.

Neither did William and Mary Jane Godwin, who continued to publish children's books into the early 1820s. Even in 1822 a new title appeared, a *History of Greece* by one Edward Baldwin, Esq.—still one of Godwin's pseudonyms. That year, though, desperately short of cash, they were evicted from their Skinner Street home

and shop. Pleas amounting almost to blackmail did not extract
more money from Godwin's son-in-law, Percy Bysshe Shelley.
Charles Lamb organized a fund drive that provided enough
money for them to relocate their business. In three years' time,
though, the Godwins declared bankruptcy. The entire Juvenile
Library stock was sold off—but the texts lived on, some
reprinted as late as the 1840s. Through his Juvenile Library collection Godwin may well have influenced the minds of British citizens in the nineteenth century as deeply as he had in the
eighteenth century through his two adult masterpieces, *Political
Justice* and *Caleb Williams*.[11]

Thomas Noon Talfourd and Bryan Waller Procter, two men
new to the Lamb circle, grew to be as close as family to the sister
and brother in their waning years. Talfourd, a contemporary of
Charles's, happened to be reading the law with a barrister whose
Inner Temple quarters adjoined the Lambs'. Talfourd fancied himself a connoisseur of arts and letters, and in 1815 he published an
appreciation of contemporary poets that included Charles Lamb.
The flattery triggered a lifelong friendship. Called to the bar in
the Middle Temple in 1821, Talfourd served Reading as a Whig
member of Parliament through most of the 1840s. He wrote the
first biography of Charles Lamb, revised it just after Mary's death,
and became a friend and legal adviser to Charles Dickens.

Like Talfourd, Procter was educated in the law but eager to
join literary circles. He wrote poems and plays prolifically from
1819 into the early 1820s, using the pen name Barry Cornwall.
One tragedy, *Mirandola,* staged at the Theatre Royal, Covent
Garden, in 1821 was a mild success. He also contributed to the
new *London Magazine,* but his real work lay in the law. At first a
property law specialist, Procter served for thirty years, from
1832 to 1861, on the Metropolitan Lunacy Commission, visiting
and reporting on Britain's madhouses, asylums, and mental hospitals—a specialization that made him a particularly sensitive

friend and, in the long run, guardian to Mary Lamb. After Lamb's death Procter commemorated their friendship by publishing a biography in 1866 and a collection of Elia essays, including a memoir of Lamb, in 1879.

Charles's literary star was ascending, but Mary was writing little. Her needlework essay left her feeling fatigued. Once again, as the brother gained strength, the sister retreated. This time not six months elapsed between the end of one madhouse stay and the onset of another breakdown. "I am sorry to say that my sister has been taken with one of her violent illnesses, which was so sudden as to have shaken my health a great deal," Charles wrote a friend in mid-September 1815.[12]

It worried them both that this illness came so soon after the last one. They had come to expect a relapse every other year and a madhouse confinement lasting no more than two months. "Mary has been ill and gone from home these five weeks yesterday," he wrote Sara Hutchinson in mid-October, when he received a letter written by her and intended for Mary. His tone was edgy:

> She has left me very lonely and very miserable. I stroll about, but there is no rest but at ones own fireside, and there is no rest for me there now. I look forward to the worse half being past, and keep up as well as I can. She has begun to shew some favorable symptoms. The return of her disorder has been frightfully soon this time, with scarce a six month's interval. I am almost afraid my worry of spirits about the E. I. House was partly the cause of her illness, but one always imputes it to the cause next at hand; more probably it comes from some cause we have no controul over or conjecture of.

Even after all these years Charles Lamb—and, one suspects, Mary too—questioned causes. Charles humbly took some blame for the current relapse but knew there was something more fundamental at its root.

He allowed himself to voice his sadness. He was becoming more fatalistic, and his letters took on a darker tone than those of years before:

It cuts sad great slices out of the time the little time we shall have to live together. I dont know but the recurrence of these illnesses might help me to sustain her death better than if we had had no partial separations. But I wont talk of death. I will imagine us immortal, or forget that we are otherwise, by Gods blessing in a few weeks we may be making our meal together, or sitting in the front row of the Pit at Drury Lane, or taking our evening walk past the theatres, to look at the outside of them at least, if not to be tempted in. Then we forget we are assailable, we are strong for the time as rocks, the wind is tempered to the shorn *Lambs*——.[13]

As Mary aged, the pattern of her mental illness changed. She suffered from more frequent periods of incoherence followed by long slides through depression before returning to normal again. More and more often, Charles referred to her madness as her death. Sometimes a change of scene did Mary good, but sometimes it triggered an attack. When, in 1822, Mary and Charles decided to take a summer trip to France, they hired a nurse to travel with them.

Henry Crabb Robinson visited them on June 16, the day before their departure. "The Lambs have a Frenchman as their companion, and Miss Lamb's nurse, in case she should be ill," he recorded. "Lamb was in high spirits; his sister rather nervous. Her courage in going is great."[14] The nurse traveling with them was Sarah James, one of four daughters of a Welsh clergyman, all of whom, upon the death of their father, took jobs as caretakers at

Whitmore House, Hoxton's upscale private madhouse owned by Warburton.[15] Little did Mary and Charles know at the time that Sarah James and her sisters would tend Mary Lamb until she died.

Travel that summer proved too much for Mary. She had to rest once they had made the crossing to Calais and excused herself from the planned adventures. She remained in the quiet care of Miss James in Paris while Charles visited friends in Versailles, and she was still unable to travel when it was time for Charles to return to work in London. Once she recovered, Mary Lamb and Miss James saw Paris on their own in the company of two male escorts: Henry Crabb Robinson and John Howard Payne.

Payne, an American actor seeking his fortune on the English and Continental stage, was particularly generous with his time and concern for Mary Lamb. "He has a good face," Robinson once commented.[16] Aside from his kindnesses to both Mary Lamb and the recently widowed Mary Shelley, Payne has come down in history as the author of the song "Home Sweet Home." Mary "got home safe" in the middle of September, Charles reported back to the Kenneys, his hosts in Versailles. She had "suffered only a common fatigue," he explained, but was feeling too "weakly" to write herself.

THE LAMBS sought ways to fend off the increasing menace of Mary's madness. Blaming the busy life of London—the constant flow of visitors in and out of their home, the gin-charged debates late into the night—Mary and Charles retreated to pastoral quiet just outside the city. In 1816 they spent a successful three months in Dalston, just north of Hoxton, at a "lodging we took to recruit our health and spirits," as Mary called it in retrospect.[17] The region was still open country in those days, yet no more than a two-hour walk from Charles's office on Leadenhall Street. Mary told Sara Hutchinson the plan "answered the purpose."

But country life only heightened their awareness of how much they enjoyed the nervous energy of the city. "We have had quite a rural summer," Mary wrote Sara,

> & have obtained a very clear idea of the great benifit of quiet— or early hours and time intirely at ones own disposal, and no small advantages these things are, but the return to old friends—the sight of old familiar faces round me has almost reconciled me to occasional headachs and fits of peevish weariness—even London streets, which I sometimes used to think it hard to be eternally doomed to walk through before I could see a green field, seem quite delightful.[18]

So for the time being Mary and Charles Lamb remained in the city, although something prompted them to move out of their beloved childhood home in 1817. "I thought we never could have been torn up from the Temple," Charles wrote Dorothy Wordsworth in November. "It was an ugly wrench, but like a tooth, now 'tis out and I am easy. We never can strike root so deep in any other ground." It is hard to determine why this move occurred, and whether it was of their own volition. "Our rooms were dirty and out of repair," was Mary's explanation, included in the letter to her friend, "and the inconveniences of living in chambers became every year more irksome, and so at last we mustered up resolution enough to leave the good old place that so long had sheltered us."[19]

They moved into rooms above a brazier's shop at 20 Russell Street, tucked in between Drury Lane Theatre and Covent Garden, "the individual spot I like best in all this great city," said Charles. He worried over Mary's reaction to the move out of the cloistered and familiar Inner Temple and into the thick of London street life. "She had not been here four and twenty hours before she saw a Thief," Charles reported. His description evokes Mary Lamb as a detached mantua maker, who "sits at the window working, and casually throwing out her eyes, she sees a concourse of people coming this way, with a constable to conduct the solemnity." To punctuate his housewifely portrait of her, Charles added, "These little incidents agreeably diversify a female life."

But Mary thought the new city surroundings were grand. "The hubbub of the carriages returning from the play does not annoy me in the least," she wrote Dorothy Wordsworth. "I quite enjoy looking out of the window and listening to the calling up of the carriages and the squabbles of the coachmen and linkboys. . . . It is well I am in a chearful place or I should have many misgivings about leaving the Temple."[20]

Traffic increased through their apartment as well. "I am never alone," Charles complained to Mary Wordsworth in 1818. "Except my morning's walk to the office, which is like treading on sands of gold for that reason, I am never so. I cannot walk home from office but some officious friend offers his damn'd unwelcome courtesies to accompany me." Many who accosted him on the street came home with him for dinner. Then, wrote Charles,

> up I go, mutton on table, hungry as hunter, hope to forget my cares and bury them in the agreeable abstraction of mastication, knock at the door, in comes Mrs. Hazlitt, or M. Burney, or Morgan, or Demogorgon, or my brother, or somebody, to prevent my eating alone, a Process absolutely necessary to my poor wretched digestion. O the pleasure of eating alone![21]

Mary never complained, but she undoubtedly felt the same. Even with a hired housekeeper, she bore the burden of entertaining the constant flow of guests.

Both Mary and Charles were torn between city and country. "I must confess I would rather live in Russell Street all my life, and never set my foot but on the London pavement, than be doomed always to enjoy the silent pleasures I now do," Mary wrote from

Dalston. "Late hours are life-shortening things; but I would rather run all risks, and sit every night—at some places I could name—wishing in vain at eleven o'clock for the entrance of the supper tray, than be always up and alive at eight o'clock breakfast, as I am here." They considered splitting their time evenly "between quiet rest and dear London weariness," as Mary put it.[22]

In 1819, for the one and only time in his adult life, Charles Lamb considered marriage. He and Mary had been following the progress of the young actress Frances Maria Kelly, a stage prodigy who had won London's hearts in 1814 as Ophelia to Edmund Kean's Hamlet. "This lady has long ranked among the most considerable of our London performers," Charles wrote his friend Gutch. He admired how she had worked her way up in the theater from her first "slender pretensions of chorus-singer," and he saw in her "the joy of a freed spirit, escaping from care." Both sister and brother found her stage presence uplifting.[23]

After writing glowing reviews of her work for the *Examiner,* Charles became emboldened and began writing letters to her. They can hardly be called love letters, so wrapped in witticisms are his sentiments. This one thrashes a pun to death, playing on the fact that free passes to the theater were made of bone, and sometimes called that:

> If your Bones are not engaged on Monday night, will you favor us with the use of them? I know, if you can oblige us, you will make no bones of it; if you cannot, it shall break none betwixt us. We might ask somebody else, but we do not like the bones of any strange animal. We should be welcome to dear Mrs. Liston's but then she is so plump, there is no getting at them.

He concludes this invitation by wishing that "God rest your bones," then can't resist one more pun: "I am almost at the end of my bon-mots."[24]

On July 19, Mary and Charles Lamb attended *Hamlet* at Covent Garden Theatre, with Fanny Kelly playing Ophelia once again. Charles must have left the theater smitten. The performance evoked "a train of thinking, which I cannot suppress," wrote Charles in the first of three letters passing between him and Miss Kelly that day. In short, Charles proposed marriage.

> Would to God you were released from this way of life; that you could bring your mind to consent to take your lot with us, and throw off for ever the whole burden of your Profession. . . . Think of it at your leisure. I have quite income enough, . . . I am not so foolish as not to know that I am a most unworthy match for such a one as you, but you have for years been a principal object in my mind. . . . Can you quit these shadows of existence, & come & be a reality to us?[25]

Miss Kelly replied instantly.

> . . . while I thus *frankly* & decidedly decline your proposal, believe me, I am not insensible to the high honour which the preference of such a mind as yours confers upon me—let me, however, hope that all thought upon this subject will end with this letter, & that you will henceforth encourage no other sentiment towards me than esteem in my private character and a continuance of that approbation of my humble talents which you have already expressed so much & so often to my advantage and gratification.

She signed her letter "Your obliged friend."[26]

Rebuffed, Charles responded immediately, writing with what E. V. Lucas, an editor of the Lambs' letters, called "a far less steady hand than that in which the proposal was made." "Your injunctions shall be obeyed to a tittle," he scrawled and underlined. "I had thought to have written seriously, but I fancy I succeed best in epistles of mere fun." He requested that she not "paste that last letter of mine into your Book."[27]

What Fanny Kelly did not express outright to Charles Lamb, she soon did in confidence, in a letter to her sister:

> . . . even at the peril of my decision causing him great despondency, which I rather feared, I could have no other course than to say the truth that I could not accept his offer. I could not give my assent to a proposal which would bring me into that atmosphere of sad mental uncertainty which surrounds his domestic life. Marriage might well bring to us both added causes for misery and regrets in later years.[28]

Clearly Fanny Kelly noticed that "us" in Charles Lamb's proposal. Some biographers suggest that she would not marry into a family known to be prone to madness, but she may just as likely have understood that marriage to Charles meant commitment to Mary. The muffed marriage proposal was the start of a warm friendship among the three people, though, and in fact Fanny Kelly became Mary's Latin student. Nearly ten years later, when Crabb Robinson visited Mary and Charles on Good Friday in 1828, he would find Fanny Kelly—an "unaffected, sensible, clear-headed, warm-hearted woman"—visiting them as well.[29]

A YOUNG WOMAN did soon join the family of Mary and Charles Lamb, however. It all started when they met eleven-year-old Emma Isola. They may have been introduced to her family by the Wordsworths, for her grandfather, Agostino Isola, was a wizened teacher of Spanish and Italian at Cambridge who counted William

Wordsworth among his students. In 1820, her mother having died, Emma was staying with her aunt. She visited the Lambs in London for a month over the holidays.

Instantly their life was filled with activity and focused on someone other than themselves. Emma wrote a letter to her aunt, gleefully recounting the first week's activities.

> The first night I came we went out to spend the evening. The second night Mr. Lamb took me to see the wild beasts at Exeter Change. Saturday night being twelfth night I went to a party and did not return till four in the morning. Yesterday Miss Lamb took me to the theatre at Covent Garden. I cannot tell you how much I liked it. I was so delighted.

For the two adults it must have been something of a comeuppance. All of a sudden raising children was not an abstraction or a choice between moral tales and mythologies. "Emma is a very naughty girl," wrote Charles to her aunt, adding his own message to the letter his young visitor began, "and has broken three cups, one plate and a slop-bason with mere giddiness." He could not hold a stern tone very long—one senses these two guardians were the prototypical grandparents, pushovers to a boisterous preadolescent. "If you can spare her longer than her holidays," he continued, "we shall be happy to keep her, in hopes of her amendment. . . . She is studying algebra & the languages. I teach her *dancing*." Charles added a slight amendment to Emma's own confession: "She came home at 5 o'clock in the morning with a strange gentleman on Twelfth Night."[30] Their ward might have been socially precocious for the age of eleven, but the absence of judgmental language suggests that Charles, at least, delighted in her liveliness.

After a month, as Emma prepared to go home, Charles wrote her aunt and guaranteed that "you will see your little friend, with her bloom somewhat impaired by late hours and dissipation, but

her gait, gesture, and general manners (I flatter myself) considerably improved by——*somebody that shall be nameless.*" The
unnamed tutor was, of course, Mary, or Charles, or both. Charles
had one final complaint about the young lady's behavior: "I wish I
could cure her of making dog's ears in books."[31]

Emma's visits to the Lambs grew longer and more frequent.
They treated her as a surrogate daughter and took seriously the
project of educating her. Finally Mary had the occasion to put into
practice the principles of female education that drove her three
books. She could see to the education of this one young lady and
make a difference in a palpable way. When Emma's father died in
1823, it seemed best for the fourteen-year-old to move in with
Mary and Charles. The three lived as a family until, five years
later, Emma secured a position as a governess.

The Lambs went into the parenting venture with high hopes.
As she had during her first visit, Emma probed all liberties possible. Eventually the Lambs had to lower even their intellectual
expectations. Emma was not the receptive learner they believed
every young mind could and should be. "I am teaching Emma
Latin to qualify her for a superior governess-ship: which we see
no prospect of her getting," wrote Charles in 1827. "'Tis like
feeding a child with chopped hay from a spoon." He turned his
frustration into a list of puns and wordplays on the Latin—"her
conjunctions copulative have no connection in them; her con-
cords disagree." Finally he vented: "[S]he herself is a lazy, block-
headly supine."[32]

Characteristically Mary viewed the situation through Emma's
eyes, recognizing the strain of hard work, the frustration of learning, the long hours spent without visible reward. She comforted
her tutee in a sonnet, which begins

> *Droop not, dear Emma, dry those falling tears,*
> *And call up smiles into thy pallid face,*

Pallid and care-worn with thy arduous race:
In few brief months thou hast done the work of years.

In the sonnet Mary calls forth a comparison between Emma and Coleridge's daughter, now twenty-five years old, who had inherited her father's gift for language and was proving herself a "most rare Latinist." Apparently a meeting of the two girls had only highlighted their unequal talents. Mary, abundantly encouraging, consoled Emma that in time to come, Sara Coleridge

Shall hail thee Sister Linguist. This will make
Thy friends, who now afford thee careful aid,
A recompense most rich for all their pains,
Counting thy acquisitions their best gains.[33]

In these last lines Mary also consoled herself and her brother. They deserved a reward for their efforts, too.

When the time came the Lambs worked diligently to find Emma a suitable work position. "We have a *young person domesticated* with us," Charles wrote one prospective employer, "in whose well-doing we are much interested." He recommended her as a teacher of French, Italian, music, drawing, or—"in a twelvemonth, or less," once she learned a little more—Latin.

I must mention also that as an English Reader—a not very common accomplishment—our friend Coleridge will bear witness to the very excellent manner in which she read to him some of the most difficult passages in the Paradise Lost. We are unwilling that her talents and many good qualities should be buried in some poor Boarding School, and are very desirous of recommending her to a good Family.[34]

Charles escorted Emma on interviews. Finally, after nearly a year's effort, she secured a position in the household of a Bury St. Edmunds clergyman. She visited Mary and Charles for holidays and came home to them during a worrisome bout with "brain fever," very likely an influenza of the type that debilitated Dorothy Wordsworth. After a month of bed rest Emma recovered and returned to her job.

DURING THE TIME Emma Isola was living with them, the Lambs moved to the country. "When you come Londonward you will find me no longer in Covt Gard," wrote Charles in September 1823:

> I have a Cottage, in Colebrook row, Islington. A cottage, for it
> is detach'd; a white house, with 6 good rooms; the New River
> (rather elderly by this time) runs (if a moderate walking pace
> can be so termed) close to the foot of the house; and behind is
> a spacious garden, with vines (I assure you), pears, strawber-
> ries, parsnips, leeks, carrots, cabbages, . . . I feel like a great
> Lord, never having had a house before.[35]

Colebrook Cottage still stands, back behind Essex Road, Islington's major thoroughfare, marked with a plaque commemorating the famous sister and brother who called it home. It was not even a five-minute walk from Fisher House, the madhouse of Mary's past.

The Lambs moved to the country at a time of life when they were maintaining an awkward balancing act, alternating between periods when one, then the other, suffered from some sort of illness. They struggled to adapt to a new daily routine once Charles became, as he put it in an essay by Elia, a "superannuated man." For years he had chafed over the daily humdrum of his job at East

India House. On March 29, 1825, he found release from those troubles. The court of directors resolved "that the resignation of Mr. Charles Lamb of the Accountant-General's Office, on account of certified ill-health, be accepted."[36] For his thirty-three years of faithful service, Lamb received an annual pension of £450, of which £9 went into a fund for Mary.[37]

The day he received the news Charles Lamb came home ecstatic. He called it his "emancipation,"[38] his "gaol delivery."[39] "I am free!" he cried out with glee.[40]

"But that tumultuousness is passing off," he wrote Wordsworth a week later,

> and I begin to understand the nature of the gift. Holydays, even the annual month, were always uneasy joys: their conscious fugitiveness—the craving after making the most of them. Now, when all is holyday, there are no holydays. I can sit at home in rain or shine without a restless impulse for walkings. I am daily steadying, and shall soon find it as natural to me to be my own master, as it has been irksome to have had a master. Mary wakes every morning with an obscure feeling that some good has happened to us.[41]

What Charles called "an obscure feeling" may have been Mary's silent ambivalence, born of the recognition that this new lifestyle required adaptations on her part.

Demands increased more than she could have imagined. In September 1825 Charles fell seriously ill with what he called the summer's second "nervous attack."[42] "I am very feeble, can scarce move a pen," he wrote Thomas Allsop. "Got home . . . on the Friday, and on Monday followg was laid up with a most violent nervous fever second this summer, have had Leeches to my Temples, have not had, nor can get, a night's sleep."[43] Soon Mary crumpled under the strain. "My sister has sunk under her anxieties about me," Charles reported. "She is laid up, deprived of reasons for many weeks to come, I fear." Sarah James moved in with them, and a "medical attendant" visited Charles daily.[44] Charles—recently capable of fifteen miles in one spurt—barely managed to hobble to the Angel Inn just blocks away.

Three years after they moved to Islington, they were "evuls'd from Colebrook" for reasons no one recorded, though "'twas with some pain," Charles wrote. "You may find some of our flesh sticking to the door posts."[45] They moved farther north to Enfield, a village nine miles from London on the road to Hertfordshire. They found a little house of their own, next door to a family named Westwood. Many years later Thomas Westwood, thirteen at the time, recalled his first sight of the Lambs, with a girl— Emma—and a dog—a hound named Dash.

> Leaning idly out of window, I saw a group of three issuing from the gambogey-looking [bright yellow] cottage; close at hand: a slim middle-aged man, in quaint, uncontemporary habiliments; a rather shapeless bundle of an old lady, in a bonnet like a mobcap; and a young girl. While before them, bounded a riotous dog, holding a board with "This House to Let" on it, in his jaws. Lamb was on his way back to the house-agent, and that was his fashion of announcing that he had taken the premises.[46]

Charles granted that the Enfield cottage was "no manor house," but it did have "capital new locks to every door, capital grates in every room" and cost less than Colebrook Cottage.[47]

Moving still spun Mary Lamb around. This time, instead of sending her to a madhouse to recover, Charles hired Sarah James to care for her at home. The decision may have been financial, given Charles's decreased income; it may have been practical, since Enfield was farther from the known madhouses; or it may have been an experiment on Charles's part, to discover whether, now that they lived in the quiet of the country, Mary might recover on her own.

14

HER TWILIGHT OF
CONSCIOUSNESS

WITH MARY STAYING home while she was ill, Charles could feel even more lonely than when she had stayed in a madhouse. He refused visitors, worrying that they would agitate his sister, but he was too far from London to go out for an evening. He sadly put pen to paper during the first week of October 1827. "I am settled for life, I hope, at Enfield," he wrote Crabb Robinson: "I have taken the prettiest, compactest house I ever saw, . . . but, alas! at the expense of poor Mary, who was taken ill of her old complaint the night before we got into it. So I must suspend the pleasure I expected in the surprise you would have had in coming down and finding us householders."[1]

"Our pleasant meeting[s] for some time are suspended," he wrote another friend. "My sister was taken very ill in a few hours after you left us (I had suspected it)."[2] To Fanny Kelly he wrote: "All our pleasant prospects of seeing you here are dashed. Poor Mary was taken last night with the beginning of one of her sad illnesses, which last so long. . . . What I expected to be so comfortable has opened gloomily."[3]

A month later he was still refusing visitors. "The house is so small, Mary hears every person and every knock. She is very bad yet."[4] She remained sensitive and withdrawn into the month of December. "My sister's illness is the most obstinate she ever had," Charles declared. "It will not go away, and I am afraid Miss James will not be able to stay a day or two longer. I am desperate to think of it some-times. 'Tis eleven weeks!" Mary recovered by Christmas, but Charles still turned away guests. "I think a visitor . . . might a little put us out of our way," he wrote to one, but he welcomed Emma Isola and Henry Crabb Robinson.[5]

The truth is that both the Lambs were aging. At the start of the year 1828, finally settled in Enfield, Charles was fifty-two, Mary sixty-three. His hands had begun to quiver. Her lapses could last months. More often, and without apparent triggers, she cycled into irrationality, "sadly rambling," as Charles put it. Once the mania dissipated, she would subside into periods of withdrawal, only loosely connected to the people and world around her. Twice in the eighteen months between May 1829 and October 1830, Mary was committed to Normand House in Fulham, southwest London, a new madhouse in a neighborhood far from Hoxton, Islington, or Enfield. Now, when Charles visited her, he found her "scarce showing any pleasure in seeing me, or curiosity when I should come again."[6]

Normand House cared for women only, no more than twenty patients at a time. An inspector in 1815 had found it one of the few London madhouses worthy of praise. The residents "appeared to be treated with the greatest kindness. They went to the local church, and were allowed out on walks."[7] This report appeared all the more positive in the context of the many other shocking accounts made public at this time as madhouse inspections, both philanthropic and governmental, became more frequent.

Mary Lamb returned home once her phase of irrationality had subsided, but she was still not herself. The effects of recurrent severe periods of mental disorder were accumulating. "Her state of mind is deplorable beyond any example," Charles wrote in 1830: "I almost fear whether she has strength at her time of life ever to get out of it. Here she must be nursed, and neither see nor hear of anything in the world out of her sick chamber. The mere hearing that Southey had called at our lodgings totally upset her. . . . I dare not write or receive a letter in her presence; every little task so agitates her."[8] Her sieges were coming too frequently and lasting too long. The burden was too much for Charles to bear. He began to realize that the very act of moving from home to madhouse to home again exacerbated her condition.

He learned of a couple named Walden in Edmonton, three miles southeast of Enfield. Mr. Walden had once worked at Bethlem, but he and his wife now "made their living by keeping in gentle restraint those whose attacks were harmless or intermittent, and whose friends looked for more human treatment than was obtainable in the asylums of those days," as an acquaintance of the Lambs wrote years later.[9] Mary moved in with the Waldens in 1833. Soon Charles joined her.

"After 8 weary years at Enfield I have emancipated myself," he wrote Talfourd, "and am, with my sister ill, at Mr. Walden's, Church St. Edmonton. I feel happier than I have been for all those years." It was as if, by resigning himself to the circumstances that best suited Mary, he had now found his own resting place. He no longer worried about how her phases of mental illness might disrupt normal daily life. "Now we need move no more," he was able to say.[10]

It was a private home, a tidy little cottage with a small front yard, a cast-iron gate, and a garden in the back graced by an apple tree. The house still stands today, called "Lamb Cottage." Its owners, proud of the ghosts that haunt it, have fashioned the library in the way they imagine the Lambs to have had it, a cozy room with fireplace just off the front hall—the same room remembered by J. Fuller Russell, a young poet who made a pilgrimage there to meet Charles Lamb:

I was admitted into a small and pleasantly shaded parlour. The modest room was hung round with fine engravings by

Hogarth, in dark frames. Books and magazines were scattered on the table, and on the old-fashioned window-seat. I chatted awhile with Miss Lamb—a meek, intelligent, very pleasant, and rather deaf, elderly lady, who told me that her brother had been gratified by parts of my poem, and had read them to her.

Charles offered Russell a rum and water. Mary objected. Like the little boy cared for by his big sister, Charles pleaded for "a little drop now, only a *leetle* drop?" Mary told him to "be a good boy," but he downed a drink with his visitor anyway.[11]

The present owners of Lamb Cottage also preserve the walk-in closet—a space just larger than a single bed, with a door that locks from the outside, off the second-floor dining room. Following the tradition handed down with the house itself, they identify this tiny room as the place where the Waldens would restrain Mary Lamb.

Both siblings may have needed the Waldens' attention. Thomas Westwood, their Enfield neighbor, visited them and found the whole house "gloomy." "Perhaps the shadow of what was to come brooded over it," he wrote. "Lamb's trick of jumping up and slapping his sister on the shoulder in moments of hilarity was a frequent and familiar outbreak." More than once Westwood heard Charles Lamb, proud virtuoso of English rhyme, repeat a mocking triplet:

> *I had a sister—*
> *The devil kist her,*
> *And raised a blister!*[12]

To an old friend, William Wordsworth, Charles gave these reasons for moving to the Waldens':

Mary is ill again. Her illnesses encroach yearly. The last was three months, followed by two of depression most dreadful. I look back upon her earlier attacks with longing. Nice little durations of six weeks or so, followed by complete restoration—shocking as they were to me then. In short, half her life she is dead to me, and the other half is made anxious with fears and lookings forward to the next shock. With such prospects, it seem'd to me necessary that she should no longer live with me, and be fluttered with continual removals, so I am come to live with her.[13]

With every year more of Mary's life was overtaken by her periods of dim recognition and rapid, senseless speech. When distant acquaintances died, Charles kept the knowledge from her, believing she would not even remember the person he was discussing. When those closer to them died, he held on to the news until the time was right. When he told her that their brother, John, had died, her response doubled his grief: "It does not seem much to have altered the state of her mind."[14]

THERE WERE GRACIOUS moments of lucidity. One came thanks to the good news of Emma Isola's engagement. The suitor who won her heart was a young bookseller named Edward Moxon, who worked for Longman in London and delivered books outside the city. First getting to know Moxon in 1826, Charles introduced him to Wordsworth as "one of Longman's best hands, . . . a young lad with a Yorkshire head, and heart that would do honour to a more Southern county," who, as "a friendly serviceable fellow . . . thinks nothing of lugging up a Cargo of the Newest Novels once or twice a week from the row to Colebrooke to gratify my Sister's passion for the newest things. He is her Bodley."[15] He was also, at the age of twenty-four, a published poet, and soon became a welcome guest at the Lambs'.

In the long run Edward Moxon's career would intertwine with those of other Romantics of note. He published Wordsworth and stood trial for having reprinted the infamously atheistical *Queen Mab* in Mary Shelley's 1839 edition of her husband's posthumous works. With the Lambs' dear friend Talfourd defending him, Moxon was found guilty in 1841 but received no punishment.[16]

Mary and Charles Lamb both liked Edward Moxon from the start. They considered him a likely suitor for their ward. "With my perfect approval, and more than concurrence, she is to be wedded to Moxon," Charles wrote Wordsworth in May 1833. At the time Mary was in no state to give her approval, but he knew she would agree. The wedding took place on July 30, 1833, and Charles Lamb remained appropriately ceremonial. "I tripped a little at the altar, was engaged in admiring the altarpiece, but, recalled seasonably by a Parsonic rebuke, 'Who gives this woman!' was in time to reply resolutely, 'I do.'"[17]

Mary Lamb did not attend. But that very evening, something triggered a change inside. Her mentality transformed itself within minutes, and she found herself returned to such health and awareness that she wrote the newlyweds about it. It was the first time she had put pen to paper in months.

> My dear Emma and Edward Moxon,
>
> Accept my sincere congratulations, and imagine more good wishes than my weak nerves will let me put into good set words. The dreary blank of *unanswered questions* which I ventured to ask in vain was cleared up on the wedding-day by Mrs. W. taking a glass of wine, and, with a total change of countenance, begged leave to drink Mr. and Mrs. Moxon's health. It restored me, from that moment: as if by an electrical stroke: to the entire possession of my senses—I never felt so calm and quiet after a similar illness as I do now. I feel as if all tears were wiped from my eyes, and all care from my heart.
>
> Mary Lamb.

To this Charles (ever eager to declare life normal once again) added:

> Dears Again
>
> Your letter interrupted a seventh game at Picquet which
> *we* were having, after walking to *Wright's* and purchasing
> shoes. We pass our time in cards, walks, and reading. We
> attack Tasso soon. C.L.

> Never was such a calm, or such a recovery. 'Tis her own
> words, undictated.[18]

It is interesting to note how Mary describes her problems. She
has come through a "dreary blank of *unanswered questions*," a period
when she feels others have not been responding to her. Those
around her probably ascribed the blankness to her, and rarely
engaged her; she felt it originated in them. Limited expectations
could be self-fulfilling—and, conversely, when Charles or others
believed in her capabilities, those strengths came to the fore.
While this analysis may be only partial, and unprofessional, it
does remind us that for an impressionable psyche like hers, the
caregiving atmosphere—whether Fisher House, Hoxton House,
Normand House, the Waldens, or at home with Charles—influenced her condition.

Her brother sensed this principle and did all he could to bring
forth the best in her, but her lengthier declines into incoherence
and long spells of depression afterward made it difficult. It was
harder to make jokes and exude optimism. One physician "led me
to expect that this illness would lengthen with her years," he
wrote his old friend Thomas Manning, now home in England,

> & it has cruelly, with that new feature of despondency after. I
> am with her alone now in a proper house. She is I hope recov-
> ering. We play picquet, and it is like the old times a while, then

goes off—I struggle up town rarely, and then to see London with little other motive, for what is left there hardly! The streets and shops entertaining ever, else I feel as in a desert, & get me home to my cave.[19]

Charles Lamb never gave up his affection and respect for his sister. In what could be considered an epitaph written while she was still alive, he poignantly described the state in which Mary Lamb spent these late years of her life. "Have faith in me!" he wrote to Maria Fryer, a friend of Emma's, who worried about Charles's overconcern for Mary. "It is no new thing for me to be left to my sister. When she is not violent her rambling chat is better to me than the sense and sanity of this world. Her heart is obscured, not buried; it breaks out occasionally; and one can disern [sic] a strong mind struggling with the billows that have gone over it."

"I could be nowhere happier than under the same roof with her," Charles Lamb continued, as devoted to his sister in 1834 as he had been in 1796:

Her memory is unnaturally strong; and from ages past, if we may so call the earliest records of our poor life, she fetches thousands of names and things that never would have dawned upon me again, and thousands from the ten years she lived before me. What took place from early girlhood to her coming of age principaly [sic] lives again (every important thing and every trifle) in her brain with the vividness of real presence. For twelve hours incessantly she will pour out without intermission all her past life, forgetting nothing, pouring out name after name to the Waldens as a dream.

"What things we are!" he declares to his young correspondent. "I know you will bear with me, talking of these things. It seems to ease me; for I have nobody to tell these things to now."[20]

To Charles's admiration for Mary can be added that of Talfourd, who grew closer to the Lambs as they aged. He saw the glint of creative genius in Mary Lamb. "Her ramblings often sparkled with brilliant description and shattered beauty," Talfourd wrote. "She would fancy herself in the days of Queen Anne or George the First, and describe the brocaded dames and courtly manners, as though she had been bred among them, in the best style of the old comedy." In her own way still collaborating with her brother, Mary lived out in her fantasies Charles's passion for England's antique past:

> It was all broken and disjointed, so that the hearer could remember little of her discourse; but the fragments were like the jewelled speeches of Congreve, only shaken from their setting. There was sometimes even a vein of crazy logic running through them, associating things essentially most dissimilar, but connecting them by a verbal association in strange order.

It was "extraordinary," Talfourd believed, that such intelligence showed through the madness. "It was as if the finest elements of mind had been shaken into fantastic combinations like those of a kaleidoscope."[21]

MARY AND CHARLES LAMB had once wistfully agreed that she should die first,[22] but that part of their life, as so many others, did not go as planned. The last months were painful. She struggled to give him companionship, as much as her health would allow. His own health rapidly declined, pulled down by age, waning interests, and worry. The death of Samuel Taylor Coleridge in July 1834 dealt an insuperable blow. Wordsworth believed Lamb's own death "was doubtless hastened by his sorrow for that of Coleridge."[23] Mary may not even have been told the news. She had been "violent"—Charles's word, several times over[24]—for twenty weeks already that year, and although she had recovered well enough to enjoy a book, "it puzzles her to read it above a page or so a day."[25]

Once Coleridge had died, Lamb "thought of little else" but death, wrote John Forster, a new acquaintance. In the midst of his comments, Forster injected a qualifier—"his sister was but another portion of himself"—as if to suggest that even as Lamb gazed into the grave, he was thinking of his sister. He indicated that Charles still wore that thick skin of irony to shield his melancholy from the world:

> In a jest, or a few light phrases, he would lay open the last recesses of his heart. So in respect of the death of Coleridge. Some old friends of his saw him two or three weeks ago, and remarked the constant turning and reference of his mind. He interrupted himself and them almost every instant with some play of affected wonder, or astonishment, or humorous melancholy, on the words, *"Coleridge is dead."* Nothing could divert him from that, for the thought of it never left him.[26]

Coleridge wrote in his will that "a small plain gold mourning ring, with my hair," should be presented "To my close friend and ever-beloved schoolfellow, Charles Lamb— . . . his equally-beloved sister, Mary Lamb, will know herself to be included."[27]

ON MONDAY, December 22, 1834, Charles Lamb took off for a typically long walk, down Church Street in the direction of London. Not far from home he stumbled and fell facedown. Standing up, he must have realized that his face was bleeding. One can only imagine Mary's distress as Mrs. Walden tended his wound and laid him down to rest.

By the end of the week Charles Lamb was dying. It was Christmas week, but his condition predominated over any festivities. On Boxing Day, Charles Ryle, with whom he had worked at East India House, visited. Lamb's will, written in 1830, named Ryle and Talfourd as executors. Ryle found Charles weak in bed, although able to conduct a conversation. He alerted Talfourd to their friend's condition.

Talfourd visited the next day. Charles Lamb was losing consciousness. He talked, but barely audibly, about details of little importance, such as the turkey he had received as a gift and how he longed for a pig instead. "I do not think he knew me," said Talfourd, "and having vainly tried to engage his attention, I quitted him."[28] Two hours later, on December 27, 1834, at the age of fifty-nine, Charles Lamb died. He died of erisypelas, a staphylococcus infection in the wound on his face, "but it was, in truth," Talfourd believed, "a breaking up of the constitution, and he died from mere weakness."[29]

Both executors were at the Waldens' cottage the next day. They found Mary aware yet vacant, in a state they ascribed to her mental illness. Gazing on the body of her brother, reported Ryle, "she observed on his 'beauty' when asleep and apprehended nothing further." Talfourd believed she understood the finality of his state but still responded with flat emotion. "Miss Lamb is quite insane, yet conscious of her brother's death, without feeling it, and able to point out the place for the grave," he reported to Crabb Robinson.[30]

Robinson visited Mary nine days later, and she responded with the same combination of awareness and delusion. Indeed "a stranger would have seen little remarkable about her," Robinson wrote in his diary:

> She was neither violent nor unhappy; nor was she entirely without sense. She was, however, out of her mind, as the expression is; but she could combine ideas, although imper-

fectly. On my going into the room where she was sitting with Mr. Waldron [Walden], she exclaimed with great vivacity, "Oh! here's *Crabby*." She gave me her hand with great cordiality, and said, "Now this is very kind—not merely good-natured, but very, very kind to come and see me in my affliction."

Her primary topics of conversation, Robinson recalled, were "subjects connected with insanity" and "her brother's death." She dredged up ancient memories of Charles's birth and childhood, remembering him as "a weakly, but very pretty child." She told him not to worry about her, that she could maintain herself. "I will mend your stockings and you shall pay me."[31] In fact, to add to the pension established at Charles's retirement, East India House employees banded together to create a £120 annuity on Mary's behalf from the Clerks' Fund.[32]

Talfourd believed that in her "long and dismal twilight of consciousness,"[33] Mary Lamb absorbed the finality of her brother's departure slowly, as she was able. Charles Lamb was buried in the Edmonton churchyard, just across Church Street from the Waldens' cottage. Mary's muffled response to his absence lasted five months, but in May the violent mania again overtook her. Moxon, Talfourd, and Robinson considered whether to move her into London, closer to them, but she wanted to stay in Edmonton. "*He* was there," Talfourd wrote, recalling her reasons, "asleep in the old churchyard, beneath the turf near which they had stood together, and had selected for a resting-place; to this spot she used, when well, to stroll out mournfully in the evening, and to this spot she would contrive to lead any friend who came in the summer evenings to drink tea and went out with her afterwards for a walk."[34]

Edward Moxon asked William Wordsworth to write an epitaph to be carved on Charles Lamb's tombstone. The expansive poet wrote an elegy 131 lines long. He suggested that it be carved in double columns on a stone tablet and displayed in the church's interior, and he apologized for how little, in his estimation, the poem touched upon "the most striking feature of our departed friend's character, and the most affecting circumstance of his life, namely, his faithful and intense love of his sister."[35]

In fact a good third of the poem commemorates Mary Lamb and her brother's devotion to her. After remarking that Charles never enjoyed the blessings of marriage, the poet rejoins:

> *Unto thee,*
> *Not so enriched, not so adorned, to thee*
> *Was given (say rather, thou of later birth*
> *Wert given to her) a Sister—'tis a word*
> *Timidly uttered, for she lives, the meek,*
> *The self-restraining, and the ever-kind;*
> *In whom thy reason and intelligent heart*
> *Found . . .*
> *More than sufficient recompense!*

The poem ends by comparing Mary and Charles's "*dual* loneliness" to a hermit's celibacy.

> *The sacred tie*
> *Is broken; yet why grieve? for Time but holds*
> *His moiety in trust, till Joy shall lead*
> *To the blest world where parting is unknown.*

Wordsworth must have expected Mary to appreciate his overflow of feeling toward her. Discreet sensitivities turned her eyes to other lines. "She does not like any allusion to his being a clerk, or to family misfortunes," wrote Robinson. Wordsworth had begun the poem by remarking that Charles Lamb was buried far from the city where he "humbly earned his bread, / To the strict labours of the merchant's desk / By duty chained." He also, albeit in veiled abstractions, revealed Mary and Charles's deepest secret, writing that "meekness at times gave way, / Provoked out of herself by troubles strange, / Many and strange, that hung about his life."

Mary would not have it. She stated her opinion clearly, and she got her way. "Not even dear Mary," recorded Robinson in his diary, "can overcome the common feeling that would conceal lowness of station, or a reference to ignoble sufferings."[36] A shorter, more traditional epitaph was written by the Reverend H. Francis Cary, a scholar and translator of Dante who had hosted Charles monthly for lunch at the British Museum during the last year of his life.[37] Carved beneath it, though, were three lines from the Wordsworth poem:

> At the centre of his being, lodged
> A soul by resignation sanctified . . .
> O, he was good, if e'er a good Man lived.

WITHOUT CHARLES LAMB to put it in writing, the story of Mary Lamb falls nearly silent from this point on. She lived another twelve long years, staying with the Waldens in Edmonton until 1842, then moving into London to live with nursemaids, sometimes Sarah James and sometimes Sarah's sister, Mrs. Parsons.

She enjoyed the occasional visitor—Robinson, Procter, Talfourd—and had the pleasure of accepting an invitation to visit others from time to time. She dictated an occasional greeting, a letter of thanks or condolences. Nearly a year after Charles Lamb's death, Robinson accompanied her to dinner at the

Moxons' and found her "very comfortable—not in high spirits—but calm, and she seemed to enjoy the sight of so many old friends."[38]

At other times, though, Mary's deterioration evoked shock and sorrow. In 1839 Robinson granted that although "her mind is gone, or, at least, has become inert," there was still a recognizable person inside: "She has still her excellent heart—is kind and considerate, and her judgment is sound."[39] Once deafness overtook her, it made communication nearly impossible. "She is a mere wreck of herself," Robinson noted in 1843, when Mary was close to eighty. "I took a single cup of tea with her, to while away the time; but I found it difficult to keep up any conversation."[40] She may have comprehended the news in 1843 that William Wordsworth, aged seventy-three, had become Britain's eleventh poet laureate.

Mary Lamb lived to the age of eighty-six. Those who loved her held tight to memories of her earlier self, such a contrast to her dwindling being. She died on May 28, 1847, and was laid to rest in Edmonton churchyard, at the site that she and her brother had chosen together, the site she had so often visited once he was buried there.

"Yesterday was a painfully interesting day," Crabb Robinson confided to his diary. "I attended the funeral of Mary Lamb." A coach arrived at his door at nine in the morning, then it joined two more along with the hearse carrying her remains to Edmonton. The day was joyously springlike, almost too hot to be riding inside a coach. Others in attendance, as Robinson remembered, were Talfourd and Ryle, Edward Moxon, Martin Burney, John Forster, and Thomas Allsop. Women did not attend, as was the custom of the time.

Afterward Mr. and Mrs. Walden hosted a gathering of mourners in the home where the Lambs had last lived together. "There was no sadness assumed by the attendants," wrote Robinson. "We all talked with warm affection of dear Mary Lamb, and that most delightful of creatures, her brother Charles—of all the men of genius I ever knew, the one the most intensely and universally to be loved."[41]

Even at her own funeral Mary Lamb remained in her brother's shadow.

Epilogue

WHEN MARY LAMB died, Charles Lamb was already attaining sainthood. It was a reputation that has now become legendary. Literary Victorians sang his praises as an essayist and letter writer. Walter Savage Landor wrote a poem addressed to Mary, comforting her that "His gentle soul, his genius, these are thine." William Makepeace Thackeray, the novelist best known for *Vanity Fair* (1848), extolled Lamb's language, wit, and urbane sensibility.

Edward FitzGerald, the influential translator of the Persian classic *The Rubaiyat of Omar Khayyam* (1859), considered writing a biography of Charles Lamb. A reminiscence by William Carew Hazlitt, the grandson of William and Sarah, published in 1874, frustrated FitzGerald. Hazlitt organized the letters by correspondent, making it hard to extract a chronology from them, so FitzGerald created his own. He did not swerve from the facts of 1796, when "Mary Lamb, worn out with nursing her Family, kills her Mother," or 1804, when the only letter he knew of portrayed "much drink and smoke by night, and depression by day" in Charles Lamb's life.[1]

"I have sent you many works, none better than the enclosed, though it may not be exactly accurate, Biographies differing," he wrote a literary friend to whom he sent the Lamb chronology in 1878:

I did it for myself, who felt often at a loss for some Data while
reading the dear Fellow's Letters. . . . I hesitated at expatiating
so on the terrible year 1796, or even mentioning the Drink in
1804: but the first is necessary to show what a Saint and Hero
the man was; and only a Noodle would fail to understand the
Drink, etc., which never affected Lamb's conduct to those he
loved. Bless him! "Saint Charles!" said Thackeray one day taking up one of his Letters, and putting it to his forehead.[2]

Virginia Woolf recalled that very scene in *A Room of One's Own*
(1929), her book on women and writing. "Saint Charles, said
Thackeray, putting a letter of Lamb's to his forehead"—"some
stray memory of some old essay" evoked such rapture, she imag-
ined. "Among all the dead . . . Lamb is one of the most congenial."
Yet in this book, for which she invented a sister for William
Shakespeare to portray how history obscures literary women,
Virginia Woolf does not mention Mary Lamb.

THE VICTORIANS may have known her secret, but few of Mary
Lamb's contemporaries did when she died. It took less than a year
after that, though, for the story to start circulating. Edward
Moxon published a one-volume edition of *The Works of Charles
Lamb, including his Life and Letters,* which received the attention of
the *British Quarterly Review* in February 1848. The review was
unsigned, but clearly written by someone who had known the
Lambs, for it began with the detailed and admiring description of
Wednesday evenings in the early days, the one that so gracefully
stated that "the champagne was in the talk."

The reviewer took the opportunity to analyze the character of
Charles Lamb, illustrated with an ample assortment of quotations
from his delectable letters and spiced up with a few personal

reminiscences. He applauded Lamb's wit, then turned grave, analyzing Charles Lamb's humor as "the safety-valve of a sad, earnest heart."

"It has been said that all true humour rests upon melancholy," wrote the 1848 reviewer. He proceeded to reveal the circumstances from which much of Lamb's melancholy arose:

> Little did the majority of those who saw this social, punning, gentle, frolicsome, stammering, quaint humorist, imagine the awful shadow which for ever rested upon his spirit, mingling with and deepening by contrast the brightness of its sunshine. Yes, in that queer-looking clerk—in the gentle-hearted Charles—in the delicate Elia, underneath the lightsome wit and playful fancy, there was shrouded a dark tragedy, such as would have broken many a robust spirit. The story is known but to few, and those few have hitherto, from obvious motives of delicacy, refrained from speaking of it. The time has now come, we believe, when the grave having closed over all whom it may concern, the story ought to be told as a noble example of unobtrusive heroism.

The writer proceeded to tell the story of "the well-known Mary Lamb"—those hollow words voicing the only characterization he offered on her behalf. The family was poor, and "the weight of their maintenance" fell on Mary. "Increasing infirmities" and "incessant watching" of her mother "made great inroads upon Mary Lamb's health."

> On that very afternoon—it was the 22nd Sept. 1796—while the family were preparing for dinner, Mary seized a knife which lay on the table, and making a rush at her little apprentice, pursued her round the room with fearful menaces. Her

infirm old mother, with eager and terrified calls upon her to
desist, attempted to interfere. With wild shrieks Mary turned
upon her mother, and stabbed her to the heart!

The point of the story, in the eyes of the *Quarterly* reviewer, was
that "This ghastly incident gave a new shape to all [Charles]
Lamb's subsequent career," turning him into "a brave, unselfish
man" who renounced love and marriage for "the stern austerity of
duty" and never left home without a strait waistcoat for his
unpredictable sister.[3]

This was the version of the story heard by most of literary
London. Surely certain intimate survivors knew—Talfourd,
Procter, the Moxons—but from 1796 on Mary and Charles Lamb
had in general succeeded in keeping the matricide a secret.

The review prompted Thomas Noon Talfourd to spring into
action. He had already, in 1837, while Mary Lamb was still alive,
published a commemorative volume titled *The Life and Letters of
Charles Lamb,* completed thanks to the "interest and zeal" of his
publisher, Edward Moxon, and dedicated to Mary. To his personal
memories he added information and quotations from Lamb's letters and essays and from conversations with a number of Lamb's
friends, whom he proudly listed: Wordsworth, Manning,
Robinson, "the executor of Coleridge," and "the surviving relatives of Hazlitt." He withheld any mention of Elizabeth Lamb's
death or Mary's madhouse confinements. "The recentness of the
period of some of the letters has rendered it necessary," he wrote
in his introduction, "to omit many portions of them, in which the
humour and beauty are interwoven with personal references,
which, although wholly free from any thing which, rightly understood, could give pain to any human being, touch on subjects too
sacred for public exposure."[4]

As Talfourd told the tale of the year 1796, for example, he

focused on the friendship with Coleridge and Lloyd and ended with a general nod to brotherly devotion:

> On the death of his parents, [Charles Lamb] felt himself called upon by duty to repay to his sister the solicitude with which she had watched over his infancy; and well indeed he performed it! To her, from the age of twenty-one, he devoted his existence; seeking thenceforth no connection which could interfere with her supremacy in his affections, or impair his ability to sustain and to comfort her.[5]

When the *British Quarterly Review* revealed the details of Elizabeth Lamb's death and Mary Lamb's madness, Talfourd felt upstaged. He swiftly compiled his *Final Memorials* and inserted many letters he had earlier censored. The time had finally come, he explained in the opening of the book:

> Several of his friends, who might possibly have felt a moment's pain at the publication of some of those effusions of kindness, in which they are sportively mentioned, have been removed by death; and the dismissal of the last, and to him the dearest of all, his sister, while it has brought to her the repose she sighed for ever since she lost him, has released his biographer from a difficulty which has hitherto prevented a due appreciation of some of his noblest qualities.[6]

Although he questioned the propriety of publishing passages that referred to Mary's "malady," Talfourd rationalized that to reveal Mary's secrets was to glorify Charles. "The truth, while in no wise affecting the gentle excellence of one of them, casts new and solemn lights on the character of the other."[7]

Talfourd allowed himself many more liberties the second time around. Revealing Charles Lamb's burdens, he understood, could serve to raise him in the reader's esteem:

> There was a tendency to insanity in his family, which had been more than once developed in his sister; and it was no matter of surprise that in the dreariness of his solitude it fell upon him; and that, at the close of the year [1795], he was subjected for a few weeks to the restraint of the insane. The wonder is that, amidst all the difficulties, the sorrows, and the excitements of his succeeding forty years, it never recurred.

By portraying his as "a life of self-sacrifice," Talfourd initiated the legend of Saint Charles. Twenty-five years later, when William Carew Hazlitt published his own collection of "poems, letters, and remains" of Mary and Charles Lamb, he accused Talfourd of "literary falsification," of having obfuscated or omitted the bad habits of Charles Lamb, such as drinking and speaking in expletives. "What was the object? it may be inquired," wrote Hazlitt. "Perhaps, reverence for the memory of Lamb? Was it not, rather, half-heartedness, egotism, effeminate prudery?"[8]

Talfourd may have canonized Charles, but out of the same generosity he treated Mary more kindly than did the *British Quarterly Review*. According to Talfourd, she was "remarkable for the sweetness of her disposition, the clearness of her understanding, and the gentle wisdom of all her acts and words," even more so given "the distraction under which she suffered for weeks, latterly for months, in every year."[9] As Talfourd told the story, "Miss Lamb was worn down to a state of extreme nervous misery, by attention to needlework by day, and to her mother by night, until the insanity, which had been manifested more than once, broke out into frenzy, which, on Thursday, 22nd of September, proved fatal to her mother." He alluded to Mary's "habitual serenity" in the years he knew her. He never knew her to flinch at the mention of her mother, he wrote, or to be haunted with memories or night-mares of the matricidal scene. "Some of her most intimate friends who knew of the disaster," he even suggested, "believed that she had never become aware of her own share in its horrors." While he worked to extol the virtues of Mary Lamb, Talfourd also por-trayed a woman not fully cognizant of her past—vacant and insouciant rather than aware and responsible for her past. His comments laid the foundation for an image that has sidelined Mary Lamb ever since.

WHAT DID REALLY happen on September 22, 1796, in the Lamb household? How unconscious—how lunatic—was the hand that thrust the knife into the bosom of Elizabeth Lamb? There were deep personal and societal reasons for this daughter to feel anger toward this mother, but theirs was a time when proper ladies repressed all such feelings. Some genetic tendency toward mental illness may well have marked the Lamb family, and it seems quite likely that organic factors played a significant role in triggering Mary Lamb's behavior. The awareness of oncoming episodes, the apparent absence of external causes in some cases, the pattern of increasing deterioration as Mary Lamb progressed in years: All point to the probability that she suffered from a mental illness that today would have a diagnosis, a name, and perhaps even a treatment.

Twenty-first-century psychologists will almost certainly diag-nose Mary Lamb with manic-depressive illness, or bipolar disor-der. "Manic-depressive illness, often seasonal, is recurrent by nature; left untreated, individuals with this disease can expect to experience many, and generally worsening, episodes of depres-sion and mania," writes Kay Redfield Jamison, one of today's experts on the disorder, in her book *Touched with Fire: Manic-Depressive Illness and the Artistic Temperament*. "Depression is a view of the world through a glass darkly, and mania is a shattered pattern of views seen through a prism or kaleidoscope: often brilliant but generally fractured," Jamison continues, using the same metaphor that Talfourd found to describe Mary Lamb's mental condition in her later years.[10]

"The depressive, or melancholic, states are characterized by a morbidity and flatness of mood," writes Jamison. "Mania is characterized by an exalted or irritable mood, more and faster speech, rapid thought, brisker physical and mental activity levels, . . . and impulsiveness."[11] Untreated, the periods of detachment from a normal state of mind grow longer and come more frequently over time.

Jamison explores the possibility that this psychological dysfunction may actually fuel the work of many writers, artists, and composers: "Most individuals who have manic-depressive illness are normal most of the time; that is, they maintain their reason and their ability to function personally and professionally."[12] She appends to her book a list of creative people through the ages whom she suspects of having suffered from bipolar disorder: Oliver Goldsmith, Samuel Taylor Coleridge, Mary Wollstonecraft, William Blake, Mary Shelley, Percy Bysshe Shelley, Edward FitzGerald, Virginia Woolf—and Charles Lamb. Mary Lamb belongs there, too.

Mary Lamb probably experienced mixed bipolar episodes, when manic and depressive symptoms occur simultaneously, as observed early in the twentieth century by Emil Kraepelin. "He conceptualized these mixed states as primarily transitional phenomena," writes Jamison. "They tended to occur when an individual was going into or out of a depressive or manic state. Such states . . . represent an important link between manic-depressive illness, artistic temperament, creativity, and the rhythms and temperament of the natural world. Unfortunately, they also are closely associated with the damaging and killing sides of manic-depressive illness: alcoholism, drug abuse, and suicide"[13]—and perhaps, in Mary Lamb's case, with murder.

A PSYCHIATRIC DIAGNOSIS does not entirely satisfy our fascination with Mary Lamb, however. Too many of her life's details resonate with those of women universally. In recent years feminist literary scholars have brought to light dozens of creative women who faded into the shadows, outshone by male contemporaries whose work now canonically defines their eras. Mary Lamb has enjoyed some increased recognition during this literary rescue operation, coming to be seen as an equal, if not primary, author of the Lambs' three books for children. She is the author's sister whom Virginia Woolf was seeking: a woman born with the same talents, the same strengths, and the same weaknesses as her brother. As in the case of Woolf's fictitious sister of Shakespeare, social circumstances muffled Mary Lamb's voice. Her life and her opus were restricted by the limits society set for her—limits that, granted, she internalized exceedingly well.

By the age of thirty-one Mary Lamb clearly understood the place society had assigned her. Since she had not married by then, she was destined for spinsterhood, with neither the devotion of a husband nor the affection of her own children to lighten her future. As her parents' only daughter, it was to her that all the domestic tasks were assigned. In her case those tasks were tremendous, and likely to increase in the coming years. She cared for three elders, one mentally incompetent, one physically unable, one cantankerous. She watched her brothers move out into the world, taking all the right steps to achieve the middle-class success that the times now offered to families such as theirs. Her brothers enjoyed fine classical educations, while she was lucky that her parents allowed her to learn to read and write. On top of her household obligations, she was asked to earn as much as she could by mantua making—a trade that promised not class advancement but in fact shrinking opportunities, now that middle-class women were sewing for themselves. Were Mary Lamb to continue on the path set for her by family and society, she would live another half century making little money and performing mindless chores. At worst she would live a life of scorn and solitude. At best she would serve the men around her as they advanced by day in the world of commerce and came home every evening to eat the food she prepared, smoke their pipes, drink their gin and porter, read and debate on matters political and philosophical.

One thrust of a knife changed her fate.

It could be argued that, no matter, she still spent the rest of her life in the service of her brother Charles. But in her single irreversible act, Mary Lamb stepped beyond the limits of expected behavior. She would never quite fade into the household woodwork again. She stepped outside the path of the ordinary and did what she could to stay on that course through the rest of her life.

She smoked. She drank. She contributed to discussions on matters literary and philosophical. She wrote. She published. All the while she performed the duties of a supportive woman of the house, sewing when she and Charles had little money, then assuming as best she could the role of woman of the house when they could afford to hire a maid. Most of their friends knew that Mary was as essential to the Lambs' literary circle as Charles—and not because she served a good supper.

Mary Lamb was not an iconoclast like Mary Wollstonecraft, nor did she find success through productivity and influence, as did Sarah Trimmer and Anna Laetitia Barbauld. Whether deliberately or simply for the sake of survival, she chose the middle path. She skirted the limits. She pushed beyond the boundaries set for women of her time but hovered just on the other side, choosing mild individuality rather than audacity or brilliance.

Epilogue

We will never know whether Mary Lamb consciously planned these strategies. Among the compromises she made in order to navigate her life and times were silence and anonymity. She has stood quietly behind her brilliant, chatty, unforgettable brother for nearly two centuries.

It is time for her to step out into the light.

NOTES

All the quotations attributed to Mary and Charles Lamb, when not identified otherwise, are taken from their letters, of which there is no single
authoritative edition. Edwin W. Marrs Jr.'s three volumes are the most
recent, complete, and inclusive of modern scholarly findings, but his edition was never completed and hence covers only the years through 1817.
E. V. Lucas's three volumes complete the collection chronologically but are
not as generous with commentary and scholarly cross-referencing. For correspondence through October 1817, therefore, I used the Marrs volumes,
and the Lucas volumes for correspondence thereafter. Marrs tends to allow
misspellings, grammatical oddities, and idiosyncratic punctuation to
remain, a practice I have followed, marking many with the customary "*sic*."
Charles Lamb's letters in particular are full of dots and dashes and boldface
and oversize lettering, little of which can be reproduced here. The notes
provide the date and recipient for letters cited in the text. Dates in brackets are hypotheses offered by Marrs or Lucas.

Numerous editions of *Tales from Shakespear* and Charles's essays are available, but *Mrs. Leicester's School* and *Poetry for Children* are difficult to find. See
the bibliography for a listing of the editions used here and for full publication information of works briefly cited here. Page references have not been
given for passages quoted from the Lambs' literary works or the volumes
of correspondence.

Prelude: The Dreadful Scene Imagined

1. Lopate, Foreword, *Charles Lamb: Essays of Elia,* vii.
2. Wollstonecraft, *A Vindication,* 109, 100, 108.

Chapter 1 The Only Daughter

1. To Mrs. Vincent Novello, [Spring 1820].
2. Details of Salt's will are provided in Lucas, *Life of Charles Lamb,* 90.
3. Ibid., 93.
4. Mackinnon's annotations to *Old Benchers,* 50.
5. To Samuel Taylor Coleridge, [June 29–July 1, 1796].
6. To Sarah Stoddart, [September 21, 1803].
7. To Coleridge, [June 8–10, 1796].

Chapter 2 Their Verdict: Lunacy

1. *Blackstone's Commentaries on the Laws of England,* book 1, chap. 9, "Of Subordinate Magistrates," www.yale.edu/lawweb/avalon/blackstone/bk1ch9.htm.
2. To Coleridge, [September 27, 1796].
3. The London Metropolitan Archives no longer hold any inquest papers for Holborn, Middlesex County, from the years between 1786 and 1799, according to Bridget Howlett, senior archivist, April 25, 2003.
4. *Times,* September 18, 1796.
5. *Whitehall Evening Post,* September 24–27, 1796.
6. Jones, *Women Who Kill,* 19.
7. Eigen, *Witnessing Insanity,* 19.
8. *British Lady's Magazine,* vol. 1, no. 4 (1815), 80.
9. *Blackstone's Commentaries,* book 1, chap. 8; book 4, chap. 2.
10. From West and Walk, "The Judges' Replies," *Daniel McNaughton,* 75.
11. Eigen, *Witnessing Insanity,* 44–45, quoting from the Old Bailey Session Papers.

12. Quoted in Macalpine and Hunter, *George III,* 311.

13. Ibid., 311–12.

14. Ibid., 3, 7.

15. Burney, *Diary and Letters*, vol. 4, 232.

16. *Morning Chronicle,* August 1, 1788, quoted in Macalpine and Hunter, *George III,* 10.

17. Ibid., 15.

18. Burney, *Diary and Letters,* vol. 4, 226.

19. Macalpine and Hunter, *George III*, 36, 43.

20. Porter, *Mind-Forg'd Manacles,* chap. 4 and elsewhere.

21. Macalpine and Hunter, *George III*, 61–79.

22. Burney, *Diary and Letters,* vol. 4, 333–40.

23. Ibid., vol. 5, 8.

24. The originators of this diagnosis were Macalpine and Hunter, *George III,* chap. 10.

25. To Coleridge, [October 3, 1796].

26. Ibid.

27. Ibid.

28. Ibid.

29. Ibid., [October 17, 1796].

30. Ibid., [October 3, 1796].

31. Ibid., [June 8–10, 1796].

32. Samuel Taylor Coleridge to Benjamin Flower, [December 11, 1796], in Jackson, ed., *Selected Letters.*

Chapter 3 In the Madhouse

1. Cullen, *First Lines of the Practice of Physic,* vols. 1 and 2, 2d. ed., 268.

2. To Coleridge, [October 3, 1796].

3. Cullen, *First Lines,* 268, 274, 280–81.

4. Ibid., 283.

5. Ibid., 285–86.

6. Ibid., 286.

7. Macalpine and Hunter, *George III,* 60n.

8. Cullen, *First Lines,* 287.

9. Ibid., 284.

10. "The Rehearsal Transposed, or Animadversions upon a late book," quoted in Morris, *Hoxton Madhouses,* n.p.

11. Based on archival documents reproduced in Allderidge, *Bethlem Hospital 1247–1997,* 36–37.

12. Allderidge, *Bethlem Hospital*, 9.

13. Hunter and Macalpine, editors' introduction to Battie, *A Treatise on Madness,* 7.

14. Quoted in Masters, *Bedlam,* 47.

15. Andrews, Briggs, et al., *History of Bethlem,* 384.

16. Allderidge, *Bethlem Hospital,* 39.

17. Quoted in ibid., 27.

18. Battie, *Treatise,* 2.

19. Ibid., 93–97, 68–69.

20. John Monro, *Remarks on Dr. Battie's Treatise on Madness* (bound with Battie, *Treatise),* 16.

21. Macalpine and Hunter, *George III,* 339.

22. Quoted in Morris, *Hoxton Madhouses,* n.p.

23. Ibid.; Parry Jones, *Trade in Lunacy,* 43.

24. Morris, *Hoxton Madhouses,* n.p.

25. To Coleridge, [June 8–10, 1796].

26. Ibid., July 5[–7], 1796.

27. History of Canonbury Tower, Canonbury Masonic Research Centre, http://www.canonbury.ac.uk/tower.htm.

28. Angel, Islington, www.angeltowncentre.com/BoroughHistory.htm.

29. Samuel Taylor Coleridge to Thomas Poole, quoted in Marrs, vol. 1, 61n.1.

30. To Coleridge, [October 3, 1796].

31. Ibid., [September 27, 1796].

32. Marrs, *Letters,* vol. 1, 46n.2; to Coleridge, [October 3, 1796].

33. To Coleridge, January 28, 1798.

34. Talfourd, *Final Memorials,* vol. 1, 223.

35. To Coleridge, October 28, 1796.

36. Ibid., [October 3, 1796].

37. Quoted in Ross, *Ordeal,* 170.

38. Clarke, *Recollections,* 177.

39. Ibid., 177–78.
40. Burton, *A Double Life,* 293ff.
41. Woodberry, "The Silence of the Lambs," 289.
42. To Coleridge, [October 3, 1796].
43. Ibid., [October 17, 1796].
44. Ibid.

Chapter 4 Reading, Writing, and Mantua Making

1. To Coleridge, April 7, 1797.
2. Personal communication from L. V. Troost, May 17, 2002, through 18th-Century Interdisciplinary Discussion, C18-L@lists.psu.edu.
3. To Coleridge, [October 11, 1802].
4. Earle, *Making of the English Middle Class,* 289.
5. Quoted from *London Tradesman* (1747), in Batchelor, *Dress, Distress, and Desire,* 90.
6. Mezzotint engraving, ca. 1770, in Denlinger, "A Wink from the Bagnio," fig. 3, p.77.
7. Quoted in Batchelor, *Dress, Distress, and Desire,* 103–5.
8. Figures calculated from Library History Database, http://www.r-alston.co.uk/library.htm.
9. To Barbara Betham, November 2, 1814.
10. Figures from White, *Women's Magazines 1693–1968,* 25.
11. Raven, "The Book Trades," 25.
12. Ibid.; Colley, *Britons,* 41.
13. This and all other monetary equivalencies have been calculated using John J. McCusker, "Comparing the Purchasing Power of Money in Great Britain from 1254 to Any Other Year Including the Present," Economic History Services, 2001, http://www.eh.net.hmit/ppowerbp/.
14. Beetham, *A Magazine of Her Own,* 17.
15. In *The Subjection of Women,* as quoted in Showalter, *A Literature of Their Own,* 3.
16. As suggested in Pearson, *Women's Reading in Britain 1750–1835,* ix.
17. As quoted in Showalter, *A Literature of Their Own,* 16–17.
18. Mellor, *Romanticism & Gender,* 7.

19. Hannah More, "The Practical Use of Female Knowledge . . . ," quoted from *The Works of Hannah More,* vol. 3, ed. Henry G. Bohn (1853), on the Houghton Mifflin Web site, *Mosaic: Perspectives on Western Civilization,* unit on "A Woman's Usefulness," http://college.hmco.com/history/west/mosaic/chapter13/source487.htm.

20. Quoted in Pearson, *Women's Reading in Britain,* 22.

21. Ibid., 79–80.

Chapter 5 Charles Alone

1. Coleridge to Robert Southey, October 21, 1794, *Collected Letters,* vol. 1, 114.

2. Coleridge and Southey, *The Fall of Robespierre,* Act 1, hypertext edition at http://otal.umd.edu/~msites/robespierre/robes1.html.

3. Coleridge, *Poems on Various Subjects,* xi.

4. To Coleridge, [May 27, 1796].

5. Ibid., [February 5–6, 1797].

6. Ibid., [October 3, 1796].

7. Ibid., [December 9, 1796].

8. Ibid., February 13, 1797.

9. Lucas, *Life,* 139.

10. To Coleridge, January 2, 1797.

11. Ibid., [January 7–10, 1797].

12. Ibid., [December 1, 1796].

13. Ibid.

14. John Lamb, *Poetical Pieces,* n.p.

15. To Coleridge, [December 1, 1796].

16. Ibid., [June 8–10, 1796].

17. Leigh Hunt's *Autobiography,* quoted in Lucas, *Life,* 93.

18. "Patmore's First Acquaintance with Lamb," in Stoddard, ed., *Personal Recollections,* 8.

19. De Quincey, *Biographical Essays,* 213.

20. Clarke, *Recollections,* 13.

21. Review of Charles Lamb, *Works,* in *British Quarterly Review,* 1848,

294; comment on his teachers' expectation mentioned in Marrs, *Letters,* vol. 1, xxxiii.

22. Procter, *Literary Recollections,* 76; *British Quarterly Review,* 303.

23. To Coleridge, November 8, 1796.

24. Ibid., December 10, 1796.

25. Lucas, *Life,* 128.

26. To Coleridge, January 16, 1797.

27. Coleridge, *Poems,* 2d ed., 153ff.

28. Marrs, *Letters,* vol. 1, 55n4.

29. To Coleridge, [January 28, 1798].

30. Ibid., [December 1, 1796].

31. Coleridge to Thomas Poole, [December 11, 1796], *Collected Letters,* vol. 1, 160.

32. Coleridge to Charles Lloyd, Sr., December 4, 1796, *Collected Letters,* vol. 1, 157.

33. Lloyd, *Edmund Oliver,* 292.

34. To Marmaduke Thompson, [January 1798].

35. To Coleridge, [January 28, 1798].

Chapter 6 Double Singleness

1. In his essay "Mackery End, in Hertfordshire."

2. To Sarah Stoddart, [May 30–June 2, 1806].

3. Wollstonecraft, *Vindication,* 100.

4. To Sarah Stoddart, [May 30–June 2, 1806].

5. To Robert Lloyd, [September 13, 1804].

6. To Sarah Stoddart, March 14, [1806].

7. To Robert Southey [January 23, 1799].

8. To Coleridge, [July 28, 1800].

9. Talfourd, *Memorials,* 213.

10. Quoted in Lucas, *Life,* 211.

11. To Coleridge, [May 12, 1800].

12. To Thomas Manning, [May 17, 1800].

13. Goodman, *Walking Guide to Lawyers' London,* 149.

14. To Coleridge, [July 28, 1800].

15. To Manning, [February 25, 1801].

16. To Coleridge, [July 19 or 26, 1797].

17. Ibid.

18. To Coleridge, August 6, 1800.

19. To Coleridge, August 14, [1800].

20. Marrs, *Letters,* vol. 2, 11n.1; to Southey, [August 9, 1815].

21. To Manning, [February 8, 1800].

22. Talfourd, *Final Memorials,* vol. 1, 140.

23. Godwin, *Political Justice,* 2, 25–26.

24. John Fenwick, "William Godwin," *Public Characters of 1799–1800* (1799), quoted in Marshall, *William Godwin,* 119.

25. C. Kegan Paul, *William Godwin: His Friends and Contemporaries* (1876), quoted in Marshall, *William Godwin,* 121–22.

26. Marshall, *William Godwin,* 122.

27. Mary Shelley in Abinger mss.; comment on George IV made by Thomas Northcote, both from Marshall, *William Godwin,* 154.

28. Sunstein, *A Different Face,* 114.

29. Godwin, *Memoirs of the Author,* 80.

30. Wollstonecraft, *Vindication,* 85–86.

31. Sunstein, *A Different Face,* 214.

32. Godwin, *Memoirs of the Author,* 122.

33. Both quoted in Marshall, *William Godwin,* 194.

34. To Manning, [February 18, 1800].

Chapter 7 The Circle Forms

1. Mackinnon's annotations to *Old Benchers*, 48–55.

2. To Manning, [August 31, 1801].

3. Ibid., April [?], 1801.

4. Ibid., [July 27?, 1805].

5. Details of daily housekeeping at the Temple courtesy of Clare Rider, senior archivist, Inner Temple Archives.

6. Robinson, *Diary,* vol. 1, 44.

7. Ibid.

8. To Manning, [September or October 1801].

9. To Coleridge, [August 26, 1800].

10. Robinson, *Diary,* vol. 1, 34.

11. Marrs, *Letters,* vol. 1, 37–38n.5.

12. Robinson, *Diary,* vol. 1, 34.

13. To Manning, December 27, 1800.

14. Ibid., [February 15, 1801].

15. Ibid., May 10, 1806.

16. *Narratives of . . . Manning,* 263–66.

17. To Manning, [November 3, 1800].

18. Ibid., February 19, 1803.

19. To Coleridge, June 13, 1797.

20. To Manning, [March 17, 1800].

21. Clarke, *Recollections,* 177.

22. To Coleridge, [June 8, 1796].

23. To Barbara Betham, November 2, 1814.

24. To Sarah Stoddart, July 21, 1802.

25. Ibid.

26. Ibid., August 9, 1802.

27. To Coleridge, [July 28, 1800].

28. To John Rickman, September 16, [1801].

29. Coleridge to Robert Southey, November 9, 1801, *Collected Letters,* vol. 2, 774–75.

30. Holmes, *Coleridge: Early Visions,* 125ff.

31. To Manning, September 24, 1802.

32. To Coleridge, [September 8, 1802].

33. Ibid.

34. Davies, *William Wordsworth,* 142.

35. Samuel Taylor Coleridge to Joseph Cottle, [ca. July 8, 1797], *Collected Letters,* vol. 1, 195.

36. *Dorothy Wordsworth's Illustrated Lakeland Journals,* 145–46.

37. Ibid., 202–3.

38. To Manning, September 24, 1802.

39. Ibid., February 15, 1802.

40. To Coleridge, [September 8, 1802].

41. To Robert Lloyd, [December 17, 1799]; to Rickman [early November 1801].

42. To Coleridge, [April 13, 1803].

43. To Manning, [April 23, 1802].

44. Clarke, *Recollections,* 178.

45. To Sarah Stoddart Hazlitt, [March 30, 1810].

46. To Manning, [May 17, 1800].

47. To Sarah Stoddart, [early November 1805].

48. Ibid.

49. To John Rickman, [February 14, 1802].

50. From "Memoirs of the Life of Mrs. Mary Brunton by Her Husband," preface to *Emmeline,* Edinburgh, 1819, quoted in Showalter, *A Literature of Their Own,* 17–18.

51. Samuel Taylor Coleridge to Thomas Wedgwood, September 16, 1803; quoted in Ingram, ed., *Patterns of Madness,* 221.

52. Samuel Taylor Coleridge to Sarah Coleridge, April 4, 1803, in *Collected Letters,* vol. 2, 941.

53. To Dorothy Wordsworth, July 9, [1803].

54. James Burney and Charles Lamb to John Rickman, July 27, 1803.

55. Ibid.

56. To Dorothy Wordsworth, July 9, [1803].

Chapter 8 Children's Books

1. To Coleridge, [October 23, 1802].

2. *Goody Two-Shoes,* 11, 14, 29.

3. Ibid., 3.

4. From Jackson, *Engines of Instruction,* plate 20, p. 28.

5. *The Renowned History of Giles Gingerbread* (Boston: Mein and Fleeming, 1768; first American reprint of the Newbery edition), available online at english.byu.edu/facultysyllabi/KLawrence/GILESGINGERBREAD.pdf.

6. Jackson, *Engines of Instruction,* 83.

7. Quoted in McCarthy & Kraft, Introduction, *Barbauld, Selected Poetry & Prose,* 11.

8. Samuel Taylor Coleridge to John Prior Estlin, March 1, [1800], *Collected Letters,* vol. 1, 323.

9. *Lessons for Children from Three to Four Years Old,* n.p.

10. Ibid.

11. Jackson, *Engines of Instruction,* 181.

12. Trimmer, *Charity School Spelling Book,* 16.

13. Ibid., 25ff.

14. Ibid.

15. Marshall, *Godwin,* 242.

16. Not all Godwin scholars have attributed *Bible Stories* to William Godwin. The book was published in 1802, its author identified as William Scolfield. That "Scolfield" is a pseudonym for Godwin is proposed by William St. Clair in *The Godwins and the Shelleys,* 279ff., who presents convincing evidence in the notes, 545. Godwin's authorship of *Bible Stories* is accepted as fact by Pamela Clemit in "Philosophical Anarchism in the Schoolroom," 60, citing St. Clair.

17. Quoted from Godwin's Preface to *Bible Stories* in St. Clair, *Godwins and Shelleys,* 280.

18. Godwin, *Political Justice,* 26.

19. Ibid.

20. Marshall, *William Godwin,* 249, and elsewhere.

21. To Rickman, September 16, [1801].

22. Ibid., [early December 1801].

23. Marshall, *William Godwin,* 250.

24. To Manning, February 15, 1802.

25. Ibid., September 24, 1802.

26. To William Godwin, August 11, 1803.

27. Ibid., [November 10, 1803].

28. As quoted in Clemit, "Philosophical Anarchism in the Schoolroom," 56.

29. St. Clair, *Godwins and Shelleys,* 284.

30. Clemit, "Philosophical Anarchism in the Schoolroom," 44, 56.

31. To Manning, February 15, 1802.

32. Lamb quoted the entire column in a letter to Manning, February 15, 1802.

33. Marrs, *Letters,* vol. 2, 53n.2.

34. To Rickman, [February 14?, 1802].

35. Marrs, *Letters,* vol. 2, 53n.2.

36. To Robert Lloyd, March 13, 1804.

37. To Sarah Stoddart, [March 17, 1804].

38. To Dorothy Wordsworth, [October 13, 1804].

39. "The Loss of the Indiaman, Early of Abergavenny," Maritime History and Naval Heritage Web site, http://www.cronab.demon.co.uk/aber.htm.

40. "Storm 11: All Who Struggled with the Sea," Hampshire and Dorset Shipwrecks, http://homepage.ntlworld.com/pernod/11.html.

41. To William Wordsworth, [February 18, 1805].

42. To Manning, February 23 or 24, 1805.

43. To William Wordsworth, [February 19, 1805].

44. Ibid., March 2, [1805].

45. As written in Charles Lamb's letter to William Wordsworth, [April 2, 1805].

46. To Dorothy Wordsworth [May 7, 1805].

47. Ibid.

48. To Dorothy Wordsworth, June 14, 1805.

49. Ibid.

50. Ibid. This letter has been torn, and the words presumed by Marrs have been transcribed here without his brackets.

51. To Manning, [July 28?, 1805].

52. As proposed on Andrew Roberts's Mary and Charles Lamb Web site, http://www.mdx.ac.uk/www/study/ylamb.htm.

53. To Sarah Stoddart, [early November 1805].

54. Ibid., [November 9 and 14, 1805].

55. Murphy, "Mad Farming," 251–52.

56. To William Hazlitt, November 10, 1805.

57. To Mrs. Thomas Clarkson, December 25, 1805.

Chapter 9 Tales from Shakespeare

1. To M. J. Godwin, [January or February 1806].

2. To William Hazlitt, February 19, 1806.

3. To Sarah Stoddart, [February 10, 1806].

4. Ibid., February 21, [1806].

5. Ibid., March 14, [1806].

6. To Manning, May 10, 1806.

7. To Sarah Stoddart, [May 30–June 2, 1806].

8. To William Wordsworth, June 26, 1806.

9. To Sarah Stoddart, [May 30–June 2, 1806].

10. *Taming of the Shrew* II.i.315; IV.i.22.

11. To Sarah Stoddart, [June 27 to July 2, 1806].

12. To William Wordsworth, January 29, 1807.

13. William Mulready, Clare People, County Clare Web site: www.clarelibrary.ie/eolas/coclare/people/mulready.htm.

14. Hamlyn and Phillips, *William Blake*, 20–22.

15. The Carl H. Pforzheimer Library copy of the first edition has bookseller Anderson Robinson's note, dated April 1918, pasted inside cover, stating: "In regard to the illustrations, while it is doubted if Blake executed more than one or two, he is said to have engraved all of them, but those which do not clearly bear his characteristic touch were probably drawn by Mulready and others."

16. To William Wordsworth, January 29, 1807.

17. To Sarah Stoddart, [June 27–July 2, 1806].

18. To Coleridge, [September 1806].

19. Samuel Taylor Coleridge to Sarah Coleridge, [September 29, 1806], *Collected Letters*, vol. 2, 626.

20. William Wordsworth to Sir George Beaumont, September 1806, quoted in Coleridge's *Collected Letters*, vol. 2, 625n2.

21. To Sarah Stoddart, [October 23, 1806].

22. Ibid.

23. Robinson, *Diary*, vol. 1, 120–21.

24. To William Wordsworth, December 11, [1806].

25. To Manning, February 2, 1808.

26. To Catherine Clarkson, December 23, 1806.

27. To Sarah Stoddart, December 11, [1806].

28. To Mr. and Mrs. Thomas Clarkson, [June 1807].

29. To Catherine Clarkson, [July 20, 1807].

Chapter 10 Schoolgirl Tales

1. To Sarah Stoddart, [May 30–June 2, 1806].

2. Patmore in Stoddard, *Personal Recollections,* 51–52.

3. Robinson, *Diary,* vol. 1, 35.

4. Ibid., 60, 70.

5. William Hazlitt, "Project for a New Theory of Civil and Criminal Legislation," http://www.blupete.com/Literature/Essays/Hazlitt/Civil&Criminal.htm.

6. Baker, *William Hazlitt,* 153.

7. William Hazlitt, "My First Acquaintance with Poets," in *Selected Writings,* 229.

8. To Sarah Coleridge, [October 13, 1804].

9. To Sarah Stoddart, [November 28, 1807].

10. Ibid.

11. To Sarah Stoddart, [December 21?, 1807].

12. William Carew Hazlitt, *Lamb and Hazlitt,* 66–67.

13. To Sarah Stoddart, [February 12, 1808].

14. To Manning, February 26, 1808.

15. To Sarah Stoddart, [March 16, 1808].

16. Ibid.

17. To Robert Southey, [August 1815].

18. Baker, *William Hazlitt,* 410–15.

19. W. C. Hazlitt in Stoddard, *Personal Recollections,* 204.

20. Samuel Taylor Coleridge, *Collected Letters,* vol. 1, 147.

21. Talfourd, *Final Memorials,* vol. 2, 227.

22. To Sarah Stoddart, [September 21, 1803].

23. Ibid.

24. See, for example, the works of Alice Miller, especially *The Drama of the Gifted Child* (1994).

25. From *Critical Review,* December 1808. This passage is copied from the 1809 edition of *Tales from Shakespear,* where it appeared as an advertisement for *Mrs. Leicester's School.*

26. Quoted in Lucas, *Letters,* vol. 3, 418.

27. Godwin to Charles Lamb, March 10, 1808, quoted in Marrs, *Letters*, vol. 2, 278.

28. Written by Lamb on Godwin's letter and returned, March [10], 1808.

29. To Manning, February 26, 1808.

30. Ibid.

31. Thomas De Quincey, "Recollections of Charles Lamb," chap. 2 in *London Reminiscences, 58.*

Chapter 11 Poetry for Children

1. Robert Lloyd to Hannah Lloyd, April 3, 1809, quoted in Lucas, *Lamb and the Lloyds,* 180–81.

2. To Louisa Martin, March 28, [1809].

3. To Sarah Stoddart Hazlitt, [March 30, 1810].

4. To Barbara Betham, November 2, 1814.

5. Ibid.

6. Henry Crabb Robinson, quoted in Marrs, *Letters,* vol. 3, 119n.4.

7. To Barbara Betham, November 2, 1814.

8. Robert Lloyd to Hannah Lloyd, April 3, 1809, op. cit.

9. Richard Herne Shepherd, quoted in William Macdonald, ed., *Poetry for Children by Charles & Mary Lamb,* xvi.

10. To Bernard Barton, September? 1827.

11. Macdonald, Introduction, *Poetry for Children,* xvi–xvii.

12. To Robert Lloyd and Charles Lloyd the elder, [late June–mid-July 1809].

13. To Manning, January 2, 1810.

14. In his essay "Detached Thoughts on Books and Reading."

15. Macdonald, Introduction, *Poetry for Children,* xxi.

16. To Frances Kelly, [March 18, 1820].

17. Talfourd, quoted in Lucas, *Life,* 458.

18. Lucas, *Life,* 588.

19. John Lamb, *Cruelty to Animals,* 9–11.

20. To Henry Crabb Robinson, [February 7, 1810].

21. To Coleridge, [June 7, 1809].

22. To Coleridge, [October 30, 1809].

Chapter 12 The Politics of Needlework

1. To Sarah Stoddart Hazlitt, [November 7, 1809].
2. To Louisa Martin, March 28, [1809].
3. To Coleridge, [June 7, 1809].
4. To Dorothy Wordsworth, November 13, 1810.
5. Ibid., November 23, 1810.
6. To William Wordsworth, [April 16, 1815].
7. "Introductory Address," *British Lady's Magazine,* vol. 1, no. 1 [January 1815], 1–6.
8. *British Lady's Magazine,* vol. 1, no. 4 [April 1815], 252.
9. Macalpine and Hunter, *George III,* 143.
10. Robinson, *Diary,* vol. 1, 242–43.
11. All quotations from "On Needle-work" from *British Lady's Magazine* 1, no. 4 [April 1815], 257–60.
12. To Sarah Stoddart, December 1, [1802].
13. Robinson, *Diary,* vol. 1, 242.
14. Ibid., 243.
15. "On the Melancholy of Tailors," quoted in its entirety in Marrs, *Letters,* vol. 3, 121n.1.
16. To John Scott, December 12, 1814.
17. Quoted in Marrs, *Letters,* vol. 3, 139n.1.
18. To Mrs. Joseph Hume, [March 1815].
19. Ibid.
20. To Mrs. Morgan and Charlotte Brent, [May 22, 1815].
21. Ibid.

Chapter 13 Elia Appears

1. To Barron Field, August 16, 1820.
2. "The South Sea House."
3. "The Old Benchers of the Inner Temple."

4. Review of Charles Lamb, *Works,* in *British Quarterly Review,* 1848, 292.

5. Quoted in Lucas, *Life,* 710.

6. Talfourd, *Final Memorials,* vol. 2, 171.

7. To William Wordsworth, April 26, 1816.

8. To John Payne Collier, December 10, 1817.

9. Hazlitt, "On the Conversation of Authors," in *Selected Writings,* 101–02.

10. To William Wordsworth, [September 23], 1816.

11. St. Clair, *Godwins and Shelleys,* 465ff., Clemit, "Philosophical Anarchism," 65-68.

12. To Mary Matilda Betham, [September 13, 1815].

13. To Sara Hutchinson, October 19, 1815.

14. Henry Crabb Robinson, *Diary,* vol. 1, 386.

15. To Basil Montague, n.d. [1830?], Lucas, *Letters,* vol. 3, 263.

16. Quoted in Lucas, *Life,* 604.

17. To Sara Hutchinson, November 1816.

18. Ibid.

19. To Dorothy Wordsworth, [November 21, 1817].

20. Ibid.

21. To Mary Wordsworth, February 18, 1818.

22. To Mrs. Vincent Novello, [spring 1820].

23. To John Mathew Gutch, January 1819.

24. To Frances Kelly, July 9, 1819.

25. Ibid., July 20, 1819.

26. Lucas, *Letters,* vol. 2, 255n.

27. To Frances Kelly, second letter of July 20, 1819.

28. Lucas, *Letters,* vol. 2, 256n.

29. Robinson, *Diary,* vol. 2, 52.

30. To Miss Humphreys, January 9, 1821.

31. Lucas, *Life,* 529–30.

32. To Mary Shelley, July 26, 1827.

33. Lucas, *Life,* 720–21.

34. To Robert S. Jameson, August 29, 1827.

35. To Bernard Barton, September 2, 1823.

36. Lucas, *Letters,* vol. 2, 465n.

37. To William Wordsworth, April 6, 1825.

38. To Bernard Barton, [April 6, 1825].

39. To Sara Hutchinson, [April 18, 1825].

40. To J. A. Hessey, March 29, 1825.

41. To William Wordsworth, April 6, 1825.

42. To William Ayrton, [October 3, 1825].

43. To Thomas Allsop, [September 9, 1825].

44. To William Ayrton, [October 3, 1825].

45. To Thomas Hood, [September 18, 1827].

46. Quoted in Lucas, *Life*, 725.

47. To Thomas Hood, [September 18, 1827].

Chapter 14 Her Twilight of Consciousness

1. To Henry Crabb Robinson, October 1, 1827.

2. To Edward Moxon, [October] 1827.

3. To Frances Kelly, October 1, 1827.

4. To Thomas Allsop, [November] 1827.

5. Ibid., [mid-December] 1827; to Thomas Allsop, December 20, 1827.

6. To Bernard Barton, July 25, 1829.

7. Quoted on Andrew Roberts's Mary and Charles Lamb Web site, http://www.mdx.ac.uk/www/study/ylamb.htm.

8. To Edward Moxon, November 12, 1830.

9. H. F. Cox, "Charles Lamb at Edmonton," *Globe*, 1875, quoted in Lucas, *Life*, 805.

10. To Thomas Noon Talfourd, May 8, 1833.

11. J. Fuller Russell, quoted in Lucas, *Life*, 825.

12. Quoted in Lucas, *Life*, 828.

13. To William Wordsworth, late May 1833.

14. To William Ayrton, October 30, 1821.

15. To William Wordsworth, September 6, 1826.

16. *Letters of Mary Wollstonecraft Shelley*, Bennett, ed., vol. 2, 311n.

17. To Louisa Badams, [August 20, 1833].

18. To Emma and Edward Moxon, July 1833.

19. To Thomas Manning, May 10, 1834.

20. To Maria Fryer, February 14, 1834.

21. Talfourd, *Final Memorials,* vol. 2, 228.

22. As reported by Mary Cowden Clarke in *Recollections of Writers,* 184.

23. Quoted in Lucas, *Life,* 834.

24. To Matilda Betham, April 14, 1834; to Thomas Manning, May 10, 1834.

25. To Thomas Hood, [late October], 1834.

26. Quoted in Lucas, *Letters,* vol. 3, 417n.

27. Quoted in Lucas, *Life,* 822.

28. Quoted in Lucas, *Life,* 831.

29. Henry Crabb Robinson, *Diary,* vol. 2, 155–56.

30. Quoted in Lucas, *Life,* 832.

31. From Henry Crabb Robinson's papers, cited in Jones, *Ordeal,* 203.

32. Ibid., 204–05.

33. Talfourd, *Final Memorials,* vol. 1, viii.

34. Ibid., vol. 2, 236.

35. Quoted in Lucas, *Life,* 833.

36. Henry Crabb Robinson, *Diary,* vol. 2, 162.

37. Talfourd, *Final Memorials,* vol. 2, 104, 113.

38. Henry Crabb Robinson, *Diary,* vol. 2, 162.

39. Ibid., 221.

40. Ibid., 241.

41. Ibid., 279.

Epilogue

1. FitzGerald, *Variorum and Definitive Edition,* vol. 7, 131–32.

2. FitzGerald to W. B. Donne, March 14, [1878], *Letters,* vol. 4, 107.

3. Review of Charles Lamb, *Works,* in *British Quarterly Review,* 1848, 292–311.

4. Talfourd, *Letters,* ix.

5. Talfourd, *Life and Letters,* 25.

6. Talfourd, *Final Memorials,* vol. 1, vii–viii.

7. Ibid., viii–x.

8. William Carew Hazlitt, *Mary and Charles Lamb,* 11.

9. Ibid., 226.
10. Jamison, *Touched with Fire,* 125.
11. Ibid., 18, 27.
12. Ibid., 16.
13. Ibid., 36.

BIBLIOGRAPHY

Primary Sources of Writing by the Lambs

The Old Benchers of the Inner Temple by Charles Lamb. With annotations by Sir F. D. Mackinnon, a master of the bench of the Inner Temple. Oxford: Clarendon Press, 1927.

Poetry for Children by Charles & Mary Lamb, edited with an introduction by William Macdonald. Freeport, N.Y.: Books for Libraries Press, 1903; reprint, 1970.

Lamb, Charles and Mary. *Mrs. Leicester's School.* London: Harvill Press Limited, 1948.

————. *Tales from Shakespeare.* Prague: Galley Press/Paul Hamlyn, 1962.

Lamb, John (elder). *Poetical Pieces on Several Occasions.* London: Printed for P. Shatwell, opposite Adelphi, Strand (n.d.).

Lamb, John (younger). *Cruelty to Animals: The Speech of Lord Erskine in the House of Peers on the Second Reading of the Bill for preventing Malicious and Wanton Cruelty to Animals.* Edinburgh: Alex. Lawrie, Bookseller & Stationer, 1809.

Lucas, E. V. *The Letters of Charles Lamb to which are added those of his sister Mary Lamb.* Vols. 2 and 3. New Haven: Yale University Press, 1935.

Marrs, Edwin W., Jr. *The Letters of Charles and Mary Anne Lamb.* Vols. 1–3. Ithaca and London: Cornell University Press, 1975–1978.

Other Primary Sources

Barbauld, Anna Laetitia. *Lessons for Children from Three to Four Years Old.*
Dublin: Hibernia-Press-Office for John Cumming, 1814.
————. *Selected Poetry and Prose.* Edited by William McCarthy and
Elizabeth Kraft. Toronto: Broadview Press, 2002.
Battie, William. *A Treatise on Madness.* Edited by Richard Hunter and Ida
Macalpine, bound with Monro, John, *Remarks on Dr. Battie's Treatise on
Madness.* London: Dawsons of Pall Mall, 1962.
Burney, Frances. *Diary and Letters of Madame D'Arblay [Frances Burney].*
Edited by her niece. 7 vols., London: Hurst & Blackett, 1854.
A Calendar of the Inner Temple Records. Edited by R. A. Roberts. Vol. 5,
1751–1800. London: Order of the Masters of the Bench, 1936.
Clarke, Charles, and Mary Cowden. *Recollections of Writers.* New York:
Charles Scribner's Sons, 1878.
Coleridge, Samuel Taylor. *Poems on Various Subjects by S. T. Coleridge Late of
Jesus College, Cambridge.* London: Printed for G. G. and J. Robinsons,
and J. Cottle, Bookseller, Bristol, 1796.
————. *Poems, by S. T. Coleridge, second edition to which are now added Poems
by Charles Lamb and Charles Lloyd.* Printed by N. Biggs, for J. Cottle,
Bristol, and Messrs. Robinsons, London, 1797.
————. *Collected Letters of Samuel Taylor Coleridge.* Edited by Earl Leslie
Griggs. Oxford: Clarendon Press, 1956.
————. *Selected Letters.* Edited by H. J. Jackson. Oxford: Clarendon
Press, 1987.
Cullen, William, M.D. *First Lines of the Practice of Physic.* Vols. 1 and 2. 2d
ed. revised and enlarged. Philadelphia: Edward Parker, 1822.
De Quincey, Thomas. *Biographical Essays, and Essays on the Poets.* Boston,
Mass.: James R. Osgood and Co., 1873.
————. *The Collected Writings of Thomas De Quincey.* Vol. 3. Edited by
David Masson. Edinburgh: Adam and Charles Black, 1890.
FitzGerald, Edward. *The Variorum and Definitive Edition of the Poetical and
Prose Writings of Edward FitzGerald.* Vol. 7. Edited by George Bentham.
New York: Doubleday, Page and Co., 1902. Reprint, New York:
Phaeton Press, 1967.

————. *The Letters of Edward FitzGerald.* Vol. 4, *1877–1883.* Edited by Alfred McKinley Terhune and Annabelle Burdick Terhune. Princeton, N.J.: Princeton University Press, 1980.

Godwin, William. *An Enquiry concerning Political Justice and its Influence on General Virtue and Happiness.* Vols. 1 and 2. Edited and abridged by Raymond A. Preston. New York: Alfred A. Knopf, 1926.

Hazlitt, William. *Selected Writings.* Edited by Jon Cook. Oxford and New York: Oxford University Press, 1991.

Hazlitt, William Carew. *Mary and Charles Lamb: Poems, Letters, and Remains now first collected, with reminiscences and notes.* New York: Scribner, Welford, & Armstrong, 1874.

————, ed. *Lamb and Hazlitt: Further Letters and Records Hitherto Unpublished.* New York: Dodd, Mead & Co., 1899.

The History of Goody Two-Shoes, with her means of acquiring Learning, Wisdom, and Riches. London: Printed for Darton, Harvey, and Darton, 1813.

Home, John. *The Plays of John Home.* Edited with an introduction by James S. Malek. New York and London: Garland Publishing, Inc., 1980.

Lloyd, Charles. *Edmund Oliver, 1798.* Oxford and New York: Woodstock Books, 1990.

———— and Charles Lamb. *Blank Verse.* London: Printed by T. Bensley; for John and Arthur Arch, No. 23, Grace-church Street, 1798.

Lloyd, Christopher, ed. *The Diary of Fanny Burney.* London: Roger Ingram, 1948.

Narratives of the Mission of George Bogle to Tibet and of the Journey of Thomas Manning to Lhasa. Edited by Sir Clements R. Markham. New Delhi: Manjusri Publishing House, 1971.

Paine, Thomas. *The Rights of Man.* 1791 and 1792. Reprint, New York: Dover Publications, 1999.

Pocock's Authentic Narrative of the Loss of the Abergavenny, East-Indiaman, John Wordsworth, Esq. Capt., off Portland February 5, 1805. Weymouth Diving Web site, http://www.weymouthdiving.co.uk/abergavenny.htm.

Procter, Bryan Waller. *The Literary Recollections of Barry Cornwall.* Edited by Richard Willard Armour. Boston, Mass.: Meador Publishing Company, 1936.

The Register of The Temple Church London, transcribed by G. D. Squibb. London: Inner Temple, 1979.

Bibliography

"Review of *The Works of Charles Lamb, including his Life and Letters, collected into one volume.*" *British Quarterly Review* 7, no. 14 (February and May 1848), 292–311.

Robinson, Henry Crabb. *Diary, Reminiscences, and Correspondence of Henry Crabb Robinson, Barrister-at-Law, F.S.A.* 3d edition, 2 vols. Edited by Thomas Sadler. London and New York: Macmillan & Co., 1872. Reprint, New York: AMS Press, Inc., 1967.

Shelley, Mary Wollstonecraft. *The Letters of Mary Wollstonecraft Shelley.* Vols. 1 and 2. Edited by Betty T. Bennett. Baltimore and London: Johns Hopkins University Press, 1983.

Stoddard, R. H., ed. *Personal Recollections of Lamb, Hazlitt and Others.* New York: Scribner, Armstrong, and Company, 1875.

Talfourd, Thomas Noon. *The Letters of Charles Lamb, with a Sketch of his life.* 2 vols. London: Edward Moxon, 1837; New York: Derby & Jackson, 1858.

————. *Final Memorials of Charles Lamb.* London: Edward Moxon, 1848.

Trimmer, Mrs. [Sarah]. *The Charity School Spelling Book. Part I. Containing the Alphabet, Spelling Lessons, and Short Stories of Good and Bad Boys In Words of one syllable only.* 7th ed. London: Printed for F. & C. Rivington, No. 62, St. Paul's Churchyard; & J. Hatchard, Piccadilly. 1802.

————. *The Charity School Spelling Book. Part I. Containing the Alphabet, Spelling Lessons, and Short Stories of Good and Bad Girls In Words of one syllable only.* 7th ed. London: Printed for F. & C. Rivington, No. 62, St. Paul's Churchyard; & J. Hatchard, Piccadilly. 1802.

Wollstonecraft, Mary. *A Vindiction of the Rights of Woman.* London and New York: Penguin Books, 1992.

Wordsworth, Dorothy. *Dorothy Wordsworth's Illustrated Lakeland Journals,* with an introduction by Rachel Trickett. London: Collins, 1987.

Secondary Sources

Aaron, Jane. *A Double Singleness: Gender and the Writings of Charles and Mary Lamb.* Oxford: Clarendon Press; New York: Oxford University Press, 1991.

Bibliography

Adburgham, Alison. *Women in Print: Writing Women & Women's Magazines from the Restoration to the Accession of Victoria.* London: George Allen & Unwin, 1972.

Allderidge, Patricia. *Bethlem Hospital 1247–1997: A Pictorial Record.* Chichester, West Sussex, England: Phillimore & Co., Ltd., 1997.

American Journal of Insanity. Vol. 5. Edited by the Officers of the New York State Lunatic Asylum, Utica. Utica: Printed at the Asylum, 1848–49.

Andrews, Jonathan, Asa Briggs, Roy Porter, Penny Tucker, and Keir Waddington. *The History of Bethlem.* (Volume published for 750th anniversary.) London and New York: Routledge, 1997.

Anthony, Katharine. *The Lambs: A Story of Pre-Victorian England.* New York: Alfred A. Knopf, 1945.

Armour, Richard Willard. *Barry Cornwall: A Biography of Bryan Waller Procter.* Boston, Mass.: Meador Publishing Company, 1935.

Baker, Herschel Clay. *William Hazlitt.* Cambridge, Mass.: Belknap Press, 1962.

Baker, J. H. *The Inner Temple: A Brief Historical Description.* London: Honourable Society of the Inner Temple, 1991.

Balle, Mary Blanchard. "Mary Lamb: Her Mental Health Issues." Lecture delivered to the Charles Lamb Society, January 14, 1995. In *Charles Lamb Bulletin* 93 (January 1996), 2–11.

Batchelor, Jennie. *Dress, Distress and Desire: Clothing and Sentimental Literature.* Ph.D. diss. University of London, 2002.

Belanger, Terry. "Publishers and Writers in Eighteenth-Century England." In Isabel Rivers, ed., *Books and Their Readers in Eighteenth-Century England* (Leicester, England: Leicester University Press, 1982).

Beetham, Margaret. *A Magazine of Her Own? Domesticity and Desire in the Woman's Magazine, 1800–1914.* London and New York: Routledge, 1996.

Braithwaite, Brian. *Women's Magazines: The First 300 Years* (London: Peter Owen, 1995).

Burton, Sarah. *A Double Life: A Biography of Charles & Mary Lamb.* London: Viking, 2003.

Clemit, Pamela. "Philosophical Anarchism in the Schoolroom: William Godwin's Juvenile Library, 1805–25." *Biblion* 9, no. 1/2 (Fall 2000/Spring 2001), 44–70.

Bibliography

Colley, Linda. *Britons: Forging the Nation, 1707–1837*. New Haven and London: Yale University Press, 1992.

Davidoff, Leonore, and Catherine Hall. *Family Fortunes: Men and Women of the English Middle Class, 1780–1850* (Chicago: University of Chicago Press, 1987).

Davies, Hunter. *William Wordsworth: A Biography*. London: Weidenfeld & Nicolson, 1980.

Delamar, Gloria T. *Mother Goose: From Nursery to Literature*. Jefferson, N.C., and London: McFarland and Co., 1987.

Denlinger, Elizabeth C. "A Wink from the Bagnio: Jocular Representations of Prostitutes in Prints in Late Eighteenth-century London," in *Biblion* 9:1/2, (Fall 2000/Spring 2001), 71–86.

Derry, John W. *Reaction and Reform 1793–1868: England in the Early Nineteenth Century*. London: Blandford Press, 1963.

Derry, John W. *The Regency Crisis and the Whigs 1788–9*. Cambridge: Cambridge University Press, 1963.

De Selincourt, Ernest. *Dorothy Wordsworth, A Biography*. Oxford: Clarendon Press, 1933.

Earle, Peter. *The Making of the English Middle Class: Business, Society and Family Life in London, 1660–1730*. London: Methuen, 1989.

Eigen, Joel Peter. *Witnessing Insanity: Madness and Mad-Doctors in the English Court*. New Haven and London: Yale University Press, 1995.

Farrington, Anthony. *Trading Places: The East India Company and Asia, 1600–1834*. London: British Library, 2002.

Gilchrist, Anne. *Mary Lamb*. Boston, Mass.: Roberts Brothers, 1883.

Goodman, Andrew. *The Walking Guide to Lawyers' London*. London: Blackstone Press, 2000.

Goodwin, Albert. *The Friends of Liberty: The English Democratic Movement in the Age of the French Revolution*. London: Hutchinson of London, 1979.

Hamlyn, Robert, and Michael Phillips. *William Blake*. New York: Metropolitan Museum of Art, 2000.

Harris, Bob. "Praising the Middling Sort? Social Identity in Eighteenth-Century British Newspapers." Chap. 1 in Alan Kidd and David Nicholls, eds., *The Making of the British Middle Class: Studies of Regional and Cultural Diversity Since the Eighteenth Century*. Stroud, Gloucestershire: Sutton Publishing, 1998.

Hibbert, Christopher. *George III: A Personal History*. London: Viking, 1998.

Holmes, Richard. *Coleridge: Early Visions*. London: Hodder & Stoughton, 1989.

Hussey, W. D. *The British Empire and Commonwealth, 1500–1961* Cambridge: Cambridge University Press, 1963.

Ingram, Allan, ed. *Patterns of Madness in the Eighteenth Century: A Reader*. Liverpool: Liverpool University Press, 1998.

Jackson, Mary V. *Engines of Instruction, Mischief, and Magic: Children's Literature in England from Its Beginnings to 1839*. Lincoln: University of Nebraska Press, 1989.

Jamison, Kay Redfield. *Touched with Fire: Manic-Depressive Illness and the Artistic Temperament*. New York: Free Press, 1993.

Jones, Ann. *Women Who Kill*. Holt, Rinehart & Winston, 1990.

Lopate, Phillip. Foreword, *Charles Lamb: Essays of Elia*. Iowa City: University of Iowa Press, 2003.

Lucas, E. V., ed. *Charles Lamb and the Lloyds*. Philadelphia: J. B. Lippincott Co., 1899.

Macalpine, Ida, and Richard Hunter. *George III and the Mad-Business*. London: Allen Lane/The Penguin Press, 1969. Reprint, London: Pimlico, 1993.

Marshall, Peter H. *William Godwin*. New Haven and London: Yale University Press, 1984.

Masters, Anthony. *Bedlam*. London: Michael Joseph, 1977.

McGavran, James Holt, Jr., ed. *Romanticism and Children's Literature in Nineteenth-Century England*. Athens and London: University of Georgia Press, 1991.

Mellor, Anne K., ed. *Romanticism and Gender*. New York and London: Routledge, 1993.

Miller, Alice. *The Drama of the Gifted Child: The Search for the True Self*. Translated from the German by Ruth Ward. New York: Basic Books, 1994.

Morris, H. D. *The Hoxton Madhouses*. London: Printed by March, for the author, 1958.

Bibliography

Murphy, Elaine. "Mad Farming in the Metropolis. Part 1: A Significant Service Industry in East London." *History of Psychiatry* 12 (2001), 245–82.

Murphy, Elaine, "The Mad-House Keepers of East London," *History Today,* 9/01/01, reprint online by Britannica.com Web site, http://www .britannica.com/magazine.

Newdick, Robert S. *The First Life and Letters of Charles Lamb: A Study of Thomas Noon Talfourd as Editor and Biographer.* Columbus: Ohio State University, 1935.

Parry, J. H., P. M. Sherlock, and A. P. Maingot. *A Short History of the West Indies,* 4th ed. London: Macmillan Caribbean, 1991.

Parry Jones, William L. *The Trade in Lunacy: A Study of Private Madhouses in England in the Eighteenth and Nineteenth Centuries.* London: Routledge & Kegan Paul, 1972.

Pearce, Robert R. *A Guide to the Inns of Court and Chancery.* London: Butterworths, 1855.

Pearson, Jacqueline. *Women's Reading in Britain 1750–1835: A Dangerous Recreation.* Cambridge: Cambridge University Press, 1999.

Pitfield, Robert L., M.D., "'A Pitiful, Ricketty, Gasping, Staggering, Stuttering Tomfool': The Mental Afflictions of Charles and Mary Lamb," *Annals of Medical History,* New Series, vol. 1, n.d.

Polowetzky, Michael. *Prominent Sisters: Mary Lamb, Dorothy Wordsworth, and Sarah Disraeli.* Westport, Conn. and London: Praeger, 1996.

Porter, Roy. *Mind-Forg'd Manacles: A History of Madness in England from the Restoration to the Regency.* Cambridge, Mass.: Harvard University Press, 1987.

Purdie, D. W., and N. Gow. "The Maladies of James Boswell, Advocate." *Journal of the Royal College of Physicians of Edinburgh* 32 (2002), 197–202.

Purton, Valerie. *A Coleridge Chronology.* London: Macmillan Press, 1993.

Raven, James. "The Book Trades." In Isabel Rivers, ed., *Books and Their Readers in Eighteenth-Century England: New Essays.* London and New York: Leicester University Press, 2002.

Riehl, Joseph E. *Charles Lamb's Children's Literature.* Romantic Reassessment Series 94. Salzburg, Austria: Institut für Anglistik und Amerikanistik, 1980.

Ritcheson, Charles R. *British Politics and the American Revolution.* Norman:

University of Oklahoma Press, 1954.

Roberts, Andrew. Mary and Charles Lamb Web site, http://www
.mdx.ac.uk/www.study/ylamb.htm.

———. Mental Health History Timeline Web site, http://www.mdx.ac
.uk/www.study/sshtim.htm.

Roff, Renée. *A Bibliography of the Writings of Charles and Mary Lamb: The First
Editions in Book Form by Luther S. Livingston with Appendices: The Books of the
Two John Lambs and Contributions to Periodicals by J. C. Thomson.*
Bronxville, N.Y.: Nicholas T. Smith, 1979.

Ross, Ernest C. *The Ordeal of Bridget Elia.* Norman: University of
Oklahoma Press, 1940.

Royle, Edward, and James Walvin. *English Radicals and Reformers
1760–1848.* Lexington: University Press of Kentucky, 1982.

St. Clair, William. *The Godwins and the Shelleys: The Biography of a Family.*
New York and London: W. W. Norton & Co., 1989.

Schofield, Mary Anne, and Cecilia Macheski, eds. *Fetter'd or Free? British
Women Novelists, 1670–1815.* Athens and London: Ohio University
Press, 1986.

Showalter, Elaine. *A Literature of Their Own: British Women Novelists from
Brontë to Lessing,* expanded. Princeton, N.J.: Princeton University
Press, 1977.

Spacks, Patricia Meyer, "'Always at Variance': Politics of Eighteenth-
Century Adolescence." In *A Distant Prospect: Eighteenth-Century Views of
Childhood.* Papers read at a Clark Library Seminar, October 13, 1979.
(Williams Andrews Clark Memorial Library, University of California,
Los Angeles, 1982).

Stabler, Jane. *Burke to Byron, Barbauld to Baillie, 1790–1830.* Basingstoke
and New York: Palgrave, 2002.

Stoddard, Richard Henry, ed. *Personal Recollections of Lamb, Hazlitt, and
Others.* New York: Scribner, Armstrong, and Company, 1875.

Sturgess, Ray. "Gladstone's Pick-Me-Up and Other Stories." *Pharmaceutical
Journal* 267, no. 1719 (December 22–29, 2001) 911–36.

Sunstein, Emily. *A Different Face: The Life of Mary Wollstonecraft.* New York:
Harper & Row, Publishers, 1975.

Sutherland, Zena, and May Hill Arbuthnot. *Children and Books,* 8th ed.
New York: HarperCollins, 1991.

Bibliography

Van der Kiste, John. *George III's Children*. Phoenix Mill, England: Alan
Sutton Publishing Ltd., 1992.

Vargo, Lisa. The Case of Anna Laetitia Barbauld's "To Mr C[olerid]ge."
Anna Laetitia Barbauld Web Site, http://duke.usask.ca/~vargo/
barbauld/.

Walker, Nigel, and Sarah McCabe. *Crime and Insanity in England*. Vol. 2,
New Solutions and New Problems. Edinburgh, Scotland: Edinburgh
University Press, 1975.

West, Donald J., and Alexander Walk, eds. *Daniel McNaughton: His Trial
and the Aftermath*. Ashford, Kent, England: Gaskell Books, 1977.

White, Cynthia L. *Women's Magazines 1693–1968*. London: Michael
Joseph, 1970.

Williams, Eric. *From Columbus to Castro: The History of the Caribbean,
1492–1969*. New York: Vintage Books, 1970.

Woodberry, Bonnie. "The Mad Body as the Text of Culture in the Writings
of Mary Lamb," *Studies in English Literature, 1500–1900*. Autumn 1999
[accessed through Northern Light.com].

———. "The Silence of the Lambs: Anti-maniacal Regimes in the
Writings of Mary Lamb," *Women's Writing* 5, no. 3 (1998) 289–304.

ACKNOWLEDGMENTS

THANK YOU to all who have helped along the way. Alison Louise Watkins, my sister-in-law, encouraged me early in the conception of this book. Likewise, early on Rachel Saury helped generously in our talks about psychology and mothers. I am lucky to have what every writer needs, a Ladies' Literary Luncheon group, and I thank all the LLLers, especially Bella Stander (our fearless leader), Kathleen Ringle Pond, Jeanne Nicholson Siler, and Janis Jaquith, for their interest and enthusiasm. Kathleen Mason and Kathryn Jaquette offered comments and background reading at critical times. I benefited from correspondence with Elaine Madsden, another writer inspired by Mary Lamb. Thanks to my dear Cornwall friend, Pamela Michael, for her keen eye and ear, as well as her continuing enthusiasm. In London, Clare Rider and Adrian Blunt at the Inner Temple and Patricia Allderidge and Colin Gale at the Royal Bethlem Hospital were particularly generous. My visit to the Lambs' London came alive thanks to the energy, imagination, and kindness of Andrew Roberts, who has continued ever since an active correspondent, research compatriot, dreamer, and seeker after truth. Willis Spaulding put an extraordinary amount of time and thought into the legal history of the case of Mary Lamb, and I thank him for that generosity. Much of my research was conducted at the University of Virginia's Alderman Library and Special Collections; thanks to all who helped me there, especially Bryson Clevenger. Odd questions got good answers when posted on the eighteenth-century discussion list, and I especially thank Jennie Batchelor for sharing a chapter of her dissertation. My stepmother, Janet Cox-Rearick, found me valuable contacts in the field of costume history. I enjoyed watching my father, H. Wiley Hitchcock, turn from dutiful proofreader to avid reader of the manuscript. The interest and pride shown by my husband, David Watkins, and the pleasures we shared in reading and research travels together made such a difference. My fascination with the English Romantics has been enriched over decades through literary travels and conversations with my mother. In thanks and appreciation, I dedicate this book to her. Finally, a heartfelt thanks to my agents, Miriam Goderich and Jane Dystel, who believed in this book from the beginning, and my editors, Jill Bialosky and Nomi Victor, who helped shape it into something for others to enjoy.

INDEX

madhouses (*continued*)
as holding tanks, 51–52
inhumane practices in, 152–54, 256, 257
kindness to patients in, 150–53, 154, 256
Laverstock House, 150–51
ML's confinements in, 18, 33, 40–42, 53–56, 79–80, 89, 95–97, 127–30, 149–50, 151–154, 177–78, 181, 213–14, 227–28, 229, 240–41, 256, 257, 274
moral management in, 50–52
Normand House, 256, 261
physicians at, 50–52, 55
Retreat, 52, 84
sleeping facilities in, 153
staff of, 55
St. Luke's Hospital, 49–52
treatments in, *see* medical treatments
visitation restrictions in, 56, 178
Whitmore House, 52, 241–42
see also Bethlem Hospital; Fisher House; Horton House
"Madman, The" (Dyer), 111
madness, 45–47, 84, 86, 202, 237
delirium in, 45–46, 71
of George III, 36–39, 221–22
manic behavior, 46–47
medical definitions of, 51
novels as cause of, 68, 71–72
terms for, 51
see also Lamb, Mary Ann, madness of; lunacy, lunatics
magazines, 20, 66
maidservants, 198, 217–19, 229, 280
Malta, 148, 182
Malvolio, 140, 167
"Maniac, The" (C. Lloyd), 84
manic behavior, 46–47, 55

manic depressive disorder, 39, 277–79
in creative people, 278
mixed episodes of, 278–79
Manning, Thomas, 185, 193, 274
books sent to, 204
CL's correspondence with, 113, 117, 121, 123, 141, 150, 159–60, 184, 195, 261–62
travels of, 111–12
manteau, 62
mantua makers, 27, 62–65, 107, 222–27, 243–44, 279–80
activities of, 63
derivation of term, 62
lascivious reputation of, 63–65
Margate, 116
Maria, or the Wrongs of Woman (Wollstonecraft), 68, 73
Marriage of Heaven and Hell, The (Blake), 171
marriage settlements, 174–75, 184
Marshall, James, 140, 141
Marvell, Andrew, 47
mechanical swings, 153
medical treatments, 36–37, 50–52, 58–59
blistering, 46–47, 51, 55, 59
bloodletting, 46, 51, 55, 59, 153
calomel, 39
cold bathing, 47, 59
digitalis, 39
electrical shocks, 153
of George III, 38–39, 47, 52
intimidation, 47, 55
of manic behavior, 46–47, 55
mechanical swings, 153
mineral waters, 36, 51
physical restraints, 46, 51, 52, 55, 153
purgatives, 37, 46, 51, 55, 59, 153
seclusion, 55

Index

Index